GEOGRAPHY
TOOLS AND CONCEPTS

PRENTICE HALL
Needham, Massachusetts
Upper Saddle River, New Jersey
Glenview, Illinois

Program Authors

Heidi Hayes Jacobs

Heidi Hayes Jacobs has served as an educational consultant to more than 500 schools across the nation. Dr. Jacobs is an adjunct professor in the Department of Curriculum on Teaching at Teachers College, Columbia University. She completed her undergraduate studies at the University of Utah in her hometown of Salt Lake City. She received an M.A. from the University of Massachusetts, Amherst, and completed her doctoral work at Columbia University's Teachers College in 1981.

The backbone of Dr. Jacobs' experience comes from her years as a teacher of high school, middle school, and elementary school students. As an educational consultant, she works with K–12 schools and districts on curriculum reform and strategic planning.

Brenda Randolph

Brenda Randolph is the former Director of the Outreach Resource Center at the African Studies Program at Howard University, Washington, D.C. She is the Founder and Director of Africa Access, a bibliographic service on Africa for schools. She received her B.A. in history with high honors from North Carolina Central University, Durham, and her M.A. in African studies with honors from Howard University. She completed further graduate studies at the University of Maryland, College Park, where she was awarded a Graduate Fellowship.

Brenda Randolph has published numerous articles in professional journals and bulletins. She currently serves as library media specialist in Montgomery County Public Schools, Maryland.

Michal L. LeVasseur

Michal LeVasseur is an educational consultant in the field of geography. She is an adjunct professor of geography at the University of Alabama, Birmingham, and serves with the Alabama Geographic Alliance. Her undergraduate and graduate work is in the fields of anthropology (B.A.), geography (M.A.), and science education (Ph.D.).

Dr. LeVasseur's specialization has moved increasingly into the area of geography education. In 1996, she served as Director of the National Geographic Society's Summer Geography Workshop. As an educational consultant, she has worked with the National Geographic Society as well as with schools to develop programs and curricula for geography.

Special Program Consultant

Yvonne S. Gentzler, Ph.D.
School of Education
University of Idaho
Moscow, Idaho

PRENTICE HALL
Needham, Massachusetts
Upper Saddle River, New Jersey
Glenview, Illinois

ISBN 0-13-050226-X

2 3 4 5 6 7 8 9 10   04 03 02 01 00

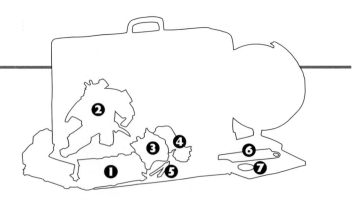

On the Cover

❶ Model of locomotive and freight cars
❷ Antique sextant
❸ Conch shell
❹ Mineral samples
❺ Calipers
❻ Thermometer
❼ Compass

Content Consultants for the World Explorer Program

Africa
Barbara Brown
Africa Studies Center
Boston University
Boston, Massachusetts

Ancient World
Maud Gleason
Department of Classics
Stanford University
Stanford, California

East Asia
Leslie Swartz
Harvard University
East Asian Outreach
Program at the
Children's Museum
of Boston
Boston, Massachusetts

Latin America
Daniel Mugan
Center for Latin American
Studies
University of Florida
Gainesville, Florida

Middle East
Elizabeth Barlow
Center for Middle
Eastern and North
African Studies
University of Michigan
Ann Arbor, Michigan

North Africa
Laurence Michalak
Center for Middle East
Studies
University of California
Berkeley, California

Religion
Michael Sells
Department of Religion
Haverford College
Haverford, Pennsylvania

**Russia, Eastern Europe,
Central Asia**
Janet Valliant
Center for Russian,
Eastern European, and
Central Asian Studies
Harvard University
Cambridge,
Massachusetts

South Asia
Robert Young
South Asia Regional
Studies
University of
Pennsylvania
Philadelphia,
Pennsylvania

Western Europe
Ruth Mitchell-Pitts
Center for West European
Studies
University of North
Carolina
Chapel Hill, North
Carolina

Teacher Advisory Board

Jerome Balin
Lincoln Junior High
School
Naperville, Illinois

Elizabeth Barrett
Tates Creek Middle
School
Lexington, Kentucky

Linda Boaen
Baird School
Fresno, California

Nikki L. Born
Harllee Middle School
Bradenton, Florida

**Barbara Coats
Grabowski**
Russell Middle School
Omaha, Nebraska

Stephanie Hawkins
Jefferson Middle School
Oklahoma City, Oklahoma

Fred Hitz
Wilson Middle School
Muncie, Indiana

William B. Johnson
La Mesa Junior High
School
Canyon Country,
California

Kristi Karis
West Ottawa Middle
School
Holland, Michigan

Kristen Koch
Discovery Middle School
Orlando, Florida

Peggy McCarthy
Beulah School
Beulah, Colorado

Cindy McCurdy
Hefner Middle School
Oklahoma City, Oklahoma

Deborah J. Miller
Department of Social
Studies
Detroit Public Schools
Detroit, Michigan

Lawrence Peglow
Greenway Middle School
Pittsburgh, Pennsylvania

Lyn Shiver
Northwestern Middle
School
Alpharetta, Georgia

Mark Stahl
Longfellow Middle
School
Norman, Oklahoma

TABLE OF CONTENTS

GEOGRAPHY TOOLS AND CONCEPTS

1

O F S P E C I A L
I N T E R E S T

A hands-on approach to learning and applying social studies skills

Step-by-step activities for exploring important topics in geography

Literature selections that help geographic concepts come to life

HEROES

Profiles of people who made a difference in their country

Detailed drawings show how the use of technology makes a country unique

A view of a country through the eyes of a student artist

MAPS

CHARTS, GRAPHS, AND TABLES

READ ACTIVELY

How can I get the most out of my social studies book? How does my reading relate to my world? Answering questions like these means that you are an active reader, an involved reader. As an active reader, you are in charge of the reading situation!

The following strategies tell how to think and read as an active reader. You don't need to use all of these strategies all the time. Feel free to choose the ones that work best in each reading situation. You might use several at a time, or you might go back and forth among them. They can be used in any order.

BEFORE YOU READ

Give yourself a purpose

The sections in this book begin with a list called "Questions to Explore." These questions focus on key ideas presented in the section. They give you a purpose for reading. You can create your own purpose by asking questions like these: How does the topic relate to my life? How might I use what I learn at school or at home?

Preview

To preview a reading selection, first read its title. Then look at the pictures and read the captions. Also read any headings in the selection. Then ask yourself: What is the reading selection about? What do the pictures and headings tell about the selection?

Reach into your background

What do you already know about the topic of the selection? How can you use what you know to help you understand what you are going to read?

Ask questions

Suppose you are reading about the continent of South America. Some questions you might ask are: Where is South America? What countries are found there? Why are some of the countries large and others small? Asking questions like these can help you gather evidence and gain knowledge.

Predict

As you read, make a prediction about what will happen and why. Or predict how one fact might affect another fact. Suppose you are reading about South America's climate. You might make a prediction about how the climate affects where people live. You can change your mind as you gain new information.

Connect

Connect your reading to your own life. Are the people discussed in the selection like you or someone you know? What would you do in similar situations? Connect your reading to something you have already read. Suppose you have already read about the ancient Greeks. Now you are reading about the ancient Romans. How are they alike? How are they different?

Visualize

What would places, people, and events look like in a movie or a picture? As you read about India, you could visualize the country's heavy rains. What do they look like? How do they sound? As you read about geography, you could visualize a volcanic eruption.

Respond

Talk about what you have read. What did you think? Share your ideas with your classmates.

Assess yourself

What did you find out? Were your predictions on target? Did you find answers to your questions?

Follow up

Show what you know. Use what you have learned to do a project. When you do projects, you continue to learn.

GEOGRAPHY
TOOLS AND CONCEPTS

Are you curious about our Earth? Do you want to know why some places in the world are cold and some are hot? Have you wondered why more people live in cities and fewer people live in other places? Would you like to find mountaintops or valleys to explore? If you answered *yes* to any of these questions, you want to know more about geography. Farmers grow corn, traders cross the ocean, and you walk or take a bus to school. Geography explains all of these activities— and many more.

Guiding Questions

The readings and activities in this book will help you discover answers to these Guiding Questions.

- What is the Earth's geography like?
- Where do the world's people live?
- What is a culture?
- How do people use the world's resources?

Project Preview

You can also discover answers to the Guiding Questions by working on projects. Preview the following projects and choose one that you might like to do. For more details, see page 126.

The Geography Game Create a team game the whole class can play. Write clues about the unique physical features, climate, population, culture, and natural resources of a country.

World News Today Prepare a short speech about a country's economy and natural resources. Use a collection of newspaper articles.

Focus on Part of the Whole Set up a classroom map and picture display based on your research of the geography, climate, and population of a country.

Desktop Countries Make a desktop display. Include food samples, a flag, souvenirs, and other items typical of a country from which your ancestors came.

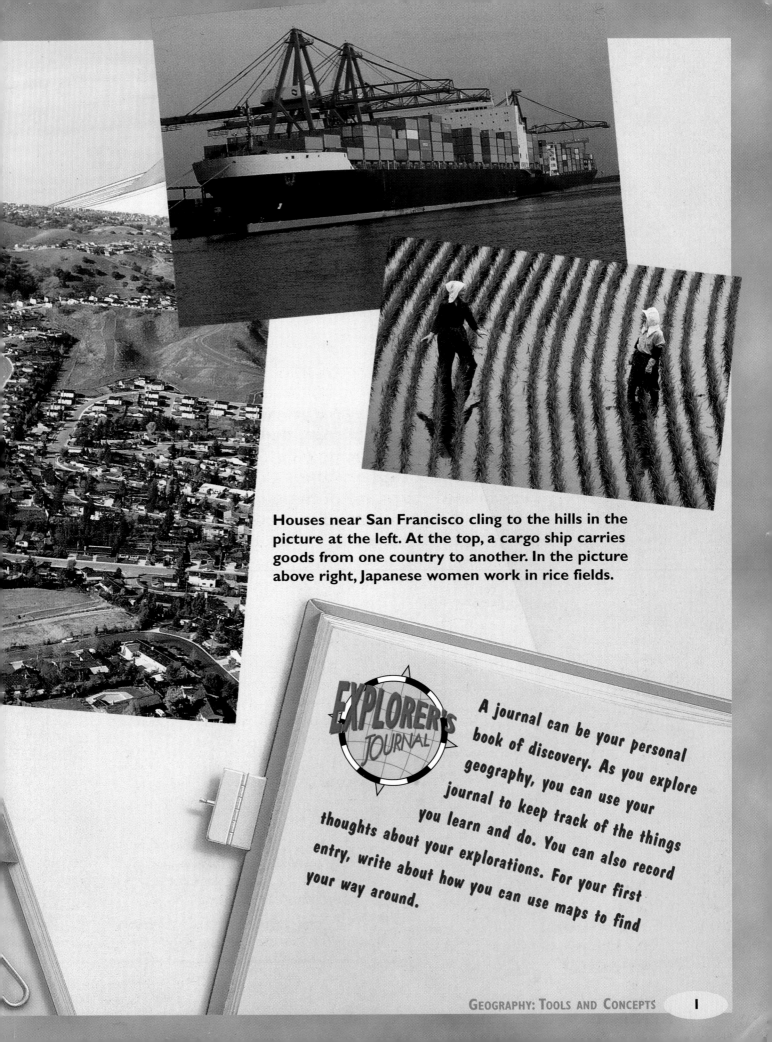

Houses near San Francisco cling to the hills in the picture at the left. At the top, a cargo ship carries goods from one country to another. In the picture above right, Japanese women work in rice fields.

EXPLORER'S JOURNAL

A journal can be your personal book of discovery. As you explore geography, you can use your journal to keep track of the things you learn and do. You can also record thoughts about your explorations. For your first entry, write about how you can use maps to find your way around.

DISCOVERY ACTIVITIES ABOUT

Geography

Learning about geography tools and concepts means being an explorer, and no explorer would start out without first checking some facts. Use the activities on the following pages to begin exploring the world of geography. They will help you learn what geography is and how it can help you.

World: Physical

▲ Why do people in this place wear this type of clothing?

▼ Why do relatively few people live in this area?

PLACE

1. Explore the Meaning of Geography Think about the word *geography*. The word part *geo* comes from a Greek word meaning "earth." *Graphy* means "science of," from an earlier word that meant "to write." How would you define *geography*?

People who are interested in geography are very curious about our world. They often ask questions such as "Where are things?" and "Why are they where they are?"

Look at the pictures on these two pages. The question that accompanies each picture is the type of question that geographers ask. For each picture, write another question a geographer might ask.

▲ Why did ancient people in this area become expert sailors?

▶ Why do visitors to this area become short of breath easily?

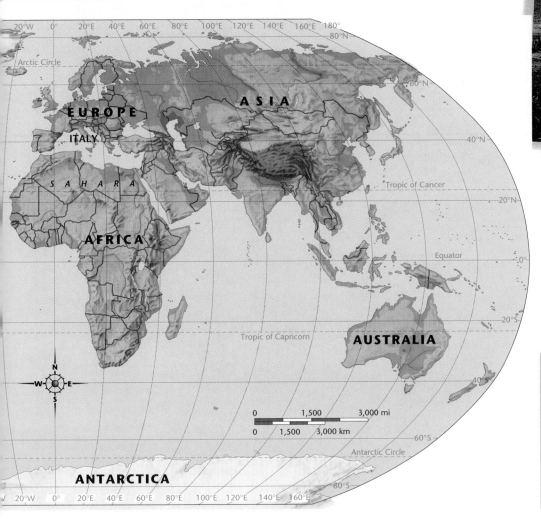

20°W 0° 20°E 40°E 60°E 80°E 100°E 120°E 140°E 160°E 180°
80°N
Arctic Circle
60°N
EUROPE   ASIA
ITALY
40°N
Tropic of Cancer
SAHARA
20°N
AFRICA
Equator 0°
20°S
Tropic of Capricorn
AUSTRALIA
0 1,500 3,000 mi
0 1,500 3,000 km
60°S
Antarctic Circle
ANTARCTICA
80°S
20°W 0° 20°E 40°E 60°E 80°E 100°E 120°E 140°E 160°E

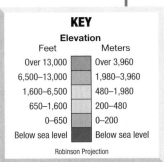

KEY

Elevation	
Feet	Meters
Over 13,000	Over 3,960
6,500–13,000	1,980–3,960
1,600–6,500	480–1,980
650–1,600	200–480
0–650	0–200
Below sea level	Below sea level

Robinson Projection

LOCATION

2. What Kinds of Maps Does Geo Leo Need?

Geographers do more than ask questions about the Earth. They also gather, organize, and analyze geographic information. Geographers use many different types of maps to do this work.

Examine the map below and the maps on the next page. Be sure to read the title of each map so you know what the map is about. Then help Geo Leo plan a trip to South Asia, an area that includes the countries of Afghanistan, India, Pakistan, and Bangladesh.

A. *"If I wanted to find out how many people live in the city of Mumbai, India, which map would I use?"*

B. *"On my trip to South Asia, I want to search for gigantic insects that live in tropical rain forests. Which map do I use to find the tropical rain forests?"*

C. *"South Asia is a region that has many different types of climate. Which map will help me bring the right gear for Pakistan's arid climate?"*

GEO LEO

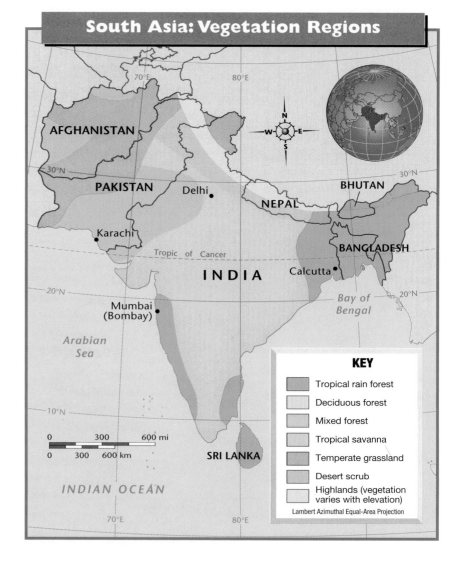

South Asia: Vegetation Regions

AFGHANISTAN

PAKISTAN

Delhi

NEPAL

BHUTAN

Karachi

Tropic of Cancer

BANGLADESH

INDIA

Calcutta

Bay of Bengal

Mumbai (Bombay)

Arabian Sea

SRI LANKA

INDIAN OCEAN

0   300   600 mi
0   300   600 km

KEY

- Tropical rain forest
- Deciduous forest
- Mixed forest
- Tropical savanna
- Temperate grassland
- Desert scrub
- Highlands (vegetation varies with elevation)

Lambert Azimuthal Equal-Area Projection

BONUS

Which type of vegetation grows in only one South Asian country?

South Asia: Climate Regions

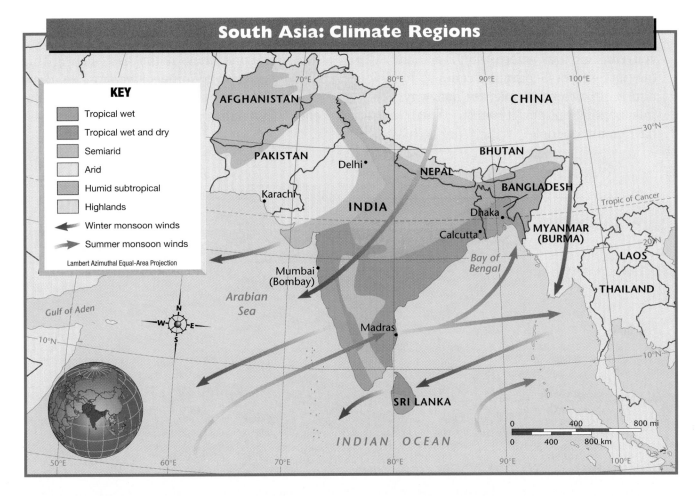

KEY

- Tropical wet
- Tropical wet and dry
- Semiarid
- Arid
- Humid subtropical
- Highlands
- ← Winter monsoon winds
- → Summer monsoon winds

Lambert Azimuthal Equal-Area Projection

AFGHANISTAN
CHINA
PAKISTAN
Delhi
BHUTAN
NEPAL
BANGLADESH
Karachi
INDIA
Dhaka
MYANMAR (BURMA)
Calcutta
LAOS
Mumbai (Bombay)
THAILAND
Arabian Sea
Bay of Bengal
Madras
Gulf of Aden
SRI LANKA
INDIAN OCEAN
Tropic of Cancer

0   400   800 mi
0   400   800 km

South Asia: Population Density

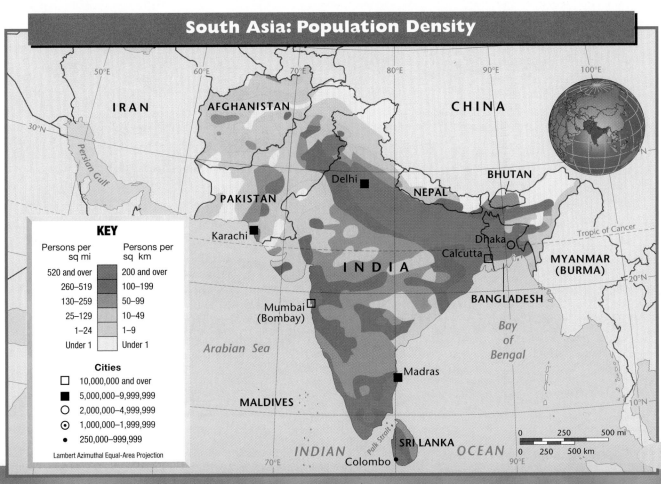

IRAN
AFGHANISTAN
CHINA
Delhi
BHUTAN
NEPAL
PAKISTAN
Karachi
Dhaka
Calcutta
MYANMAR (BURMA)
INDIA
BANGLADESH
Mumbai (Bombay)
Bay of Bengal
Arabian Sea
Madras
MALDIVES
SRI LANKA
Colombo
INDIAN OCEAN
Persian Gulf
Polk Strait
Tropic of Cancer

KEY

Persons per sq mi	Persons per sq km
520 and over	200 and over
260–519	100–199
130–259	50–99
25–129	10–49
1–24	1–9
Under 1	Under 1

Cities

- □ 10,000,000 and over
- ■ 5,000,000–9,999,999
- ○ 2,000,000–4,999,999
- ◉ 1,000,000–1,999,999
- • 250,000–999,999

Lambert Azimuthal Equal-Area Projection

0   250   500 mi
0   250   500 km

5

3. Analyze Density As you explore geography, you can find out where things are and why they are there. Geography can also help you figure out where people are and why. Study this population density map. Which places have many people? Which areas have the fewest? Why do you think people live where they do? Look back at the first map in this Activity Atlas for some clues. Try to draw conclusions about how physical features influence where cities are located.

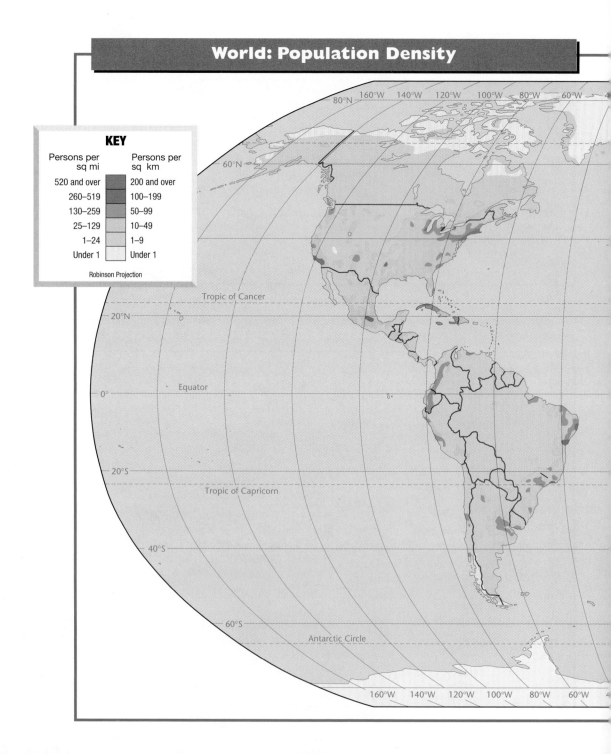

World: Population Density

KEY

Persons per sq mi	Persons per sq km
520 and over	200 and over
260–519	100–199
130–259	50–99
25–129	10–49
1–24	1–9
Under 1	Under 1

Robinson Projection

MOVEMENT

4. Create a "Mental Map" Mental maps exist in people's minds, not on paper. Each of us has a file of mental maps, which show the routes to and around places such as school, home, or the mall. To put a mental map on paper, simply choose somewhere you like to go, and draw a map of how you get there. Include as many details as you can—landmarks, streets, buildings, and other details. Then, test the map by giving it to another person to follow. Is it clear? If not, make corrections. Finally, compare it with the maps on the previous pages. What is different? What is the same?

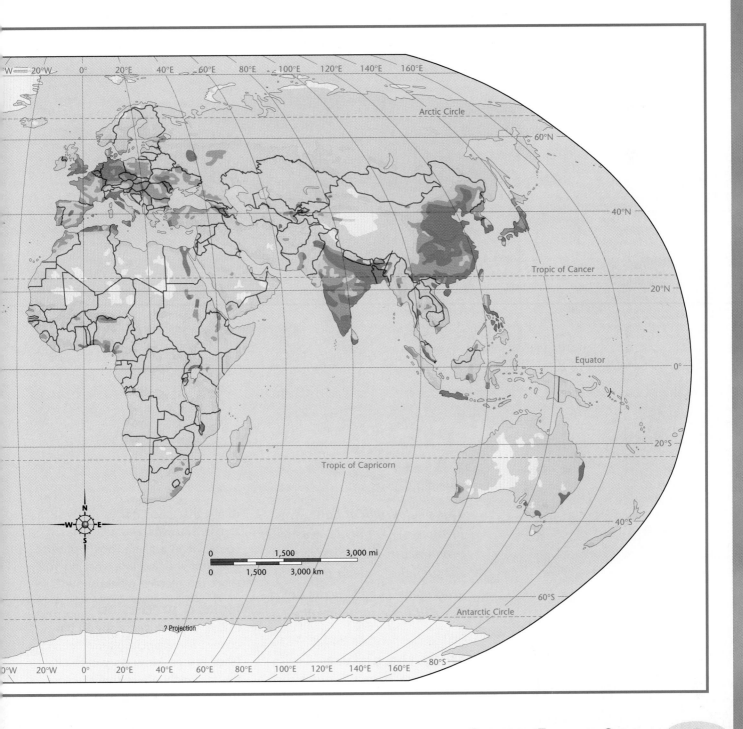

The World of Geography

PICTURE ACTIVITIES

This photograph of San Francisco, California, was taken from the air. Pictures like this tell something about the world of geography. The following activities will help you understand how.

Study the picture

Find several natural features such as forests, hills, or oceans. Notice things that people have made such as roads, towns, and industries. If someone in a plane took a photograph of your region, what do you think the picture would show?

Make a prediction

In this picture, dense fog all but covers San Francisco's Golden Gate Bridge. How do you think the fog might affect traffic across the bridge and ships in the water?

The Five Themes of Geography

Reach Into Your Background

If you were going to tell someone how to get to your school from where you live, what would you say? You might say something like "Go six blocks north and one block east." Or you might say your school is next to a local park or shopping center. These directions are examples of geography at work in your everyday life.

Questions to Explore

1. What is geography?

2. How can the five themes of geography help you understand the world?

Key Terms

geography
latitude
parallel
degree
Equator
longitude
meridian
Prime Meridian
plain

What would it be like to look at the Earth from a spaceship? Michael Collins, an astronaut who went to the moon, did just that. In his book *Carrying the Fire,* Collins described what he saw in July 1969 from his space capsule, 200 miles above the Earth. Even that far away, Collins could see natural features of the planet and evidence of the Earth's people.

"The Indian Ocean flashes incredible colors of emerald jade and opal in the shallow water surrounding the Maldive Islands; then on to the Burma [Myanmar] coast and nondescript green jungle, followed by mountains, coastline, and Hanoi. We can see fires burning off to the southeast, and we scramble for our one remaining still camera to record them. Now the sun glints in unusual fashion off the ocean near Formosa [Taiwan]. There are intersecting surface ripples just south of the island, patterns which are clearly visible and which, I think, must be useful to fishermen who need to know about these currents. The island itself is verdant—glistening green the color and shape of a shiny, well-fertilized gardenia leaf."

▼ From hundreds of miles in space, huge clouds drifting over the Indian Ocean look like haze. What features can you see on the land?

The Study of the Earth

From his high perch, Michael Collins described the colors of the ocean and the plant life on the land. He wrote about how land and water looked. He saw fires set by human beings. Collins was looking at the world as a geographer does.

Geography is the study of the Earth, our home. Geographers analyze the Earth from many points of view. They may discuss how far one place is from another. You do this when you tell someone directions. But they also study such things as oceans, plant life, landforms, and people. Geographers study how the Earth and its people affect each other.

The Themes of Geography: Five Ways to Look at the Earth

In their work, geographers are guided by two basic questions: (1) Where are things located? and (2) Why are they there? To find the answers, geographers use five themes to organize information. These themes are location, place, human-environment interaction, movement, and regions.

Location Geographers begin to study a place by finding where it is, or its location. There are two ways to talk about location—its absolute location and its relative location. Absolute location describes a place's exact position on the Earth. You might call absolute location a geographic address. Geographers identify the absolute location by

Predict What do you think each of the five geographic themes means?

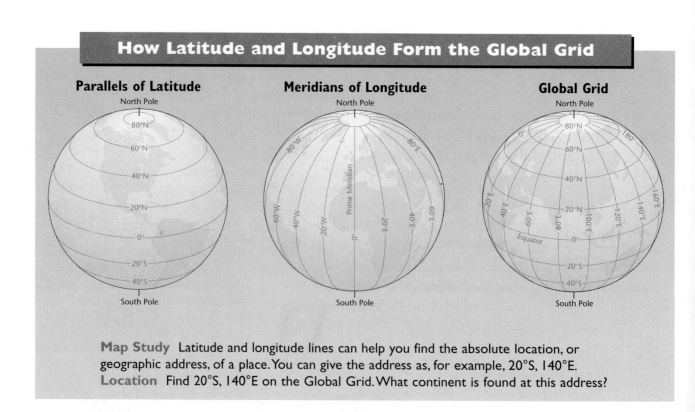

How Latitude and Longitude Form the Global Grid

Parallels of Latitude

North Pole
80°N
60°N
40°N
20°N
0°
20°S
40°S
South Pole

Meridians of Longitude

North Pole
80°W · 80°E
60°W · 40°W · 20°W · Prime Meridian · 20°E · 40°E · 60°E
0°
South Pole

Global Grid

North Pole
0° · 80°N · 180°
60°N
40°N
20°E · 40°E · 60°E · 80°E · 20°N · 100°E · 120°E · 140°E · 160°E
Equator · 0°
20°S
40°S
South Pole

Map Study Latitude and longitude lines can help you find the absolute location, or geographic address, of a place. You can give the address as, for example, 20°S, 140°E.
Location Find 20°S, 140°E on the Global Grid. What continent is found at this address?

The Hemispheres

Map Study The Equator and the Prime Meridian both divide the Earth in two. Each half is called a hemisphere. The Equator divides the Earth into Northern and Southern hemispheres. The Prime Meridian divides the Earth into Eastern and Western hemispheres. **Location** The United States is in North America. In which of the hemispheres is the United States located?

North Pole

Northern Hemisphere

NORTH AMERICA

ATLANTIC OCEAN

Equator

PACIFIC OCEAN

SOUTH AMERICA

Southern Hemisphere

South Pole

Eastern Hemisphere

EUROPE

ATLANTIC OCEAN

Prime Meridian

AFRICA

Western Hemisphere

---

using two kinds of imaginary lines around the Earth: latitude and longitude. With these lines, they can pinpoint any spot on the Earth.

Lines of **latitude** are east-west circles around the globe. They are also called **parallels,** because they are parallel to one another. They never meet. These circles divide the globe into units called **degrees.** In the middle of the globe is the parallel called the **Equator,** which is 0 degrees latitude. Geographers measure locations either north or south of the Equator. The farthest latitude north of the Equator is 90° north, the location of the North Pole. The farthest latitude south of the Equator is 90° south, the location of the South Pole.

Geographers also must pinpoint a place from east to west. For this they use lines of **longitude.** These lines, also called **meridians,** circle the globe from north to south. All meridians run through the North and South poles. The **Prime Meridian,** which runs through Greenwich, England, is 0 degrees longitude. Geographers describe locations as east or west of the Prime Meridian. The maximum longitude is 180°, which is halfway around the world from the Prime Meridian.

Geographers also discuss relative location. This explains where a place is by describing places near it. Suppose you live in Newburg, Indiana. You might give Newburg's relative location by saying: "I live in Newburg, Indiana. It's about 180 miles southwest of Indianapolis."

Place Geographers also study place. This includes a location's physical and human features. To describe physical features, you might say the climate is hot or cold. Or you might say that the land is hilly. To emphasize human features, you might talk about how many people live in a place and the kinds of work they do.

LINKS TO MATH

Using Latitude
Latitude can be used to measure distance north or south. One degree of latitude is equal to about 69 miles. For example, Fort Wayne, Indiana, is located 6 degrees north of Chattanooga, Tennessee. Therefore, we can determine that Fort Wayne is located about 414 miles north of Chattanooga (6 × 69 = 414).

Predict What two things about the environment of a place do you think the theme of interaction stresses?

Human-Environment Interaction   The theme of interaction stresses how people affect their environment, the physical characteristics of their natural surroundings, and how their environment affects them. Perhaps they deliberately cut trails into the mountainside. Perhaps they have learned how to survive with little water.

Geographers also use interaction to discuss the consequences of people's actions. For instance, because farms in Turkey receive little rain, people have built dams and canals to irrigate the land. On the good side, everyone in the region has more food. On the bad side, irrigation makes salt build up in the soil. Then farmers must treat the soil to get rid of the salt. As a result, food could become more expensive.

Movement   The theme of movement helps geographers understand the relationship among places. Movement helps explain how people, goods, and ideas get from one place to another. For example, when people from other countries came to the United States, they brought traditional foods that enriched the American way of life. The theme of movement helps you understand such cultural changes.

Regions   Geographers use the theme of regions to make comparisons. A region has a unifying characteristic such as climate, land, population, or history. For instance, the Nile Valley region is a snake-shaped region on either side of the Nile River. The region runs through several countries. Life in the valley is much different from life in the regions alongside the valley. There the landscape is mostly desert.

The Rift Valley—Lake Naivasha

Edwin Rioba
Age 16
Kenya
The Great Rift Valley of East Africa was formed over millions of years by earthquakes and volcanic eruptions. Running from Syria in Asia to Mozambique in Africa, it stretches some 4,500 miles (7,200 km). **Place** Based on this picture, what landforms do you think are commonly found in the Great Rift Valley?

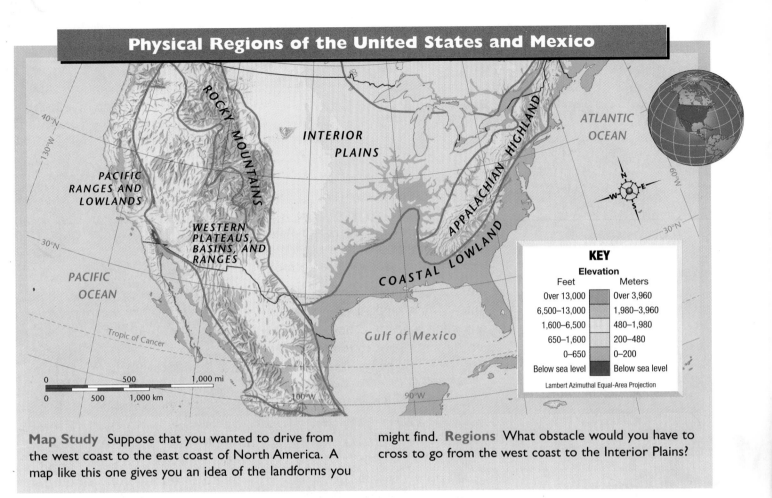

INTERIOR PLAINS

ROCKY MOUNTAINS

APPALACHIAN HIGHLAND

ATLANTIC OCEAN

PACIFIC RANGES AND LOWLANDS

WESTERN PLATEAUS, BASINS, AND RANGES

COASTAL LOWLAND

PACIFIC OCEAN

Tropic of Cancer

Gulf of Mexico

KEY

Elevation

Feet		Meters
Over 13,000		Over 3,960
6,500–13,000		1,980–3,960
1,600–6,500		480–1,980
650–1,600		200–480
0–650		0–200
Below sea level		Below sea level

Lambert Azimuthal Equal-Area Projection

Map Study Suppose that you wanted to drive from the west coast to the east coast of North America. A map like this one gives you an idea of the landforms you might find. **Regions** What obstacle would you have to cross to go from the west coast to the Interior Plains?

On maps, geographers use color and shape or special symbols to show regions. One map may show a **plain,** a region of flat land. The map above shows different regions of elevation, to show the height of land above sea level. A place can be part of several regions at the same time. For example, Houston, Texas, is in both a plains region and an oil-producing region.

SECTION 1 REVIEW

1. **Define** (a) geography, (b) latitude, (c) parallel, (d) degree, (e) Equator, (f) longitude, (g) meridian, (h) Prime Meridian, (i) plain.

2. What are two questions geographers ask when they study the Earth?

3. List the five themes of geography.

4. Give an example of how each theme can be used.

Critical Thinking

5. **Identifying Central Issues** You decide to start a geography club. When you invite a friend to join, she tells you she thinks geography is boring. She would rather learn about people, not just places. What could you say to change her mind?

Activity

6. **Writing to Learn** Make a chart listing the five geography themes. Find the location of your town or city on a map. Write down a relative location that tells where your city or town is. Then, take a walk around your neighborhood and think about the other four themes. Complete the chart by adding descriptions of your neighborhood that relate to each theme.

The Geographer's Tools

BEFORE YOU READ

Reach Into Your Background

Skulls-and-crossbones. Ships with black sails. Cannons. Swords. Treasure maps. That's right, MAPS. These things are all tools in great pirate tales. Maps are also one of the most important tools geographers use. Geographers and movie pirates aren't the only ones who use them. You do too!

Questions to Explore

1. What are some of the different ways of showing the Earth's surface and why do geographers use them?
2. What are the advantages and disadvantages of different kinds of maps and globes?

Key Terms

globe
scale
distortion
projection
compass rose
cardinal direction
key

Key People

Gerhardus Mercator
Arthur Robinson

You might expect a map to be printed on a piece of paper. But hundreds of years ago, people made maps out of whatever was available. The Inuit (IN oo it) people carved detailed, accurate maps on pieces of wood. The Inuits were once called Eskimos. These Native Americans have lived in northern regions of the world for centuries. They needed maps that were portable, durable, and waterproof. Carved maps remind us that making maps is not just an exercise in school. People rely on maps, sometimes for their very survival.

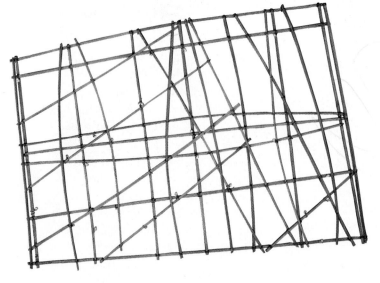

▼ The Marshall Islanders made wood maps of the southwest Pacific Ocean. Curved palm sticks show ocean currents and shells show islands.

Globes and Maps

Hundreds of years ago, people knew very little about the land and water beyond their own homes. Their maps showed only the areas they traveled. Other places either were left out or were only an empty space on their maps. Sometimes they filled the empty spaces with drawings of lands, creatures, and people from myths and stories.

As people explored the Earth, they collected information about the shapes and sizes of islands, continents, and bodies of water. Mapmakers wanted to present this information accurately. The best way was to put it on a **globe,** a round ball like the Earth itself. By using the same shape, mapmakers could show the continents and oceans of the Earth much as they really are. The only difference would be the **scale,** or size.

But there is a problem with globes. Try putting a globe in your pocket every morning. Try making a globe large enough to show the details of your state or community. A globe just cannot be complete enough to be useful and at the same time be small enough to be convenient. People, therefore, invented flat maps.

Flat maps, however, present another problem. The Earth is round. A map is flat. Can you flatten an orange peel without tearing it? There will be wrinkled and folded sections. The same thing happens when mapmakers create flat maps. It is impossible to show the Earth on a flat surface without some **distortion,** or change in the accuracy of its shapes and distances. Something is going to look larger or smaller than it is.

READ ACTIVELY

Predict Why do you think it would be hard to make an accurate map of the world on a flat sheet of paper?

An Orange Peel Map

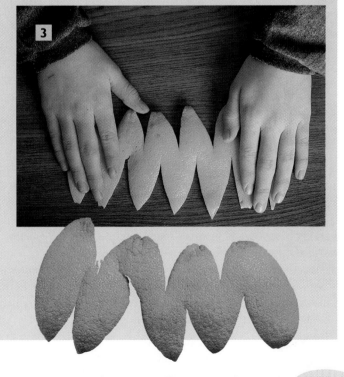

Chart Study It is almost impossible to flatten an orange peel. The peel tears, wrinkles, and stretches. Mapmakers can make a flat map of an orange—or of the Earth—by using mathematics. But even a map laid out to look like this flattened orange peel is not accurate. **Critical Thinking** Look carefully at the photographs. As the orange peel is flattened, what distortions do you think might occur?

Getting It All on the Map

In 1569, a geographer named Gerhardus Mercator (juh RAHR duhs muhr KAYT uhr) created a flat map to help sailors navigate long journeys around the globe. To make his map flat, Mercator expanded the area between the longitudes near the poles. Mercator's map was very useful to sailors. They made careful notes about the distortions they found on their journeys. More than 400 years after he made it, those notes and the Mercator **projection,** or method of putting a map of the Earth onto a flat piece of paper, is used by nearly all deep-sea navigators.

When Mercator made his map, he had to make some decisions. He made sure that the shape of the landmasses and ocean areas was similar to the shapes on a globe. But he had to stretch the spaces between the longitudes. This distorted the sizes of some of the land on his map. Land near the Equator was about right, but land near the poles became much larger than it should be. For example, on Mercator's map Greenland looks bigger than South America. Greenland is actually only one eighth as large as South America.

Geographers call a Mercator projection a conformal map. It shows correct shapes but not true distances or sizes. Other mapmakers used other techniques to try to draw an accurate map. For instance, an equal area map shows the correct size of landmasses but their shapes are altered. The Peters projection on the next page is an equal area map.

Mapmakers have tried other techniques. The interrupted projection (see next page) is like the ripped peel of an orange. By creating gaps in the picture of the world, mapmakers showed the size and shape of land accurately. The gaps make it impossible to figure distances correctly. You could not use this projection to chart a course across an ocean.

Today, many geographers believe Arthur Robinson's projection is the best world map available. This projection shows the size and shape of most of the land quite accurately. Sizes of the oceans and distances are also fairly accurate. However, even a Robinson projection has distortions, especially in areas around the edges of the map.

There are many other types of projections. Each has advantages and draw-backs. It all depends on how you want to use each one. The illustrations on this page and the next page show several projections.

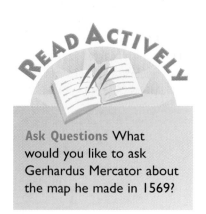

Ask Questions What would you like to ask Gerhardus Mercator about the map he made in 1569?

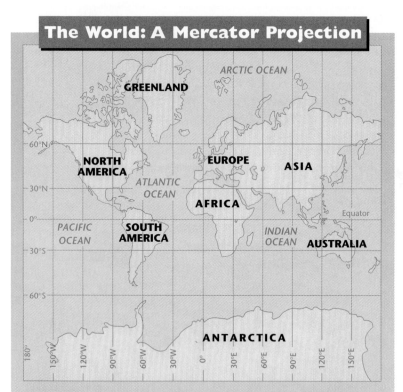

The World: A Mercator Projection

Map Study Mercator maps make areas near the poles look bigger than they are. This is because on a globe, the lines of longitude meet at the poles, but on a flat Mercator map, they are parallel. However, Mercator maps are useful to navigators because the longitude and latitude lines appear straight. Navigators can use these lines and a compass to plot a ship's route. **Place** Here Greenland looks bigger than it really is. It actually is about the size of Mexico. What other areas do you think might look larger than they should? Why?

Interrupted Projection

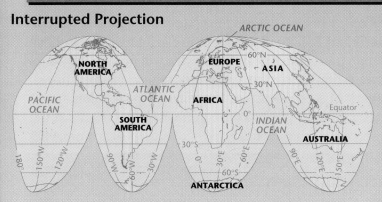

Map Study There are many ways to show a globe on a flat map. The interrupted projection map, on the left, shows the real sizes and shapes of continents. The equal area map, below left, shows size accurately. The Peters projection, below, shows land and ocean areas and correct directions accurately. **Location** Compare each projection with the more accurate Robinson projection below. What do each of these three projections distort?

Equal-Area Projection

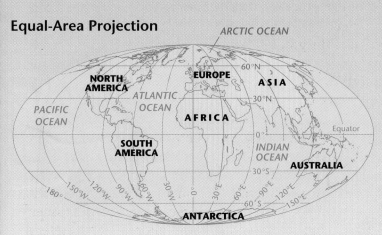

Peters Projection

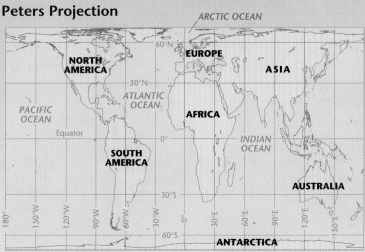

The World: A Robinson Projection

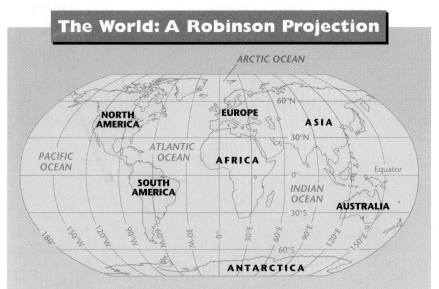

Map Study In 1988, the National Geographic Society adopted the Robinson projection as its official projection for world maps. While the Robinson projection does distort the globe a little, it shows the sizes and shapes of countries most accurately. **Movement** Do you think the Robinson projection would be as useful to a navigator as the Mercator projection? Why or why not?

The Parts of a Map

Look at the two maps below. One is an imaginary pirate map. The other is a map of the Grand Bahama Island, in the Caribbean Sea. Believe it or not, the pirate map has some features that you will find on any map. Of course, regular maps don't have the X that tells where the treasure is, but you will find a mark of some sort that shows your destination.

A Pirate Map and a Road Map

Map Study Almost all maps have some things in common. A compass rose shows direction. A key explains special symbols. A grid often shows longitude and latitude. The road map below has a grid of numbers and letters to help locate places.

Location What airport is located at B-1?

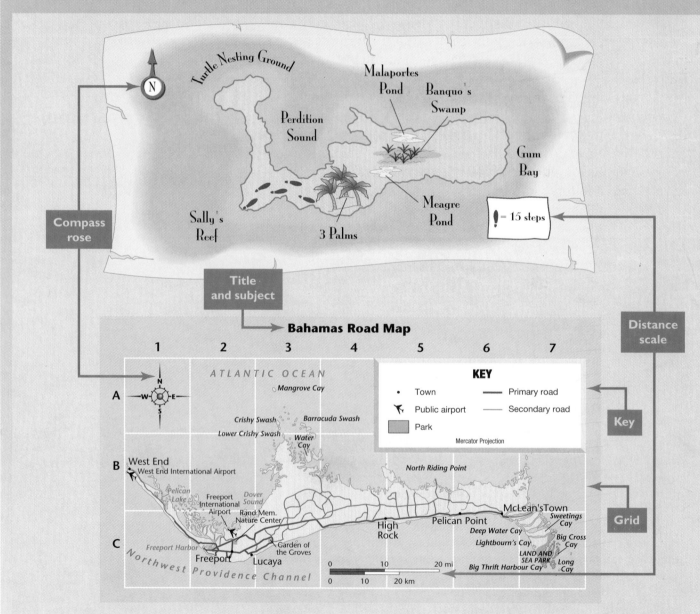

The pirate map has an arrow pointing north. On the regular map, you will find what geographers call a **compass rose,** which is a model of a compass. It tells the **cardinal directions,** which are north, south, east, and west.

On a pirate map, marks will tell you how many paces to walk to find the treasure. On a conventional map, an indicator for scale tells you how far to go to get to your destination. The scale tells you that one inch on the map represents a particular distance on the land. Scales vary, depending on the map. On one map, an inch may equal one mile. On another map, an inch may equal 100 miles.

On the pirate map, special symbols indicate landmarks such as trails, an oddly shaped rock, a tree with a broken branch, a small stream, or a cave. Regular maps also have symbols. They are explained in the section of the map called the **key,** or legend. It may include symbols for features such as national and state parks, various types of roads, sizes of towns and cities, or important landmarks.

A regular map includes some things that the pirate map doesn't. For instance, the pirate map doesn't have a map title. On a regular map, a title tells you the subject of the map.

A treasure map does not have a grid, either. Some maps use a grid of parallels and meridians. Remember that parallels show latitude, or distance north and south of the Equator. Meridians show longitude, or distance east and west of the Prime Meridian. On some maps, the area is too small for longitude and latitude to be helpful. These maps usually have a grid of letters and numbers to help people find things.

Every part of a map has a very simple purpose. That is to make sure that people who use maps have accurate information they need. The more you know about maps, the easier it will be for you to use them well—even if you're hunting for buried treasure!

READ ACTIVELY

Connect What parts of a map do you think are most helpful to you?

SECTION 2 REVIEW

1. **Define** (a) globe, (b) scale, (c) distortion, (d) projection, (e) compass rose, (f) cardinal direction, (g) key.

2. **Identify** (a) Gerhardus Mercator, (b) Arthur Robinson.

3. What are some advantages and disadvantages of using a globe to show the Earth's surface?

4. Why are there so many different types of map projections?

5. How can knowing the parts of a map help you?

Critical Thinking

6. **Making Comparisons** You are planning a hiking trip with your family to a nearby state park. Your family uses two maps: a road map and a map of the park. What advantages does each map have?

Activity

7. **Writing to Learn** Think of a place that you like to visit. How would you tell a friend to get there? Make some notes about directions and landmarks you could include in a map. Then make a map that shows your friend how to get there.

SKILLS ACTIVITY

Expressing Problems Clearly

eographers know that geography is not just about maps and where places are. Geography is about change. After all, the Earth is always being changed by natural forces. You and the nearly six billion other people on the planet also change it. Geographers use geography to view and understand these changes.

"Geography," as one of the world's leading geographers put it, "turns out to be much more, and much more significant, than many of us realized."

Are you still having a problem understanding what geography is? You can help yourself by expressing that problem clearly.

Get Ready

One way geographers help organize their study of the Earth is to use the five themes of geography. Look for them in Chapter 1. Understanding the five themes will help you express the meaning of geography.

▲ What can a geography walk teach you about your surroundings?

Try It Out

A. Identify the problem. You may think that geography is only about maps and the names of countries. You need to know what geography really is.

B. Think about exactly what the problem is. You know that the five geography themes should help you figure out what geography is. But maybe you have trouble understanding the five themes.

C. Put the problem into words. Write a sentence that tells the problem. There are many sentences that will work. Perhaps you will think of one something like this.

> What are the five geography themes, and how are they connected to what I know about the world?

Apply the Skill

Practice understanding the five themes of geography by going for a geography walk. Find out how the themes are reflected in the world around you. You don't have to walk near mountains or rivers. You can walk near your home or school.

1 Take a notebook and a pencil. You will need to take notes on your walk. Put into the notebook a list of the five geography themes and their definitions.

2 Take someone with you. Walk with a family member or a friend. Be sure to walk in a safe place.

3 Look for geography. As you walk, look for examples of the five themes. Does a delivery truck drive by? That is an example of movement. Is it carrying bread? Wheat for the bread was grown on a farm. That's human-environment interaction.

4 Record the geography around you. Find as many examples of each theme as you can. Record each one in your notebook.

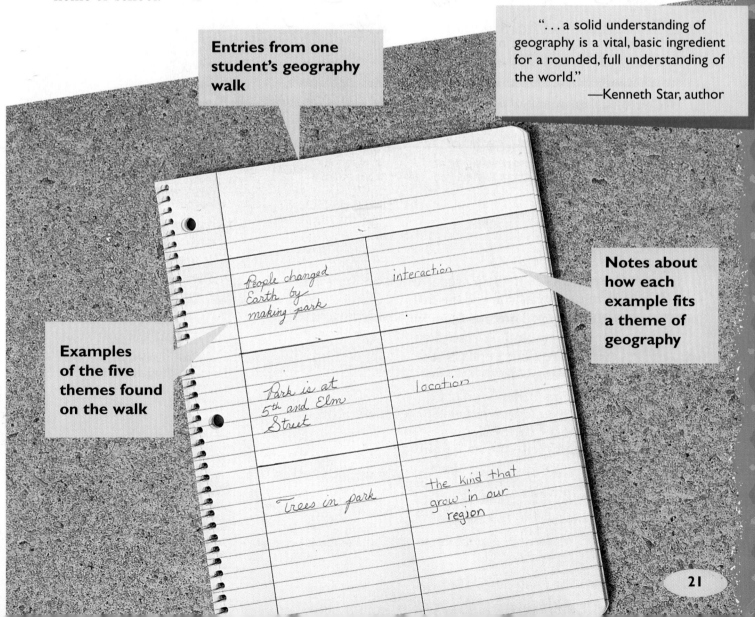

Entries from one student's geography walk

"...a solid understanding of geography is a vital, basic ingredient for a rounded, full understanding of the world."
—Kenneth Star, author

Notes about how each example fits a theme of geography

Examples of the five themes found on the walk

People changed Earth by making park — interaction

Park is at 5th and Elm Street — location

Trees in park — the kind that grow in our region

21

Review and Activities

Reviewing Main Ideas

1. (a) What two questions do geographers always ask about a place? (b) What do geographers use to help answer the questions?
2. Explain how geographers locate any spot on the Earth.
3. You read in the newspaper that geographers are part of a team of people planning a new highway in your area. List and describe three geography themes that the team might use.
4. If you had to make a map, how would you show the Earth so that the size and shape of its features and the distances between them were accurate?
5. An ocean navigator uses one particular map to determine the best route from New Hampshire to Florida. An official who must solve an argument about which country owns a certain piece of land uses a different kind of map. Why do these two people use different maps?

Reviewing Key Terms

Use each key term below in a sentence that shows the meaning of the term.

1. geography
2. latitude
3. parallel
4. degree
5. Equator
6. longitude
7. meridian
8. Prime Meridian
9. plain
10. globe
11. scale
12. distortion
13. projection
14. compass rose
15. cardinal direction
16. key

Critical Thinking

1. **Recognizing Cause and Effect** Explain why today's maps are more accurate than maps drawn hundreds of years ago.
2. **Expressing Problems Clearly** Explain why there are so many different types of map projections.

Graphic Organizer

Choose a place that interests you. It might be a place you know very well or a place you have never seen. Fill in the web chart on the right. Write the name of the place in the center oval. If you know the place well, list facts or information under each theme. If you don't know the place, list questions that would fit each theme.

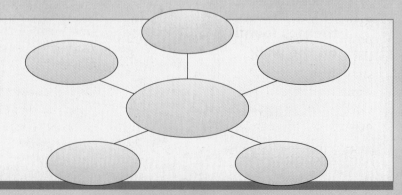

Map Activity

The Globe
For each place listed below, write the letter from the map that shows its location.

1. Prime Meridian

2. Equator

3. North Pole

4. South Pole

5. Europe

6. Africa

7. South America

8. North America

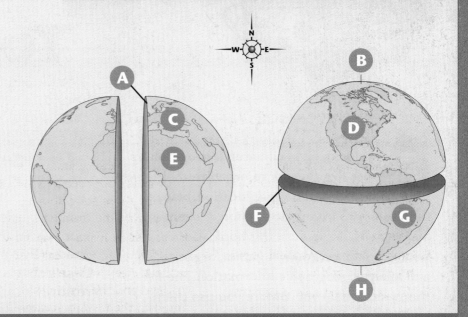

Writing Activity

Writing a Paragraph
Write a paragraph describing ways that you have seen people use maps. You may include such things as road maps, maps for seats in a sports arena or areas in a museum, or even hand-drawn maps to a friend's house.

Internet Activity
Use a search engine to find the **National Geographic Society** site. Find the link to the **Map Machine,** and click on it. Choose **Political Maps** or **Physical Maps.** Click on the different regions to see the maps. With a partner, make a physical or a political map of the region of your choice.

Skills Review

Turn to the Skills Activity.

Review the steps for expressing problems clearly. Then complete the following: (a) Name one strategy you can use to help you express problems clearly. (b) How can expressing problems clearly help you to solve problems?

How Am I Doing?
Answer these questions to help you check your progress.

1. Can I list the five themes of geography and describe how they are used?

2. Do I understand the advantages and disadvantages of different ways of showing the Earth's surface?

3. What information from this chapter can I use in my book project?

A Five-Theme Tour

As discussed in Chapter 1, geographers use five themes to organize their study of the world and its people: location, place, human-environment interaction, movement, and regions. As you use this book, you will also be a geographer. You will gather, organize, and analyze geographic information. The five themes can help you. Before you use them, however, it helps to thoroughly know what they mean. A good way to explore the themes is through real-life examples.

Purpose

In this activity, you will plan a world tour. Your destination is either the world's mountains or the world's rivers. As you plan your tour, you will also explore the five geography themes.

Decide Where You Will Go

First, select the mountain tour or the river tour. Then, use a physical map of the world to choose five places you will visit along the way. Research each place so you can describe its relative location. That is, you will be able to write down descriptions such as "The Nile River in northeast Africa flows through Sudan and Egypt." This is an example of the theme of location, which answers the question "Where is this place?"

◀▲ Tourists enjoy the Nile River and the sights of Egypt.

Describe the Places on Your Tour

Use the theme of place to write an exciting description of each place on your tour. The theme of place answers the question "What is this place like?" Include both physical and human characteristics. Physical characteristics are the natural features of the Earth. Things related to people are human characteristics. Your research will help you focus on what makes your places unique.

Next, focus on the theme of human-environment interaction. This theme answers the questions: "How do people use this place? How and why have people changed this place?" For each place on your tour, gather information that answers these two questions. Add the information to your descriptions.

Plan a Travel Route

The theme of movement answers the question "How has this place been affected by the movement of people, goods, and ideas?" To explore this theme, choose just one place. Do research to plan a travel route from your community to that place.

Call or visit a travel agent to find the number of miles for each section of the journey. Add the distances together to find the total number of miles for the trip.

Learn About the Language

The theme of regions answers the question "How is this place similar to and different from other regions?" To help you learn about this theme, focus on the same one special place. Do research to find out what languages people speak there. Then find other places in the world where people speak the same languages. This activity will show you one type of region—a

Links to Other Subjects

Writing descriptions
of places .... **Language Arts**

Adding distances in miles .... **Math**

Creating a brochure .... **Art**

language region. Your place belongs to a group of places that share something similar: the same language.

Do additional research to make a chart of some common words in the languages spoken in your place. For instance, you might find the words for "hello," "good-bye," "thank you," and "please." These are words a visitor will need to know.

Create a Travel Brochure

Now, use the information you have gathered to create a brochure about the places you will visit on your tour. The brochure will tell everyone about your plans. Include the descriptions you wrote for each place on the tour. Also include your travel route and language chart. Decorate the brochure with drawings or magazine pictures.

ANALYSIS AND CONCLUSION

Write a summary that tells which type of tour you planned—mountains or rivers. Be sure to answer the following questions in your summary.

1. How did the process of planning your tour help you learn about the five themes?

2. Which of the five themes do you think are most important in your tour?

Earth's Physical Geography

PICTURE ACTIVITIES

Before we had satellites in space, people could only imagine how the Earth truly looked. Now, satellites let people see the Earth's land and water beneath a swirling mix of clouds. The following activities will help you get to know your planet.

Be a global weather forecaster

Weather forecasters use satellite pictures like the one above to see weather patterns. The white areas in the picture are clouds. What land areas do you recognize? How do you recognize them? On the day this picture was taken, what areas seem cloudier? Swirling patterns may indicate storms. Do you see any storm patterns?

Become an Earth expert

Watch especially for one of these topics as you read this chapter: Beneath the Earth's Surface, On the Earth's Surface, and Beyond the Earth's Atmosphere. Which one would you like to be an expert on?

Our Planet, the Earth

BEFORE YOU READ

Reach Into Your Background

What is spring like where you live? What is winter like? How long do these seasons last

where you live? If you can answer these questions, consider yourself an amateur geographer. You have noticed the changes in your region at different times of the year.

Questions to Explore

1. How does the Earth move in space?
2. Why do seasons change?

Key Terms

orbit
revolution
axis
rotation

low latitudes
high latitudes
middle latitudes

Key Places

Tropic of Cancer
Tropic of Capricorn
Arctic Circle
Antarctic Circle

"The Sky Father opened his hand. Within every crease there lay innumerable grains of shining maize [corn]. In his thumb and forefinger he took some of the shining grains and placed them in the sky as brilliant stars to be a guide to humans when the bright sun was hidden."

This is part of an ancient myth of the Pueblos, who lived in what today is the southwestern United States. They used the story to explain the appearance of the night sky.

▼ Thousands of years ago, Native Americans laid this wheel out in Wyoming's Bighorn Mountains. They may have used it to track the movements of the stars.

The Earth and the Sun

The Earth, the sun, the planets, and the twinkling stars in the sky are all part of a galaxy, or family of stars. We call our galaxy the Milky Way because the lights from its billions of stars look like a trail of spilled milk across the night sky. Our sun is one of those stars. Although the sun is just a tiny speck in the Milky Way, it is the center of everything for the Earth.

Predict What causes day to change into night?

Understanding Days and Nights   The sun may be about 93 million miles (150 million km) away, but it still provides the Earth with heat and light. The Earth travels around the sun in an oval-shaped path called an **orbit.** It takes $365\frac{1}{4}$ days, or one year, for the Earth to complete one **revolution,** or circular journey, around the sun.

As the Earth revolves around the sun, it is also spinning in space. The Earth turns around its **axis**—an imaginary line running through it between the North and South poles. Each complete turn, which takes about 24 hours, is called a **rotation.** As the Earth rotates, it is daytime on the side facing the sun. It is night on the side away from the sun.

Understanding Seasons   At certain times of the year, days are longer than nights, and at other times, nights are longer than days. This happens, in part, because the Earth's axis is at an angle. At some points in the Earth's orbit, the tilt causes a region to face toward the sun for more hours than it faces away from the sun. Days are longer. At other times, the region faces away from the sun for more hours than it faces toward the sun. Days are shorter.

The Earth's tilt and orbit also cause changes in temperatures during the seasons. The warmth you feel at any time of year depends on how directly the sunlight falls upon you. Some regions receive a great deal of fairly direct sunlight, while other regions receive no direct sunlight. Special latitude lines divide up these regions of the world. You can see them on the map on the next page.

How Night Changes Into Day

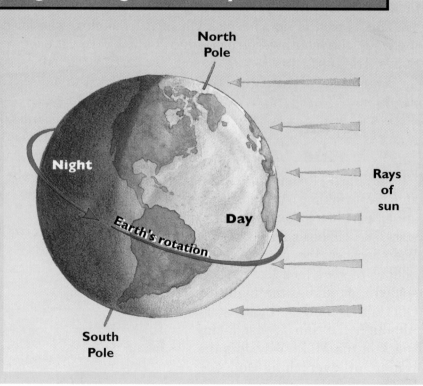

Chart Study This diagram shows how places on the Earth move from night into day. Today, it takes almost 24 hours for the Earth to make one complete rotation. But when the Earth first formed millions of years ago, it spun 10 times faster. A full cycle of day and night on the Earth lasted just over two hours. **Critical Thinking** As time passes, the Earth spins more and more slowly. What will eventually happen to the length of a day? Find North America on the globe. Which coast gets daylight first?

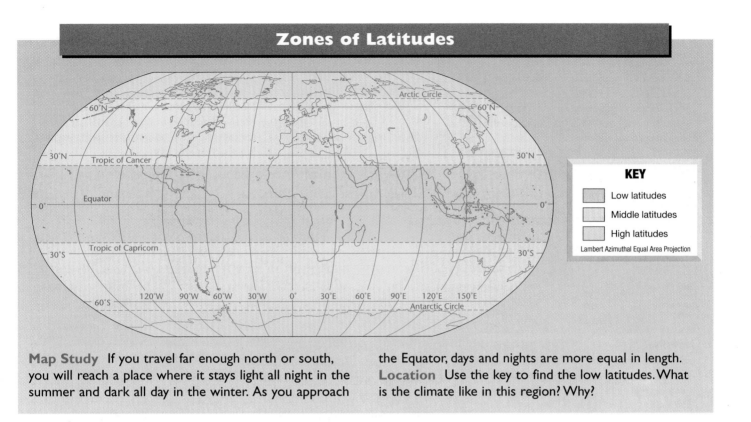

Map Study If you travel far enough north or south, you will reach a place where it stays light all night in the summer and dark all day in the winter. As you approach the Equator, days and nights are more equal in length. **Location** Use the key to find the low latitudes. What is the climate like in this region? Why?

Looking at Latitudes

Look at the diagram on the next page. In some places on the Earth, the sun is directly overhead at particular days during the year. One place is the Equator, an imaginary latitude line that circles the Earth at 0°, exactly halfway between the North Pole (90°N) and the South Pole (90°S). On about March 21 and September 23, the sun is directly over the Equator. On those days, all over the Earth, days are almost exactly as long as nights. People call these days the spring and fall equinoxes.

Two other imaginary latitude lines lie $23\frac{1}{2}°$ north and $23\frac{1}{2}°$ south of the Equator. At $23\frac{1}{2}°$N is the Tropic of Cancer. Here, the sun shines directly above on June 21 or 22. This is the first day of summer, or the summer solstice (SOHL stiss), in the Northern Hemisphere. At $23\frac{1}{2}°$S is the Tropic of Capricorn. Here, the sun shines directly above on December 21 or 22. This is the first day of winter, or the winter solstice, in the Northern Hemisphere. The seasons are reversed in the Southern Hemisphere. When would the summer solstice occur there?

The area between the Tropic of Cancer and the Tropic of Capricorn is called the **low latitudes,** or the tropics. Any location in the low latitudes receives direct sunlight at some time during the year. In this region, it is almost always hot.

Two other latitude lines set off distinct regions. To the north of the Equator, at $66\frac{1}{2}°$N, is the Arctic Circle. To the south of the Equator, at $66\frac{1}{2}°$S, is the Antarctic Circle. The regions between these circles and the poles are the **high latitudes,** or the polar zones. The high latitudes receive no direct sunlight. It is very cool to bitterly cold.

Midnight Sun Earth's axis is at an angle, which makes the Earth seem to lean. When the North Pole leans toward the sun, the sun never sets. At the same time, the South Pole leans away from the sun, so at the South Pole, the sun never rises. This lasts for six months. When the South Pole leans toward the sun, this pole has six months of continuous sunlight. Sunlight at the poles falls at an angle, so the poles receive very little heat.

Seasons of the Northern Hemisphere

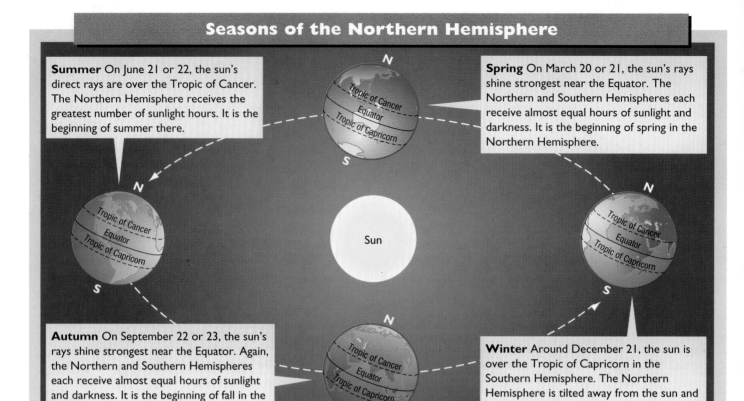

Summer On June 21 or 22, the sun's direct rays are over the Tropic of Cancer. The Northern Hemisphere receives the greatest number of sunlight hours. It is the beginning of summer there.

Spring On March 20 or 21, the sun's rays shine strongest near the Equator. The Northern and Southern Hemispheres each receive almost equal hours of sunlight and darkness. It is the beginning of spring in the Northern Hemisphere.

Autumn On September 22 or 23, the sun's rays shine strongest near the Equator. Again, the Northern and Southern Hemispheres each receive almost equal hours of sunlight and darkness. It is the beginning of fall in the Northern Hemisphere.

Winter Around December 21, the sun is over the Tropic of Capricorn in the Southern Hemisphere. The Northern Hemisphere is tilted away from the sun and it is the beginning of winter there.

Chart Study As the Earth moves around the Sun, summer changes to fall and fall changes to winter. But the warmest and coldest weather does not start as soon as summer and winter begin. Why? Oceans and lakes also affect the weather, and they warm up and cool off slowly. **Critical Thinking** Australia lies in the Southern Hemisphere. What is the season in Australia when it is winter in the United States?

Two areas remain: the **middle latitudes,** or the temperate zones. At some times of the year, these areas receive fairly direct sunlight. At other times, they receive fairly indirect sunlight. So, the middle latitudes have seasons: spring, summer, winter, and fall. Each lasts about three months and has distinct patterns of daylight, temperature, and weather.

SECTION 1 REVIEW

1. **Define** (a) orbit, (b) revolution, (c) axis, (d) rotation, (e) low latitudes, (f) high latitudes, (g) middle latitudes.

2. **Identify** (a) Tropic of Cancer, (b) Tropic of Capricorn, (c) Arctic Circle, (d) Antarctic Circle.

3. The Earth revolves and the Earth rotates. Explain the difference between the two.

4. Why are seasons different in the Northern and Southern hemispheres?

5. What causes the Earth to have seasons?

6. Describe conditions in the high, middle, and low latitudes.

Critical Thinking
7. **Drawing Conclusions** What would happen to plant and animal life if the Earth did not tilt on its axis? Why?

Activity
8. **Writing to Learn** Write a storybook for a young child explaining the relationship between the Earth and the sun.

Land, Air, and Water

BEFORE YOU READ

Reach Into Your Background
Think of one of your favorite outdoor activities, such as skiing, cycling, or hiking. Tell how the shape of the land helps you enjoy it.

Questions to Explore
1. What forces shape the land?
2. What are the Earth's major landforms?

Key Terms

landform	plate
mountain	weathering
hill	erosion
plateau	atmosphere
plain	
plate tectonics	

Key Places
Ring of Fire
Pangaea

Listen to the words of Megumi Fujiwara, a Japanese medical student who lived through the Great Hanshin Earthquake in 1995.

"Early that morning, I had awakened hearing explosions and feeling my body rising. I knew immediately that it was an earthquake and expected the shaking to last only a moment. It didn't, and after landing back on my futon [bed], I lay frozen, listening to windows rattling and breaking [and] seeing objects flying above. Then everything blacked out. I awoke some time later, inhaling dust and unable to see anything. [I] found myself outside at ground level, rather than in my second-story apartment. Open sky had replaced my ceiling."

Fujiwara was lucky. The Great Hanshin Earthquake killed 5,500 people when it struck Kobe (KOH bay), Japan, on January 17, 1995.

Forces Inside the Earth

Japan knows about earthquakes because it is part of what geographers call the "Ring of Fire." About 90 percent of the world's earthquakes and many of the world's active volcanoes occur on the Ring, which circles the Pacific Ocean. Earthquakes and volcanoes are two forces that shape and reshape the Earth. They provide clues about the Earth's structure, and they are one reason why the Earth's surface constantly changes.

What Is the Earth Made Of?   To understand events like volcanoes and earthquakes, you must study the Earth's structure. Pictures of the Earth show a great deal of water and some land. The water covers about 75 percent of the Earth's surface in lakes, rivers, seas, and oceans. Only 25 percent of the Earth's surface is land.

In part, continents are unique because of their **landforms,** or shapes and types of land. **Mountains** are landforms that rise usually more than 2,000 feet (610 m) above sea level. They are wide at the bottom and rise steeply to a narrow peak or ridge. **Hills** are lower and less steep than mountains, with rounded tops. A **plateau** is a large, mostly flat area that rises above the surrounding land. At least one side of a plateau has a steep slope. **Plains** are large areas of flat or gently rolling land. Many are along coasts. Others are in the interiors of some continents.

Pangaea: The Supercontinent   For hundreds of years, as geographers studied the Earth's landforms, they asked "where" and "why" questions. When they looked at the globe, they thought they saw a relationship between landforms that were very far apart.

Predict Why do scientists think the Earth once had only one, large landmass?

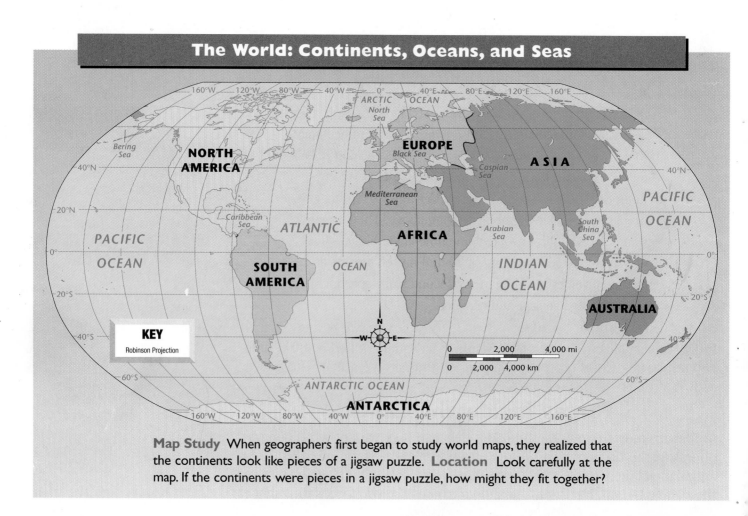

The World: Continents, Oceans, and Seas

Map Study When geographers first began to study world maps, they realized that the continents look like pieces of a jigsaw puzzle. **Location** Look carefully at the map. If the continents were pieces in a jigsaw puzzle, how might they fit together?

The Movement of the Continents

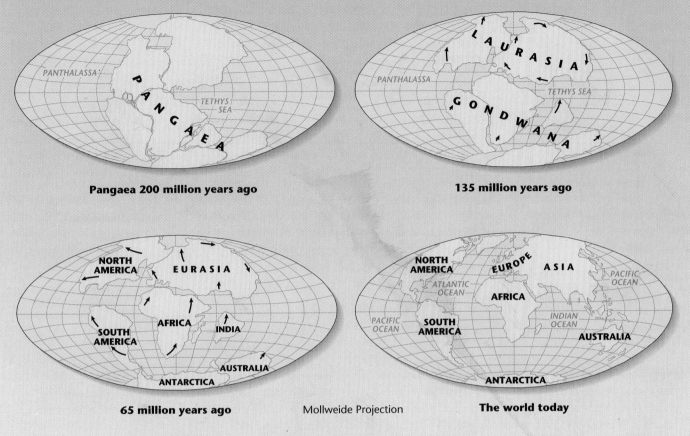

Pangaea 200 million years ago

135 million years ago

65 million years ago

Mollweide Projection

The world today

Map Study The first animals to walk on land lived on Pangaea. Birds and dinosaurs first appeared on Laurasia and Gondwana, and dinosaurs died not long after the continents began to separate. Humans did not appear until two million years ago. **Movement** If you were a scientist trying to prove the theory of plate tectonics, what clues would you look for?

Today, geographers theorize that millions of years ago the Earth had only one huge landmass. They called it Pangaea (pan JEE uh). Scientists reasoned that about 200 million years ago, some force made Pangaea split into several pieces, and it began to move apart. Over millions of years, the pieces formed separate continents.

But why did the continents separate? To explain this question, geographers use a theory called **plate tectonics.** It says the outer skin of the Earth, called the crust, is broken into huge pieces called **plates.** The continents and oceans are the top of the crust. Below the plates is a layer of rock called magma, which is hot enough to be fairly soft. The plates float on the magma, altering the shape of the Earth's surface. Continents are part of plates, and plates shift over time. We cannot see them move because it is very slow and takes a long time. When geographers say a plate moves quickly, they mean it may shift two inches (five cm) a year.

The World: Plate Boundaries

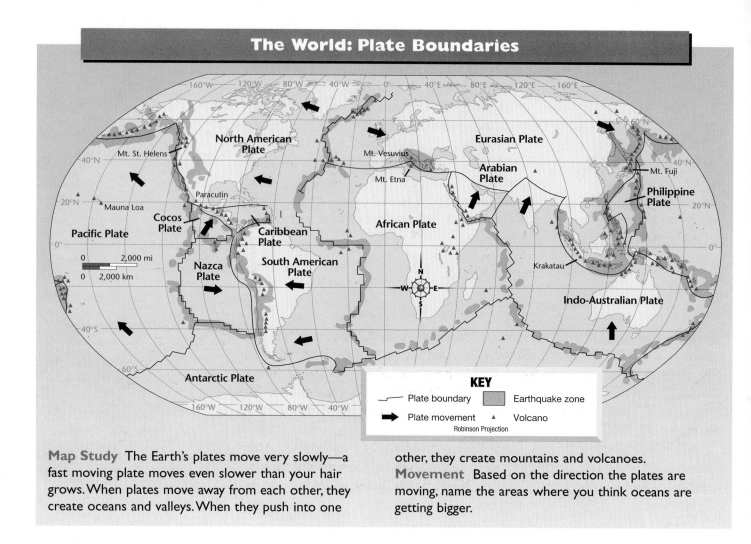

KEY

— Plate boundary   ▨ Earthquake zone

➜ Plate movement   ▲ Volcano

Robinson Projection

Map Study The Earth's plates move very slowly—a fast moving plate moves even slower than your hair grows. When plates move away from each other, they create oceans and valleys. When they push into one other, they create mountains and volcanoes.

Movement Based on the direction the plates are moving, name the areas where you think oceans are getting bigger.

A New Island For thousands of years, magma from underwater volcanoes built up until it rose above sea level to create the Hawaiian islands. Today, a new island, named Loihi (low EE hee), is forming. Already two miles (3.2 km) high, it has 3,000 feet (914 m) to go before it breaks the ocean's surface. Loihi erupts almost all the time. It causes earthquakes and tidal waves that threaten the other islands.

Volcanoes, Earthquakes, and Shifting Plates Look at the map of plate boundaries on this page. It shows that plates move in different directions. In some places, plates move apart, and magma leaks out through cracks in the crust. In the oceans, over time, the cooling rock builds up to form lines of underwater mountains called ridges. On either side of the line, the plates move away from each other.

In other places, the plates push against one another, forcing one plate under the other. Tremendous pressure and heat builds up. Molten rock races upward, exploding onto the surface and producing a volcano.

Along plate boundaries, there are many weak places in the Earth's crust. When plates push against one another, the crust cracks and splinters from the pressure. The cracks are called faults. When the crust moves along faults, it releases great amounts of energy in the form of earthquakes. These movements can cause dramatic changes.

Forces on the Earth's Surface

Forces like volcanoes slowly build up the Earth; other forces slowly break it down. Often, the forces that break the Earth down are not as dramatic as volcanoes, but the results can last just as long.

Weathering is a process that breaks rocks down into tiny pieces. Three things cause weathering: wind, rain, and ice. Slowly but surely, they wear away the Earth's landforms. Hills and low, rounded mountains show what weathering can do. The Appalachian Mountains in the eastern United States once were as high as the Rocky Mountains of the western United States. Wind and rain weathered them into much lower peaks. Weathering helps create soil, too. Tiny pieces of rock combine with decayed animal and plant material to form soil.

Once this breaking down has taken place, small pieces of rock may be carried to new places by a process called **erosion.** Weathering and erosion slowly create new landforms.

Air and Water:
Two Ingredients for Life

The Earth is surrounded by a thick layer of special gases called the **atmosphere.** It provides life-giving oxygen for people and animals and life-giving carbon dioxide for plants. The atmosphere also acts like a blanket. It holds in the amount of heat from the sun that makes life possible. Winds, as you can see in the map below, help to distribute this heat around the globe.

About 97 percent of the Earth's water is found in its oceans. This water is salty. Fresh water, or water without salt, makes up only a tiny percentage of all the Earth's water. Most fresh water is frozen at the

Predict What two things do people, other animals, and plants need to survive?

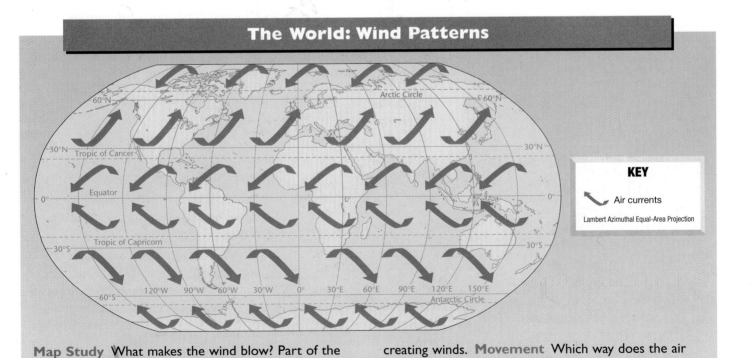

The World: Wind Patterns

KEY

Air currents

Lambert Azimuthal Equal-Area Projection

Map Study What makes the wind blow? Part of the answer is that the sun warms some areas of the Earth more than others. Since heat always flows toward cooler areas, warm air moves into areas of cooler air, creating winds. **Movement** Which way does the air flow between the Tropic of Cancer and the Arctic Circle—toward the tropics or toward the Arctic Circle? Why?

The Water Cycle

Chart Study Ocean water is too salty to drink or to irrigate crops. However, the oceans are a source of fresh water. How does this happen? When water evaporates from the ocean's surface, salt is left behind. The water vapor rises and forms clouds. The rain that falls to the Earth is fresh. **Critical Thinking** Once rain has fallen, how does water return to the ocean?

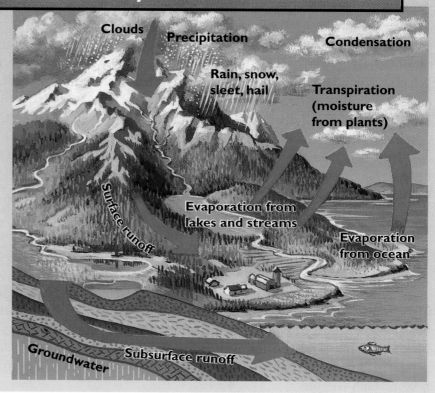

Clouds
Precipitation
Condensation
Rain, snow, sleet, hail
Transpiration (moisture from plants)
Surface runoff
Evaporation from lakes and streams
Evaporation from ocean
Groundwater
Subsurface runoff

North and South poles. People need fresh water for many things. This fresh water comes from lakes, rivers, and rain. Also, much fresh water, called groundwater, is stored in the soil itself. The diagram above shows the movement of all the water on the Earth's surface, in the ground, and in the air. The Earth does have enough water for people. However, some places have too much water and other places have too little.

SECTION 2 REVIEW

1. **Define** (a) landform, (b) mountain, (c) hill, (d) plateau, (e) plain, (f) plate tectonics, (g) plate, (h) weathering, (i) erosion, (j) atmosphere.

2. **Identify** (a) Ring of Fire, (b) Pangaea.

3. Why are there earthquakes and volcanoes?

4. What forces on the Earth's surface break down rocks?

5. Why is the atmosphere important?

Critical Thinking

6. **Distinguishing Fact From Opinion** What facts support the theory of plate tectonics?

Activity

7. **Writing to Learn** Suppose you were able to see the region you live in 10,000 years from now. Describe how the landforms might look. Explain what might have caused those changes.

Climate and What Influences It

Reach Into Your Background

Thunderstorms can knock down power lines and trees. Hurricanes can destroy whole communities. What is the worst weather you have experienced? How did you feel? How did you stay safe?

Questions to Explore

1. What is climate?
2. How do landforms and bodies of water affect climate?

Key Terms

weather
temperature
precipitation
climate

Key Names and Places

Gulf Stream
Peru Current
California Current
St. Louis
San Francisco

In late May 1996, a tornado's furious winds tore down the movie screen of a drive-in theater in St. Catherine's, Ontario, Canada. Ironically, the week's feature movie was *Twister,* a film about tornadoes.

Richard and Daphne Thompson spend their time tracking tornadoes in Oklahoma. Daphne Thompson recalls one particular storm: "The car was hit by 50- to 70-mile-per-hour gusts," she says. "Tumbleweeds were blowing so hard one left a dent in the car."

Weather or Climate?

These two stories show that weather like tornadoes can be dangerous. Or is it "climate" like tornadoes? What is the difference between weather and climate?

Every morning, most people check the temperature outside before they get dressed. But in some parts of India, people have very serious reasons for watching the **weather,** or the day-to-day changes in the air. In this region, it rains only during one period of the year. No one living there wants the rainy days to end too soon. That rain must fill the wells with enough fresh water to last through the coming dry spell.

▼ Tornadoes can easily flatten buildings. Tornado winds are the most powerful and violent winds on the Earth.

Map Study Many factors, including nearness to the Equator and to bodies of water, affect climate.
Regions What are the two major climate regions of South America? What is the major climate region of North Africa?

KEY

Tropical
- Tropical wet
- Tropical wet and dry

Dry
- Semiarid
- Arid

Mild
- Mediterranean
- Humid subtropical
- Marine west coast

Continental
- Humid continental
- Subarctic

Polar
- Tundra
- Ice cap
- Highlands
- Ice pack

Robinson Projection

ATLANTIC OCEAN

PACIFIC OCEAN

80°N
60°N
40°N
Tropic of Cancer
20°N
Equator
0°
Tropic of Capricorn
60°S
Antarctic Circle
160°W   120°W   80°W   40°W

Predict What do you think influences the climate of an area?

Weather is measured primarily by temperature and precipitation. **Temperature** is how hot or cold the air feels. **Precipitation** is water that falls to the ground as rain, sleet, hail, or snow.

Climate is not the same as weather. The **climate** of a place is the average weather over many years. Weather is what people see from day to day. A day is rainy or it is dry. Climate is what people know from experience happens from year to year.

Latitude, Landforms, and Climate The Earth has many climate regions. Some climates are hot enough that people rarely need to wear a sweater. In some cold climates, snow stays on the ground most of the year. And there are places on the Earth where between 30 and 40 feet (9 and 12 meters) of rain fall in a single year. Geographers know climates are different in the low, middle, and high latitudes, because latitude affects temperature. Major landforms such as mountains also affect climates in neighboring areas. Wind and water also play a role.

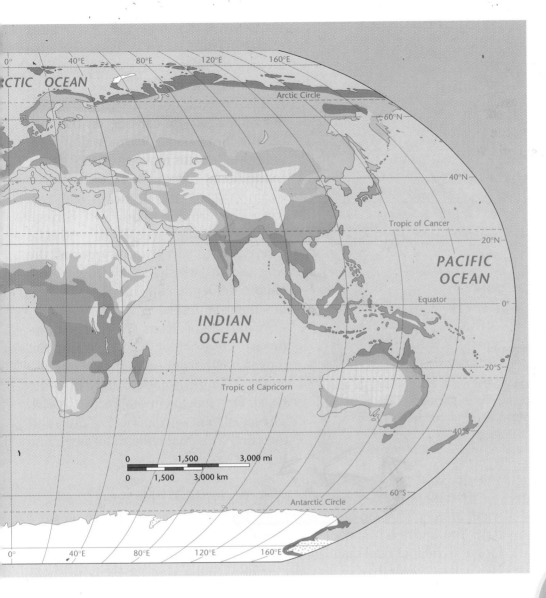

Map labels:
ARCTIC OCEAN
Arctic Circle
60°N
40°N
Tropic of Cancer
20°N
PACIFIC OCEAN
Equator
0°
INDIAN OCEAN
20°S
Tropic of Capricorn
40°S
Antarctic Circle
60°S
0°, 40°E, 80°E, 120°E, 160°E

0 1,500 3,000 mi
0 1,500 3,000 km

Wind and Water

Without wind and water, the Earth would overheat. If you sit in the sun for a while on a hot day, you will feel warmer and warmer. The same thing could happen to the tropical regions of the Earth if wind and water did not help spread the sun's heat.

The Blowing Winds   In part, the Earth's rotation creates our winds. Because of it, air moves in an east-west direction, as the map at the end of the last section shows. Two other factors make air move in a north-south direction: (1) Hot air rises and circulates toward regions where the air is not as hot. (2) Cold air sinks and moves toward regions where the air is warmer. As a result, hot, moist air from the Equator rises in the atmosphere, then moves toward the North Pole or the South Pole. Cold, dry air from the poles moves toward the Equator. This movement helps keep the Earth from overheating.

LINKS TO SCIENCE

Smog Normally, air is cooler at higher altitudes. During a temperature inversion, however, a layer of warm air sits on top of the cooler air. The warm air traps pollution near the ground. This mixture of dangerous smoke and fog is called smog. The brown air seen in cities such as Los Angeles and Denver is smog caused by car exhaust.

Relief and Precipitation

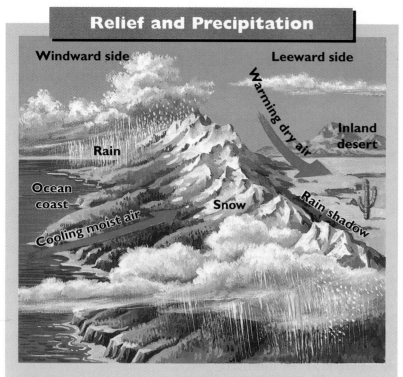

Windward side

Leeward side

Warming dry air

Inland desert

Rain

Ocean coast

Snow

Rain shadow

Cooling moist air

Chart Study As moist air blowing from the ocean rises up a mountain, it cools and drops its moisture. **Critical Thinking** Describe the climate on a mountain's leeward side—or side away from the wind.

Ocean Currents: Hot and Cold The Earth's rotation also creates ocean currents, which are like fast-moving rivers in the oceans. Like winds, ocean currents travel great distances. As you can see on the map on the next page, warm water from near the Equator moves north or south. In the Atlantic Ocean, the Gulf Stream, a warm current, travels north and east from the tropics. The Gulf Stream merges with the North Atlantic Current to to carry warm water all the way to the British Isles. People there enjoy a milder climate than people living in similar latitudes.

Cold water from the poles flows toward the Equator. The Peru Current moves north from Antarctica, along the coast of South America, and on to the Galapagos Islands in the Pacific Ocean. These islands sit on the Equator, but the current is cold enough for penguins to live there.

The Ocean's Cooling and Warming Effects Bodies of water affect climate in other ways, too. Have you gone to a beach on a hot day? You learned it is cooler by the water. That is because water takes longer to heat or cool than land. So in summer, a place near the ocean or a lake will be cooler than an area farther away. In the winter, it will be warmer.

For example, consider two places in the United States—San Francisco, California, and St. Louis, Missouri. Both cities have an average annual temperature of about 55°F (13°C). Their climates, however, are quite different. San Francisco borders the Pacific Ocean. The California Current passes by the city, carrying cool water from the waters off Alaska. In winter, the ocean current is warmer than the air, so the current gives off warmth and the air temperature rises. A San Franciscan traveling to St. Louis in December would find it much colder there than at home. In summer, the current is colder than the air, so the current absorbs heat, making the air temperature fall. A San Franciscan probably would find the summer months in St. Louis uncomfortably warm.

Raging Storms Wind and water can make climates milder, but they also can create storms. Some storms cause great destruction. Hurricane Andrew, for example, struck south Florida in the early morning hours of August 24, 1992, and left 160,000 people homeless. Julius Keaton recalls what happened:

READ ACTIVELY

Ask Questions What would you like to know about the raging storms that are part of the Earth's climate?

"I heard one window break, so I jumped up and put a mattress against it. But I guess that storm really wanted to get in, 'cause it blew out another window and beat down the front door.**"**

Hurricanes are wind and rain storms that form over the tropics in the Atlantic Ocean. The whirling winds at the center of a hurricane travel over 73 miles (122 km) per hour and can reach speeds of more than 100 miles (160 km) an hour. Hurricanes produce huge waves called storm surges, which flood over shorelines and can destroy homes and towns. Typhoons are similar storms that take place in the Pacific Ocean.

Hurricanes and typhoons affect large areas. One single hurricane can threaten islands in the Caribbean Sea, the east coast of Mexico, and the southern coast of the United States. Other storms are just as dangerous, but they affect smaller areas. Tornadoes, for example, are swirling funnels of wind that can reach 200 miles (320 km) per hour. The winds and the vacuum they create in their centers can wreck almost

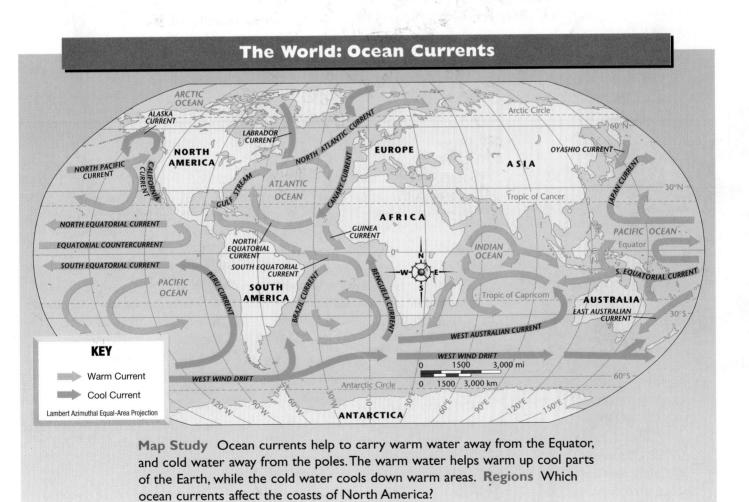

The World: Ocean Currents

KEY

→ Warm Current
→ Cool Current

Lambert Azimuthal Equal-Area Projection

Map Study Ocean currents help to carry warm water away from the Equator, and cold water away from the poles. The warm water helps warm up cool parts of the Earth, while the cold water cools down warm areas. **Regions** Which ocean currents affect the coasts of North America?

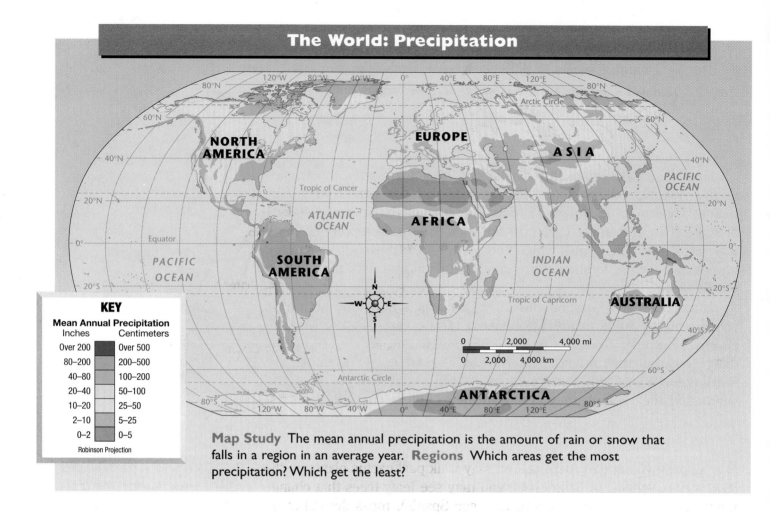

The World: Precipitation

Map Study The mean annual precipitation is the amount of rain or snow that falls in a region in an average year. **Regions** Which areas get the most precipitation? Which get the least?

KEY

Mean Annual Precipitation

Inches	Centimeters
Over 200	Over 500
80–200	200–500
40–80	100–200
20–40	50–100
10–20	25–50
2–10	5–25
0–2	0–5

Robinson Projection

everything in their path. However, tornadoes only average about one-half mile in diameter. Therefore, they affect a more limited area than hurricanes.

Some storms are less severe. In winter, blizzards dump huge amounts of snow on parts of North America. And severe rainstorms and thunderstorms strike the continent most often in spring and summer.

SECTION 3 REVIEW

I. Define (a) weather, (b) temperature, (c) precipitation, (d) climate.

2. Identify (a) Gulf Stream, (b) Peru Current, (c) California Current, (d) St. Louis, (e) San Francisco.

3. Explain the difference between weather and climate.

4. How does latitude affect climate?

5. How do mountains affect neighboring climates?

Critical Thinking

6. Recognizing Cause and Effect Explain how currents from the tropics affect climates far away.

Activity

7. Writing to Learn Check a newspaper's local weather forecasts for the last several weeks. Make a chart. Then write a paragraph about your climate. Use what you know about your region's climate to describe the weather as normal or abnormal for this time of year.

How Climate Affects Vegetation

BEFORE YOU READ

Reach Into Your Background
Make a list of some plants and trees native to your area. How much rain and sunlight do they seem to need? How do they react to unusual weather?

Questions to Explore
1. Where are the Earth's major climate regions?
2. What kinds of vegetation grow in each climate region?

Key Terms
vegetation
canopy
tundra
vertical climate

Key Place
Great Plains
Arctic Circle

Suppose you live in Arizona. You may walk past cactus plants on the way to school. In Minnesota, you may see leafy trees that change color in the fall. In Georgia, you may see Spanish moss draped along bald cypress trees. All these differences are related to climate.

▼ Cacti have waxy skins that hold water in. Prickly spines protect a cactus from being eaten by animals that want its water.

Climate and Vegetation

A climate must provide plants with water, sunlight, and certain nutrients, or elements, plants use as food. Also, plants have features, called *adaptations,* that enable them to live in their particular climate. That means that over a very long time, small, accidental changes in a few individual plants made them better able to survive in a particular place.

How do geographers use such information? They can predict the kinds of plants they will find in a climate. Geographers discuss five broad types of climates: tropical, dry, moderate, continental, and polar. Each has its unique **vegetation,** or plants that grow there naturally.

Tropical Climates In the low latitudes, you will find two types of tropical climates. Both are hot and wet. A tropical wet climate has two seasons—one with a great deal of rain and one with a little less rain. A tropical wet and dry climate also has two seasons: one with much rain and one with very little rain. The vegetation associated with these climates is tropical rain forest.

Because growing conditions are so perfect—there is so much light, heat, and rain—thousands of kinds of plants grow in a rain forest. Some trees rise 130 feet (40 meters) into the air. Their uppermost branches create a **canopy.** Little sunlight can break through this dense covering of leafy branches. Other types of trees, which are adapted to the shade, grow to lower heights. Thousands of kinds of vines and ferns thrive in the rain forest.

Dry Climates Arid and semiarid climates are very hot but receive very little rain. Since there is so little moisture, vegetation in dry regions is sparse. Plants grow far apart in sandy, gravelly soil. Their shallow roots are adapted to absorb scarce water before it evaporates in the heat. Some plants have small leaves, which lose little moisture into the air through evaporation. Other plants flower only when it rains so that as many seeds survive as possible.

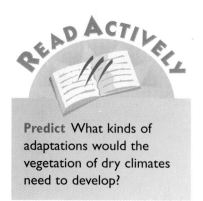

Predict What kinds of adaptations would the vegetation of dry climates need to develop?

The World: Natural Vegetation

Map Study Cacti do not grow in the rain forest, and you will not find oak trees growing in the desert. The kind of plants that grow in a place depend on climate. **Regions** Compare this map with the climate map in Section 3. What similarities do you see? **Location** What areas of the world have little or no vegetation at all? How does the climate of these areas explain the lack of plant life?

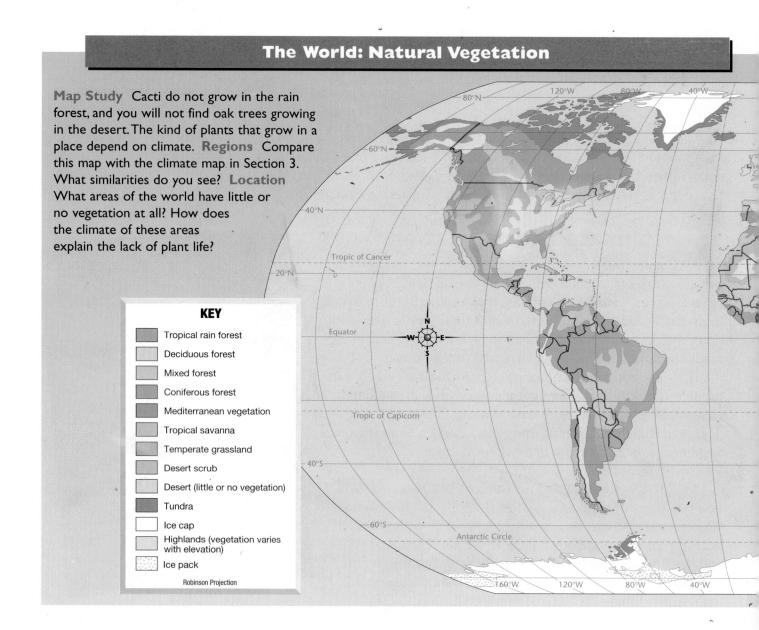

KEY

- Tropical rain forest
- Deciduous forest
- Mixed forest
- Coniferous forest
- Mediterranean vegetation
- Tropical savanna
- Temperate grassland
- Desert scrub
- Desert (little or no vegetation)
- Tundra
- Ice cap
- Highlands (vegetation varies with elevation)
- Ice pack

Robinson Projection

Moderate Climates Moderate climates are found in the middle latitudes. There are three types: Mediterranean, marine west coast, and humid subtropical. In all three climate types, rain is moderate. There are seasonal changes, but temperatures hardly ever fall below freezing.

Moderate climates have a wide variety of vegetation. Forests of deciduous trees, which lose their leaves in the fall, grow here. So do tall shrubs, low bushes—or scrub—wildflowers, and a variety of grasses. The Mediterranean climate receives most of its rain in winter and summers are hot and dry. In this climate, plants have leathery leaves, which hold in moisture during the dry summers. Of the three moderate climates, the humid subtropical climate has the most precipitation, heat, and humidity. It supports many types of vegetation. Most marine west coast climates are mountainous and are cooled by ocean currents. Therefore, they support more forests than grasses.

To Be a Leader
In the 1970s, Michael Stewartt was a charter airplane pilot in Alaska. Every day he flew over its vast forests, where he could see the damage to national forests from clear-cut logging. Lawmakers should see this for themselves, he thought. So, Stewartt founded LightHawk, an environmental plane service that took people on educational "tours" in the air. LightHawk continues today. It also creates plans for change.

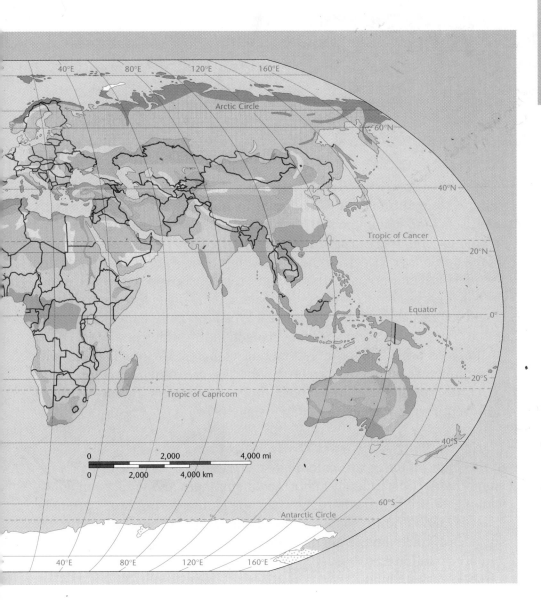

A Study in Contrasts

Antarctica (right) is an "icy desert"—a world of permanent ice and snow. In contrast, Oregon (below) is a world of constant green, teeming with life. **Critical Thinking** How do you think humans could adapt to living in each of these environments?

LINKS ACROSS TIME

Plant Fossils In ancient rocks in Wyoming, scientists have found fossils of palm trees. Centuries ago, sediments such as sand or ash buried the plants quickly. Over thousands of years, the buildup continued. Slowly, the plants turned to rock. Scientists study fossils to learn about ancient climate and vegetation. Scientists also learn how climate and vegetation have changed over time.

Continental Climates In a humid continental climate, summer temperatures are moderate to hot, but winters can be very cold. This kind of climate supports grasslands and forests. Grasses tend to be tall. The first European settlers on the Great Plains of the United States noted that the grass there was high enough to hide a horse and its rider! Certain areas in this climate region support large deciduous forests. In areas where winters are colder, coniferous forests are found. Coniferous trees have needles, not leaves, and have cones to produce seeds. These adaptations provide protection through the winter.

Regions with subarctic continental climates are much drier, with cool summers and cold winters. Grasses are much shorter. Some subarctic continental areas have huge coniferous forests. Others, however, have few trees.

Polar Climates and Their Vegetation The polar climates of the high latitudes are cold all year around. The **tundra**, which lies along the Arctic Circle, has short, cold summers and long, even colder winters. No trees grow here. Low shrubs bloom during brief summers. Mosses and strange plants called lichens (LY kuhns) grow on the surfaces of rocks. In the northern regions of the tundra, it is even colder and precipitation is very scarce. Only low grasses, mosses, lichens, and a few flowering plants grow.

A Vertical Climate

The climate at the top of Mount Everest, in Nepal in Southeast Asia, is like Antarctica's. But Mount Everest is near the Tropic of Cancer, far from the South Pole. Why is it so cold at the top of the mountain? A mountain is an example of **vertical climate,** where the climate changes according to the mountain's height.

Picture yourself on a hike up a mountain in a moderate climate. Grasslands surround the base of the mountain, and temperatures are warm. You begin to climb and soon enter a region with less precipitation than below. There are short grasses, like those in a continental climate. As you climb higher, you move through deciduous forests. It is cooler and drier here. Slowly the forests change to coniferous trees.

As you continue to climb, you find only scattered, short trees. Finally, there are only low shrubs and short grasses. Soon it is too cold and dry even for them. Mainly you see only the mosses and lichens of a tundra. And at the mountain top, you find an icecap climate, where no vegetation grows.

Vertical Climate Zones

Vertical climate zones determine land use. At an elevation of 6,762 feet (2,061 m), this Swiss village can grow hay and graze cattle. **Critical Thinking** What activities do you think happen at the higher elevations seen in this photograph?

SECTION 4 REVIEW

1. **Define** (a) vegetation, (b) canopy, (c) tundra, (d) vertical climate.

2. **Identify** (a) Great Plains, (b) Arctic Circle.

3. Why do polar climates have sparse vegetation?

4. What climate region has the most varied vegetation? Why?

5. How are continental climates different from moderate climates?

Critical Thinking

6. **Drawing Conclusions** Choose a climate region. Explain why certain kinds of plants do *not* grow there.

Activity

7. **Writing to Learn** Research three different cities. Find out what climate and vegetation regions they are in. Write an essay explaining how climate and vegetation affects everyday life in these cities.

Using Special Geography Graphs

"**E**verybody talks about the weather,**"** Mark Twain is supposed to have said, **"but nobody does anything about it." The great humorist was both right and wrong. People have always talked about the weather. Where we live and what we do are all affected by weather and climate.**

Because weather is such a big part of life, people have tried to do something about it. For example, hundreds of years ago people in Europe tried to get rid of thunderstorms by ringing church bells. Today, people "seed" clouds with chemicals to try to cause rainfall.

Trying to "do something" about the weather is not very successful. Geographers have managed to do one thing very well, however. That is to gather information about weather and climate. One of the ways geographers do this is by making a climate graph. It usually shows average precipitation and average temperature.

Get Ready

A climate graph is really two graphs in one. Look at the climate graph on this page, for the city of São Paulo, Brazil.

The graph has two parts: a line graph and a bar graph. The line graph shows temperature. The scale for temperature is along the graph's left side. The bar graph shows precipitation. The scale for average precipitation in inches is along the right side of the graph. Finally, along the bottom of the graph are the labels for months of the year.

A good way to learn more about climate graphs is to make one of your own. You will need:

- a sheet of graph paper
- a lead pencil
- two different colored pencils

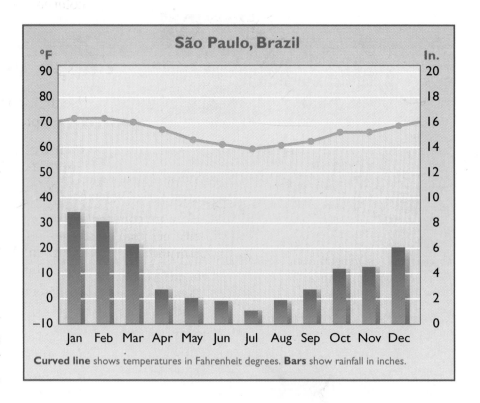

São Paulo, Brazil

Curved line shows temperatures in Fahrenheit degrees. **Bars** show rainfall in inches.

► During which months do you think most thunderstorms occur in South Carolina?

Try It Out

A. Draw a grid. Use the graph paper and the lead pencil to draw a large square. Divide the square into 10 horizontal rows and 12 vertical rows.

B. Label the grid. At the top of the graph, write Charleston, the name of the city you will graph. Using the lead pencil, copy the labels on the climate graph as shown on the previous page. Put labels for temperature on the left side of the graph. Put labels for precipitation on the right side. Finally, put labels for the months of the year along the bottom of the graph.

C. Make a line graph. The data on this page is for Charleston, South Carolina. Use the temperature data to plot a line graph. Use the climate graph on the opposite page as a model. Plot your line graph with one of the colored pencils.

D. Make a bar graph. Now use the data for precipitation to make a bar graph. Use the climate graph on the opposite page as a model. Plot your bar graph with the other colored pencil.

Apply the Skill

Use the steps below to practice reading your climate graph.

❶ **Compare differences in temperature.** (a) Which month has the highest temperature in Charleston? (b) Which month has the lowest?

❷ **Compare differences in precipitation.** (a) Which months have the highest precipitation? (b) Which month has the lowest?

❸ **Describe the climate.** Temperature and precipitation are two major factors that determine a climate. Using the information presented in the climate graph, how would you describe Charleston's climate?

Charleston, South Carolina		
	Temperature (Fahrenheit)	Precipitation (inches)
January	48	3.5
February	51	3.5
March	58	4.5
April	65	3.0
May	73	4.0
June	78	6.5
July	82	7.0
August	81	7.0
September	76	5.0
October	67	3.0
November	58	2.5
December	51	3.0

Review and Activities

Reviewing Main Ideas

1. What causes day and night?
2. Why are the seasons at higher latitudes different from seasons at latitudes near the Equator?
3. How do plate tectonics shape the Earth?
4. What is the difference between weathering and erosion?

5. Why can two places have the same average temperatures but still have different climates?
6. How are climates closer to the poles similar to the tops of vertical climates?

7. (a) List five major climate regions in the world. (b) Then choose one of them and describe plants that live there.

Reviewing Key Terms

Use each key term below in a sentence that shows the meaning of the term.

1. orbit
2. revolution
3. axis
4. rotation
5. plate tectonics
6. weathering
7. erosion
8. atmosphere
9. weather
10. temperature
11. precipitation
12. climate
13. vegetation
14. tundra
15. vertical climate

Critical Thinking

1. **Identifying Central Issues** How does water affect a region's landforms and climate?
2. **Recognizing Cause and Effect** Why is the Earth continually changing form?

Graphic Organizer

Copy the chart on a separate sheet of paper. Select three climates from tropical, dry, moderate, continental, or polar. Write one term in each box of column 1. In column 2, write temperature, precipitation, plus other important information.

Climate

Map Activity

North America

For each place listed below, write the letter on the map that shows its location. Use the Atlas at the back of the book to complete the exercise.

1. Tropic of Cancer

2. Appalachian Mountains

3. Rocky Mountains

4. Arctic Circle

5. Great Plains

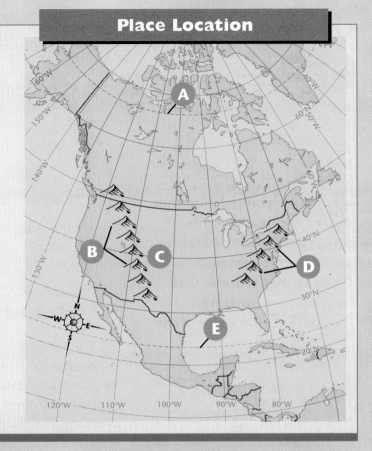

Place Location

Writing Activity

Writing a News Report
Choose a well-known natural disaster such as Hurricane Mitch or the eruption of Mount St. Helens. Find out where it happened, why it happened, and what were the immediate and long-term effects. Then, write a news report that explains the natural disaster in geographic terms.

Skills Review

Turn to the Skills Activity.
Review the steps for understanding special geography graphs. Then complete the following: (a) What two kinds of information are included in a climate graph? (b) How does a line graph help geographers describe a climate?

Internet Activity
Use a search engine to find the **Weather Underground** site. Enter your community's zip code in the **Fast Forecast** search box to find current local weather information. Make a chart showing the temperature, humidity, wind, pressure, and weather throughout the day. What does the chart tell you about today's weather patterns?

How Am I Doing?
Answer these questions to help you check your progress.

1. Do I know how the Earth's movements through space create day, night, and seasons?

2. Do I understand the forces that shape the Earth?

3. Can I explain the influences on the Earth's weather and climate?

4. Do I know why the Earth's climates support a variety of vegetation?

5. What information from this chapter can I use in my book project?

ACTIVITY SHOP

The Earth's Seasons

e take seasons for granted. Summer always follows spring, and winter follows fall. Anywhere in the United States, you can usually tell when the seasons begin to change. Two factors cause seasons. One is the way the Earth revolves, or travels around the sun. The other is the angle of the Earth's axis.

Purpose

In this activity, you will make a model that shows how the revolution of the Earth around the sun causes the seasons.

Materials

- masking tape
- marker
- lamp
- globe

Procedure

STEP ONE

   Make a model of the Earth's path around the sun. Use masking tape to mark a spot on the floor for the "sun." Following the diagram, use the tape to mark the Earth's orbit around the sun. Next, label the tape where each season begins. Now, tape the globe firmly to its frame. Because the Earth's rotation does not

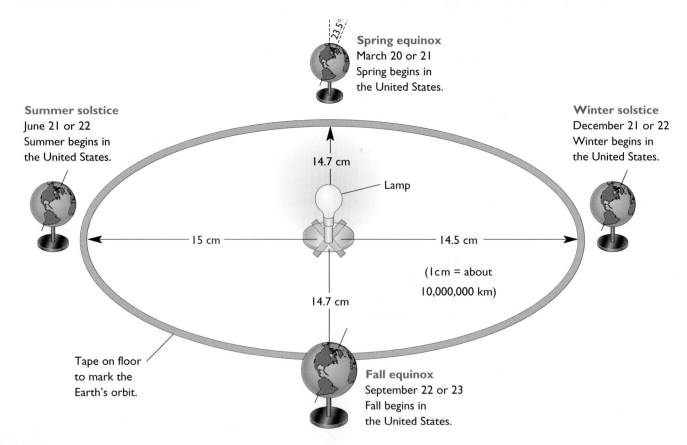

23.5°

Spring equinox
March 20 or 21
Spring begins in
the United States.

Summer solstice
June 21 or 22
Summer begins in
the United States.

Winter solstice
December 21 or 22
Winter begins in
the United States.

14.7 cm

Lamp

15 cm

14.5 cm

(1cm = about
10,000,000 km)

14.7 cm

Tape on floor
to mark the
Earth's orbit.

Fall equinox
September 22 or 23
Fall begins in
the United States.

affect the seasons, the globe can remain in place. Put a lamp on the mark for the sun. Remove the shade and turn on the lamp.

STEP TWO

Show winter in the United States. Move the globe to the spot in the orbit where the season is winter in the United States. Be sure that the Earth's axis matches the position in the diagram. Notice that at other times of the year the Earth will be farther from the sun. Something besides distance must cause the season to be winter.

Let the globe sit for five minutes. Study how the sun's light hits the globe. Then, feel it by placing one hand on the Northern Hemisphere and the other on the Southern Hemisphere. Because of the tilt of the Earth's axis, the Northern Hemisphere gets less direct sunlight from the sun than the Southern Hemisphere. That means that the Northern Hemisphere receives less energy from the sun. So temperatures are cooler in the United States than in the Southern Hemisphere.

STEP THREE

Show spring in the United States. Place the globe on the floor at the spot where it is spring in the United States. Line up the Earth's axis correctly. Let the globe sit for five minutes. Place one hand on the Northern Hemisphere and the other on the Southern Hemisphere. Both hemispheres should feel about the same. Notice how the sun's light strikes the Earth. All parts of the Earth get about the same amount of energy.

STEP FOUR

Show summer in the United States. Place the globe at the spot where the season is summer in the United States. Notice that the Earth is farther from the sun than it was in winter. Line up the axis correctly. Let the globe sit for five minutes. Study the effect of the sun on both the Northern and Southern hemispheres. This time, because of the tilt of the axis, the Northern Hemisphere gets more direct sunlight from the sun, and therefore energy, than the Southern Hemisphere. Now, it is summer in the United States.

STEP FIVE

Show fall in the United States. Place the globe on the floor at the spot where it is fall in the United States. Line up the axis correctly. Let the globe sit for five minutes. Study both the Northern and the Southern hemispheres. Again, both hemispheres should feel about the same because all parts of the Earth get about the same amount of energy.

Observation

1 Which affects the seasons more—the angle at which the sun's rays hit the Earth or its distance from the sun? Explain your answer.

2 Which season does the Southern Hemisphere have when it is winter in the Northern Hemisphere?

3 When will you have about the same amount of daylight as night—January 8, July 20, or September 22? Explain your answer.

ANALYSIS AND CONCLUSION

1. If the Earth was not tilted on its axis, how do you think the seasons would be affected? Explain your answer.

2. In a science fiction story, the Earth's orbit is disturbed. The planet travels in a straight line, not around the sun. How would this affect the seasons?

CHAPTER 3

Earth's Human Geography

PICTURE ACTIVITIES

Many people live in New York City, Los Angeles, and other large American cities. To learn more about these people, carry out the following activities.

Study the picture
Look at this crowd of people hurrying along a busy New York City street. Many have come from other countries. List some places you think people in New York City might be from.

Rename the city
With a population of over seven million, New York City has more people than many small countries. The city has enough business and industry to be a country. What would you name the crowded "country" of New York City? Why?

Where Do People Live?

BEFORE YOU READ

Reach Into Your Background
Would you like to live in a city or in the country? List some interesting things you could do if you lived far from a city. List the things you would enjoy most about city life.

Questions to Explore
1. Where do most of the world's people live?
2. How is the world's population changing?

Key Terms
population
population distribution
demographer
population density

Key Places
Nile River valley

Imagine that you go to school in Tokyo, the capital of Japan. Every day you ride the Tokyo "bullet train" to school. What is it like? You probably must stand up for your two-hour ride. Every day more and more people jam the train. Often the car is so crowded that special station guards push people inside so the doors can close behind them.

This is not an exaggeration. The country of Japan is smaller than California. But it is home for 125 million people. Over 26.5 million of them live in Tokyo and its suburbs. Public transportation, roads, and living space are extremely crowded.

▲ At rush hour in Tokyo, white-gloved guards jam two more passengers onto an already full train.

What Is Population Distribution?

The world's **population**, or total number of people, is spread unevenly over the Earth's surface. Some places have large numbers of people. In other places, the population is very small. **Population distribution** describes the way the population is spread out over the Earth.

The reasons population is distributed as it is may seem unclear. Scientists called demographers try to figure it out. **Demographers** study the populations of the world. They examine such things as rates of birth, marriage, and death. And they look at the reasons why people choose to live in certain areas.

Why Is Population Distribution Uneven? To answer this question, demographers start with the idea that people are choosy. Recall an important fact about the Earth's surface. Many of the Earth's landforms are rugged mountains, hot deserts, and dry land with little vegetation. Few people can live in these places.

Many factors make a location a good place for people to live. Most major civilizations of world history began along bodies of water. Rivers and lakes form natural "roads" for trade and travel. Also, rivers and lakes supply fresh water for drinking and farming. People also prefer areas of flat, fertile soil. There they can grow food and build easily. Therefore, plains and valleys are easy to settle. Flat coastal areas make it easy for people to trade by ship with other countries. Look at the maps on this page and the opposite page to see how landforms affect where people live.

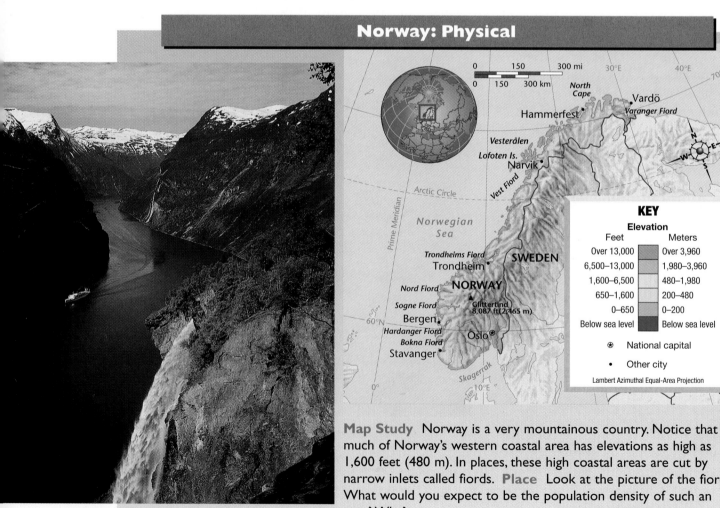

Norway: Physical

KEY

Elevation

Feet	Meters
Over 13,000	Over 3,960
6,500–13,000	1,980–3,960
1,600–6,500	480–1,980
650–1,600	200–480
0–650	0–200
Below sea level	Below sea level

⊛ National capital
• Other city

Lambert Azimuthal Equal-Area Projection

Map Study Norway is a very mountainous country. Notice that much of Norway's western coastal area has elevations as high as 1,600 feet (480 m). In places, these high coastal areas are cut by narrow inlets called fiords. **Place** Look at the picture of the fiord. What would you expect to be the population density of such an area? Why?

Other factors affect where people live. People prefer areas where the climate is not too hot or too cold, and where there is adequate rainfall. These places make it easier to raise food crops and animals. People also prefer places with natural resources to build houses and make products. For instance, few trees grew on the America's Great Plains. Few people settled there at first. They went on to other regions.

Continents Populous and Not Populous These reasons explain why more than 81 percent of the Earth's people—about 4.5 billion—live in Asia, Europe, and North America. These continents total only about 35 percent of the world's land. However, they have fertile soil, plains, valleys, and other favorable landforms. They also have fresh water, rich natural resources, and good climates.

Other continents have smaller populations partly because it is harder to live there. For example, Australia is about three million square miles, about as large as the continental United States. Only about 18 million people live in Australia, however. About the same number of people live in just the state of New York. Australia's environment is mostly desert or dry grassland. There are few rivers and little rainfall. As a result, most people live along the coasts, where conditions are better.

In Africa, too, landforms and climates limit population. Africa has about 15 percent of the world's land. But it has only 12 percent of the world's population. Africa has two of the world's largest deserts, one in the

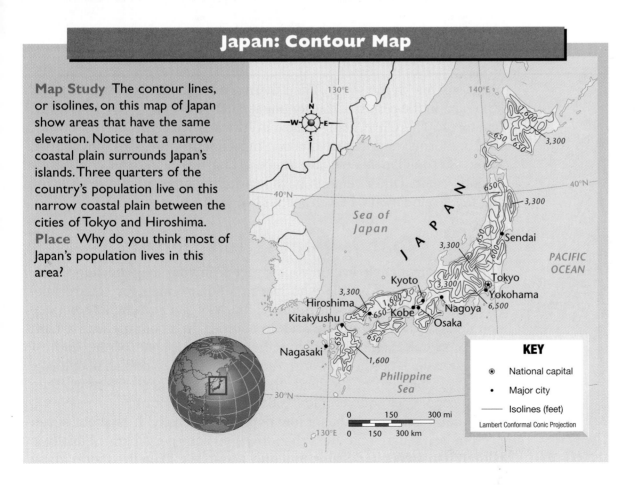

Japan: Contour Map

Map Study The contour lines, or isolines, on this map of Japan show areas that have the same elevation. Notice that a narrow coastal plain surrounds Japan's islands. Three quarters of the country's population live on this narrow coastal plain between the cities of Tokyo and Hiroshima.
Place Why do you think most of Japan's population lives in this area?

KEY
⊛ National capital
·   Major city
—   Isolines (feet)
Lambert Conformal Conic Projection

In many countries, people can choose to live in very different places. For example, these photographs show apartments in Boston's Back Bay (above), houses in a Texas suburb (above right), and farms dotting the rich land near Lancaster, Pennsylvania (right). **Critical Thinking** What factors might cause people to choose homes in the city, the suburbs, or the country?

north and one in the south. Then there are broad bands of land that get little rain. In the center of the continent, along the Equator, there is a vast rain forest. Therefore, many people in Africa live along its narrow coasts.

Landforms and climates also limit South America's population. About 309 million people live there. Most live along the continent's Atlantic coast. Other regions have soaring mountains, vast dry plains, and thick rain forests. Fewer people live in these areas.

What Is Population Density?

How many people live on your street or in your neighborhood? The average number of people who live in a square mile (or square kilometer) is called **population density.** In every city and country, population density varies from one area to another. In a country with a high density, people are crowded together. Japan has one of the highest population densities in the world. Almost all of its 125 million people live on only 16 percent of the land. In Tokyo alone, there are more than 25,000 people per square mile (9,664 people per sq km).

In contrast, Canada has a low population density. It is about seven persons per square mile (less than three persons per sq km). Canada is bigger than the United States. But only about 28 million live there. Many factors affect Canada's population. For instance, its cool climate has a short growing season. This limits farming.

Studying Population Density How do demographers measure population density? They divide the number of people living in a place by the number of square miles (or sq km) of that place. For example, California's population is 31,430,697 people. Its land area is 155,973 square miles (403,970 sq km). Therefore, California's average population density is 201.5 persons per square mile (77.8 persons per sq km).

Remember that population density is an *average*. People are not evenly distributed over the land. New York City has a very dense population. However, New York state has many fewer people per square mile. Even in the city, some areas are more densely populated than others.

On a world population density map, different colors show how world population is distributed. Darker colors show areas with heavy population. Find this map in the Activity Atlas. Find the most densely populated areas of each continent. Now, find these places on the world physical map in the Activity Atlas. Compare the landforms to the population density. Notice that people tend to live on level areas near bodies of water.

Find the Nile River valley in Egypt. This region is very densely populated. In some areas the population density is about 5,000 people per square mile (1,930 per sq km). This is one of the highest population densities in the world. Why do so many people live here? If you think it is because the Nile is a great source of water and the land around it is flat and fertile, you are right. The land beyond the river is desert. Life there is difficult.

Some people do live in areas most of us would find uncomfortable. The Inuit and the Sami people live in frozen Arctic regions. Herders in desert regions of Africa and Asia survive in places that would challenge most people. Over many generations, these people have developed ways of life suited to their environments.

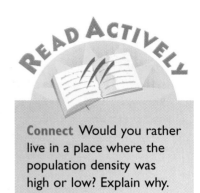

READ ACTIVELY

Connect Would you rather live in a place where the population density was high or low? Explain why.

SECTION 1 REVIEW

1. **Define** (a) population, (b) population distribution, (c) demographer, (d) population density.

2. **Identify** Nile River valley.

3. How do the physical characteristics of a country tend to affect its population distribution?

4. Why is it important to understand that population density is an average?

Critical Thinking

5. **Making Comparisons** A large percentage of the world's population lives on a small percentage of the world's land. How do the population distributions in Japan and Canada reflect this fact?

Activity

6. **Writing to Learn** You are a demographer studying your community. Make a list of questions to ask and possible sources for answers. Include in your list some population issues that are important to your community.

2

A Growing Population

BEFORE YOU READ

Reach Into Your Background

If you called a hospital in your community, you could find out how many babies were born last week. Multiply that number by all the hospitals in the world. Then, add the number of babies who were not born in hospitals. Subtract from this figure the number of people who died both in and out of hospitals. That's one way to find out how much the world's population increased in seven days.

Questions to Explore

1. How fast is the world's population growing?
2. What challenges are created by the world's growing population?

Key Terms
birthrate
death rate
life expectancy
Green Revolution

I magine that all the years from A.D. 1 to the year A.D. 2000 took place in just 24 hours. Now you have an imaginary clock to measure how fast the world's population is growing. The list below shows that the Earth's population doubled several times in those 24 hours.

12:00 AM	200 million people in the world
7:48 PM	Population doubles to 400 million
10:12 PM	Population doubles to 800 million
11:00 PM	Population doubles to 1.6 billion
11:36 PM	Population doubles to 3.2 billion
11:59 PM	Population will double to 6.4 billion

How large was the world population at 12:00 AM (A.D. 1)? At 10:12 PM? During the 24 hours, how many times has the world's population doubled? How long did it take for the world population to double the first time? The last time?

Population Growth Is Worldwide

The example above makes it easy to see that world population has grown rapidly. Even more important, the rate of growth has increased greatly in modern times. For example, in 1960 the world population was 3 billion. By 2000—only 40 years later—it will climb to 6.4 billion people.

Population Birthrate and Death Rate During different historical periods, populations grew at different rates. Demographers want to understand why. They know that population growth depends on the birthrate and the death rate. The **birthrate** is the number of live births each year per 1,000 people. The **death rate** is the number of deaths each year per 1,000 people. By comparing birthrates and death rates, demographers can figure out population growth.

For centuries, the world population grew slowly. In those years, farmers worked without modern machinery. Food supplies often were scarce. Many thousands died of diseases. As a result, although the birthrate was high, so was the death rate. The **life expectancy,** or the average number of years that people live, was short. A hundred years ago in the United States, men and women usually lived less than 50 years.

Better Health Care for the Young

A mother and baby await medical help at the Kenyatta National Hospital in the East African country of Kenya. **Critical Thinking** How has modern medical care helped to increase the world's population growth?

Reasons for Population Growth Today Today, things have changed. The birthrate has increased dramatically. The death rate has slowed. As a result, populations in most countries have grown very fast. In some countries, the population doubles in less than 20 years. People live longer than ever. In the United States, for example, the average life expectancy for women is about 80 years and for men about 73 years.

Two scientific developments have made this possible. First, new farming methods have greatly increased the world's food supply. Starting in the 1950s, scientists developed new varieties of important food crops and new ways to protect crops against insects. Scientists developed new fertilizers to enrich the soil so farmers can grow more crops. Scientists also discovered ways to raise crops with less water. These changes in agriculture are called the **Green Revolution.**

The second set of scientific advancements came in medicine and health. Today, new medicines and types of surgery treat health problems that used to kill people, such as heart disease and serious injuries. Researchers also have created vaccines to fight diseases such as smallpox, polio, and measles, and antibiotics to fight infections. As a result, many more babies are born and stay healthy, and people live many more years.

LINKS TO SCIENCE

Hydroponics How can you grow a plant without soil? People called hydroponics farmers grow plants in water and necessary nutrients. The techniques are used where there is no soil, such as on ships. Today some groceries sell hydroponic vegetables. Some scientists say hydroponics may help feed the world's rapidly growing population.

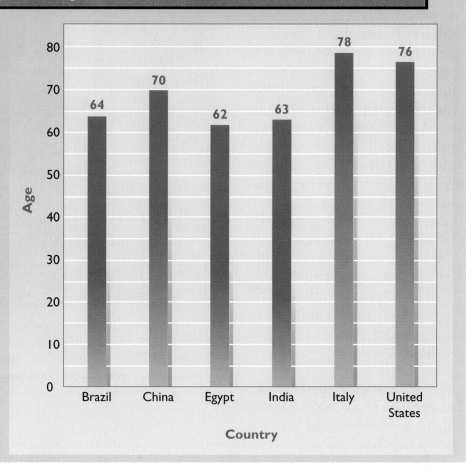

Life Expectancy in Selected Countries, 1998

Graph Study Life expectancy, or the number of years a newborn baby can expect to live, has soared in many countries since 1900. In some countries, however, life expectancy remains low. Which countries on this chart have the highest life expectancies? Which have the lowest? **Critical Thinking** What has contributed to the rise in life expectancy over the last few years?

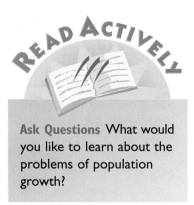

Ask Questions What would you like to learn about the problems of population growth?

The Challenges of Population Growth

Today, food supplies have increased and people live longer. Even so, the people in many countries still face very serious problems. Growing populations use resources much faster than stable populations. Some nations, like those in Southwest Asia, face shortages of fresh water and energy. In Asia and Africa, food supplies cannot keep up with the growing population. Often, these countries do not have enough money to purchase imported food.

Population growth puts pressure on all aspects of life. The population of many countries is increasing so fast that many people cannot find jobs. There are not enough schools to educate the growing number of children. Decent housing is scarce and expensive. Public services like transportation and sanitation are inadequate.

A recent study by the World Bank describes the situation.

> **"T**oday, South Asia is home to a quarter of the world's population, but it accounts for 39 percent of the world's poor [people] . . . . Out of every 12 children born, at least one is expected to die before reaching the age of one.**"**

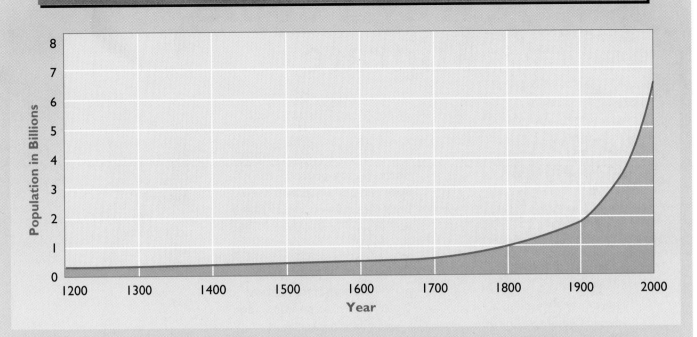

World Population Growth, A.D. 1200–2000

Population in Billions

8
7
6
5
4
3
2
1
0

1200 1300 1400 1500 1600 1700 1800 1900 2000

Year

Graph Study For hundreds of years, the world's population rose very slowly. Recently, however, the rate of growth has skyrocketed.

Critical Thinking How does the graph show the change in the growth of the world's population?

Rapid population growth also affects the environment. For instance, forests in areas of India and Pakistan are disappearing. People cut the trees to use the wood for building and for fuel. Cutting forests affects the supply of clean air. Before, tree roots held soil in place. Now heavy rainfall may wash away the soil.

Look at the population changes indicated in the graph on this page. It shows how rapidly change has occurred in the last 300 years. The Earth's resources must now be shared by six times as many people than in earlier times. All the Earth's people must work to meet this challenge.

SECTION 2 REVIEW

1. **Define** (a) birthrate, (b) death rate, (c) life expectancy, (d) Green Revolution.

2. Why has the world's population increased so dramatically in the last four or five decades?

3. How have science and technology contributed to the growing population?

Critical Thinking

4. **Drawing Conclusions** The world's population has been growing at a fast rate. What are some of the dangers of a rapidly increasing population?

Activity

5. **Writing to Learn** World hunger is one of the major concerns caused by the rapid population growth. Write one or two suggestions to help solve this problem.

Why People Migrate

Reach Into Your Background

There may have been a time in your life when you or your family moved to a new home. Or perhaps a close friend moved away from your neighborhood. You probably felt a little sad and uncertain then. Imagine how you would feel if you moved to another country!

Questions to Explore

1. Why do people migrate?
2. What are some important population issues?

Key Terms
migration
immigrant
"push-pull" theory
urbanization
rural area
urban area

Key Places
Cuba
Vietnam
Jakarta

Roberto Goizueta was the former head of Coca-Cola, one of the largest companies in the world. Yet when he came to the United States from Cuba in 1960, he had nothing. This is how he described his escape from Cuba:

▼ On July 4, 1996—Independence Day—hundreds of people celebrate receiving their citizenship in El Paso, Texas.

66 When my family and I came to this country [the United States], we had to leave everything behind . . . our photographs hung on the wall, our wedding gifts sat on the shelves. 99

Like millions of others who came to the United States, Roberto Goizueta helped the nation become a land of prosperity.

Migration: The Movement of People

For centuries people have moved from one place to another. This is called **migration.** **Immigrants** are people who leave one country and move to another. From 1881 to 1920, almost 23.5 million Europeans moved to the United States. Since the late 1970s, more than 773,700 people migrated here from the country of

Vietnam. Over 818,000 came from El Salvador and other Central American countries, and over 3.5 million came from Mexico. More than 919,000 immigrants came from the Dominican Republic, Haiti, Jamaica, and Trinidad and Tobago.

Demographers use the **"push-pull" theory** to explain immigration. It says people migrate because certain things in their lives "push" them to leave. Often, the reasons are economic. Perhaps people cannot buy land or find work. Or changes in a government may force people to leave.

For instance, in 1959 there was a revolution in Cuba. Some Cubans lost land and businesses. Many fled to America to find safety and a better life. In the 1800s, many Scandinavians moved to Minnesota and Wisconsin. They wanted their own land, which was scarce in Scandinavia. Some also left to escape religious persecution.

What about the "pull" part of the theory? The hope for better living conditions "pulls" people to a country. Cubans settled in Florida because it was near their former home. It already had a Spanish-speaking population. Also, Florida's climate and vegetation are similar to Cuba's. Scandinavians were "pulled" by the United States government's offer of free land for immigrants willing to set up farms. They also moved to a familiar place. The long, cold winters in Minnesota and Wisconsin were similar to those in northwestern Europe.

Connect Did you or any members of your family or your ancestors immigrate to the United States? Why?

Cuba and Florida: Climate Regions

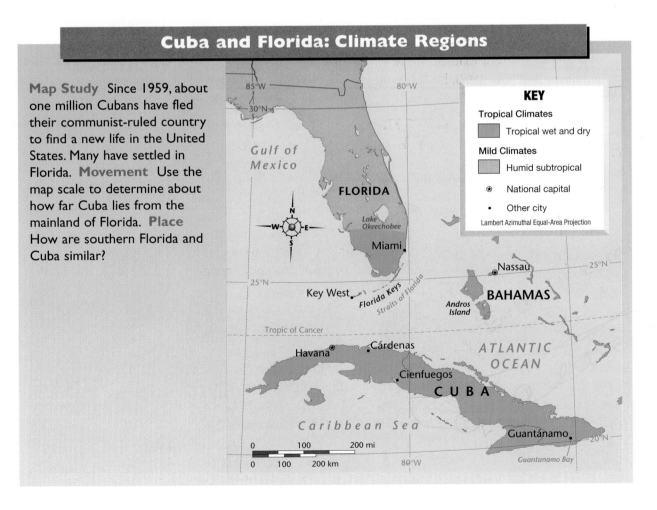

Map Study Since 1959, about one million Cubans have fled their communist-ruled country to find a new life in the United States. Many have settled in Florida. **Movement** Use the map scale to determine about how far Cuba lies from the mainland of Florida. **Place** How are southern Florida and Cuba similar?

KEY

Tropical Climates
- Tropical wet and dry

Mild Climates
- Humid subtropical
- ⊛ National capital
- • Other city

Lambert Azimuthal Equal-Area Projection

Gulf of Mexico

FLORIDA

Lake Okeechobee

Miami

Key West

Florida Keys

Straits of Florida

Nassau

Andros Island

BAHAMAS

Tropic of Cancer

Cárdenas

Havana

Cienfuegos

ATLANTIC OCEAN

CUBA

Caribbean Sea

Guantánamo

Guantanamo Bay

0   100   200 mi
0   100   200 km

Settlement of Polynesia
Not all people end up in a location by choice. Thousands of years ago people settled in Polynesia, a group of islands in the Pacific Ocean. Scholars theorize that these people left eastern Asia in search of new land. Then violent storms blew them off course. Ocean currents carried these people to the islands they now call home.

Irish Immigrants in the United States   Demographers use the push-pull theory to explain the great Irish immigration in the 1840s and 1850s. In those years, 1.5 million people left Ireland for the United States. Why did so many Irish people come to America? Ireland was a farming nation. In the 1840s, disease destroyed its main crop—potatoes. Hunger and starvation pushed people to migrate. Also, England ruled Ireland very harshly. There were very few ways for Irish people to improve their lives. These things also pushed people to move. Job opportunities pulled Irish families to the United States.

Vietnamese Come to the United States   The push-pull theory also explains Vietnamese immigration. These people came from southeastern Asia to the United States. After many years of war between North and South Vietnam, peace came in 1975. North Vietnam had won. Soon, it extended its communist form of government to South Vietnam. This was a serious change for many South Vietnamese. Thousands left the country. They were not welcome in nearby Asian countries. But the United States and the South Vietnamese had been allies during the war. The United States accepted the immigrants. That pulled the Vietnamese here.

An Irish-American President

John Fitzgerald Kennedy was elected President of the United States in 1960. His great-grandfather migrated to the United States from Ireland. Like many other immigrants to this country, Irish Americans have made many important contributions. President Kennedy is shown here delivering a speech at the University of California, Berkeley, in 1962.

▲ Sometimes war forces people to migrate. In 1995, thousands of refugees fled a brutal civil war in the Central African country of Rwanda.

Other Kinds of Immigration Sometimes, people are forced to migrate. Australia was colonized by the English. Some were convicts serving their sentences in Australia. When their sentences were done, they stayed. War also forces people to migrate. In the mid-1990s, war broke out among three ethnic groups in the former Yugoslavia, in Eastern Europe. Many refugees fled to escape the warfare. Also, victorious soldiers of one group often forced entire communities of other groups to leave. Millions of immigrants flooded into countries in Eastern and Western Europe.

Other people leave their countries for a few years to help their families. Young men from Morocco and Turkey often go to Europe to find work. They leave their families behind. For a few years they work hard and save their money. Then they return home.

The World Becomes More Urban

Migration also occurs within a country. This happens in the United States. Americans migrate more than citizens of any other country, but most move from one state to another. Recently, the population has shifted from the northeastern states to the southern and southwestern states. People may be searching for better job opportunities or a better climate. This growth in urban areas of southern states has put great stress on services. Southwestern cities, for example, are developing new ways to ensure an adequate supply of fresh water.

Ask Questions What questions would you like to ask someone who plans to migrate to a city from a rural area?

One of the biggest challenges to today's nations is people migrating to cities from farms and small villages. In recent years, the population of major cities has grown tremendously. The movement of people to cities and the growth of cities is called **urbanization.** What pushes people from rural areas? What pulls people to cities?

Growing Cities, Growing Challenges   Cities in Indonesia are an example. In the past, most Indonesians were farmers, fishers, and hunters. They lived in **rural areas,** or villages in the countryside. Recently, more and more Indonesians have moved to **urban areas,** or cities and nearby towns. Its urban population is increasing rapidly. For example, in 1978, about 4.5 million people lived in the capital of Jakarta. By 1996, its population was about 9.5 million. That is an increase of 138 percent. And demographers estimate that by 2015 the population will have risen to about 21 million.

Jakarta is not unique. In South America, too, large numbers of people are moving from rural to urban areas. São Paulo, Brazil, is now the largest city in South America. The city has hundreds of tall office buildings, stores, banks, businesses, and small factories. In 1995, its population was nearly 16 million. By 2015, it is expected to be 21 million.

The problem in cities like São Paulo is that too many people are coming too fast. Cities cannot keep up. They cannot provide housing,

World Urban and Rural Populations, 1800–2000

Graph Study In countries all over the world, city populations have soared, while rural populations have fallen. What percentage of the world's population lived in cities in 1800? What percentage of the world's population lived in cities in 2000? **Critical Thinking** Based on the graph, what do you predict will happen to the world's rural and urban populations by the year 2050?

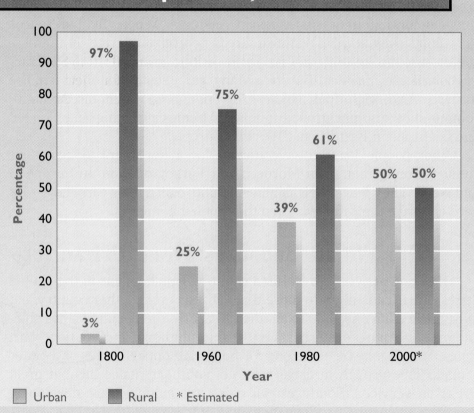

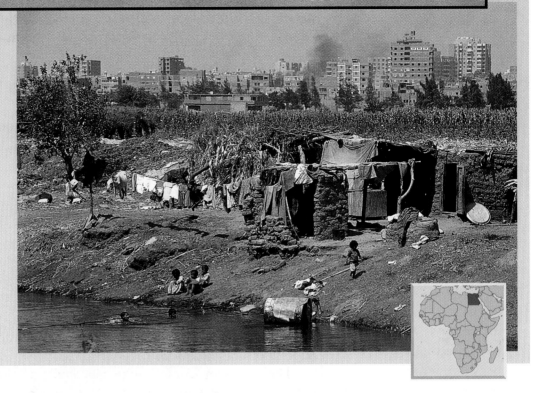

Across the world, growing cities face special challenges. Sometimes, there is not enough housing for newcomers to the cities. Sometimes, newcomers cannot afford the housing that is available. Until they find better housing, many newcomers build whatever shelters they can. These shelters are in Cairo, Egypt's capital.

jobs, schools, hospitals, and other services that people need. The country as a whole also suffers. With fewer farms, there is less food.

If you visited São Paulo, you would see why some migrants have a hard life. Schoolrooms are crowded. The city's four million cars and buses pollute the air. Traffic noise echoes day and night. Traffic jams and crowds often make it a struggle to get around.

With so many daily problems, why do immigrants flock to São Paulo and other big cities? Most are seeking a better life for their families. They are looking for jobs, decent houses, and good schools. Above all, most want more opportunities for their children.

READ ACTIVELY

Visualize Visualize what it would be like to move to a city like São Paulo, Brazil.

SECTION 3 REVIEW

1. Define (a) migration, (b) immigrant, (c) "push-pull" theory, (d) urbanization, (e) rural area, (f) urban area.

2. Identify (a) Cuba, (b) Vietnam, (c) Jakarta.

3. What are some of the reasons why people migrate from place to place?

4. Why have some immigrants left their homelands to live in the United States?

Critical Thinking

5. Making Comparisons What is the difference between migration within a country and migration from one country to another?

Activity

6. Writing to Learn When too many people migrate from rural to urban areas, it can mean hardships. List suggestions and ideas to help people decide whether to migrate to the city.

Using Distribution Maps

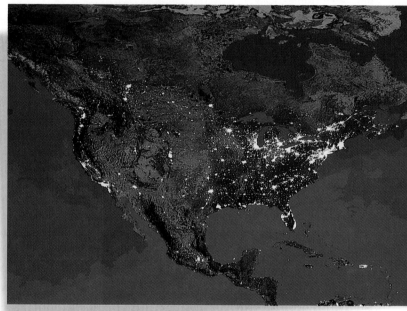

Imagine yourself in a spaceship, floating high above the Earth. Although there is no day or night in space, you can see day and night on the planet beneath you. Half the Earth is lit by the sun, and half of it is in darkness. As you begin to glide over the night side, the Earth comes between you and the sun. Looking out of the spacecraft, you see that in many places there are small smudges of light spaced across the dark land. Some huge areas are brightly lit.

You are seeing the lights of human settlement. They include firelight, street lights, floodlights in parking lots, and the combined effect of millions of lights in homes. Where there are people, there is light. The distribution of the light reflects the distribution of people on the planet. The term geographers use to refer to where people live on the planet is population distribution. Floating over the Earth, you are looking at a living population distribution map of the Earth.

Get Ready

Why do geographers study population distribution? People live all over the world, yet population is concentrated in certain places. Consider this. Nearly six billion people live in the world. Yet all of us, standing close to each other, could easily fit into the state of Connecticut! Why do we live where we do? Figuring out this answer and the reasons behind it are basic to understanding human life on the Earth. The first step is to find out where we do live. A population distribution map shows this best.

To see how population distribution maps are made and used, make and use one of your own. You will need paper, a pen, and a ruler.

Try It Out

A. **Draw a map of your school.** Use a large sheet of paper. Use the ruler to draw straight lines. Show and label classrooms, hallways, and so on.

B. **Make a key for your map.** Use stick figures as symbols. Each figure will represent five people. See the example on the next page.

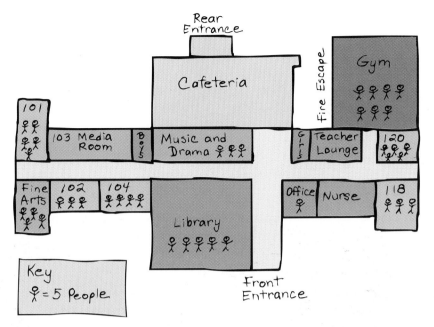

Key
👤 = 5 People

C. **Add stick-figure symbols to your map.** Remember to put the symbols where the people are. Put the right number of symbols to show how many people are in each room. If there are 24 students and 1 teacher in your classroom, for example, you would draw 5 stick-figure symbols on the part of the map that shows your classroom.

D. **Give your map an appropriate title.** You have just made a population distribution map. It answers the same two questions that any such map does: Where are the people? How many people are in each place? Your map also provides clues about another question. Why is the population distributed in the way it is? See if you can answer this question about your school map.

Apply the Skill

Now that you see how population distribution maps are made and what questions they answer, you can learn a great deal from one of Mexico. Use the map here to answer these questions.

🌗 **Read the map key.** Look at the key to get a sense of what the map is about. How is

population represented on the map? How many people does each symbol stand for?

② **Answer the "where" and "how many" questions that population distribution maps can answer.** Where do most of the people of Mexico live?

③ **Answer the "why" question that population distribution maps can address.** Why do you think the population of Mexico is distributed the way it is? Think about physical factors such as climate and landforms as well as historical factors.

④ **Think about distribution maps generally.** This map shows population distribution. Other maps show the distribution of such things as natural resources, technology, and wealth. Find another type of distribution map and share it with the class.

Mexico: Population Distribution

KEY

· One dot represents 200,000 people

Lambert Azimuthal Equal-Area Projection

Review and Activities

Reviewing Main Ideas

1. How does geography affect where people settle?

2. (a) List the three continents with the most population and the four continents with the least population. (b) Choose one continent in each group and describe its landforms. Explain how those landforms affect population.

3. What kind of region is most attractive to new settlers? Which is least attractive?

4. Why does the Nile River valley of Egypt have such a high population density?

5. What factors have caused a rapid increase in human population?

6. Explain why people in many parts of the world are moving from rural areas to cities. Name two of these cities.

7. What are some conditions that push people to leave their country and pull them to migrate to another country?

Reviewing Key Terms

Use each key term below in a sentence that shows the meaning of the term.

1. population
2. population distribution
3. population density
4. urbanization
5. rural
6. urban
7. Green Revolution
8. life expectancy
9. birthrate
10. death rate
11. migration
12. immigrants
13. demographer
14. "push-pull" theory

Critical Thinking

1. **Recognizing Cause and Effect** How have Africa's landforms and climate limited its population?

2. **Identifying Central Issues** Explain the meaning of this statement: "Today, many countries of the world are becoming more urban." What does this statement tell about the movement of people in those countries?

Graphic Organizer

Copy the organizer onto a sheet of paper. Then fill the empty ovals with other effects that are the result of population growth.

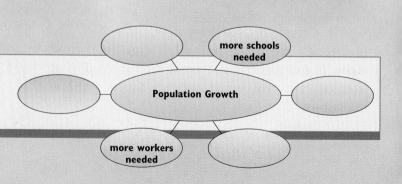

Map Activity

Continents

For each place listed below, write the letter from the map that shows its location.

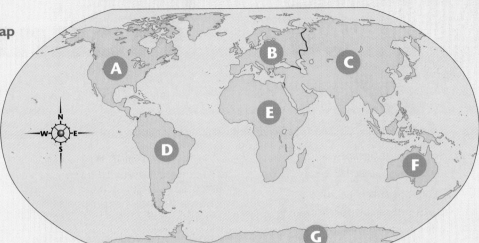

1. Asia

2. Antarctica

3. Africa

4. South America

5. North America

6. Europe

7. Australia

Writing Activity

Writing to Learn

Find out how the population of your state has changed in the last 50 years. Write a paragraph that explains the main reasons why people migrated to or from your state.

Internet Activity

Use a search engine to find the **U.S. Census Bureau** site. Click on **Estimates** next to the **People** category. Then click on **State** under the **Population Estimates** category. Find the population of your state in 1990. Then find the estimated population of your state in 1998. How did the population change? Click **Subjects A-Z** at the bottom of the page for other data about your state, such as education, income, and race statistics. Use this data to make a chart of census data for your state.

Skills Review

Turn to the Skills Activity.

Review the steps for using distribution maps. Then complete the following: (a) What can you learn from a population distribution map? (b) Would you learn more if you compared a population distribution map with a landform map or a climate map? Explain your answer.

How Am I Doing?

Answer these questions to help you check your progress.

1. Do I understand why the world's population is distributed unevenly?

2. Can I identify the continents with the highest population density? The continents where fewer people live?

3. Can I describe how the Earth's landforms and climates affect where people live?

4. Do I understand why many people move from rural to urban areas?

5. What information from this chapter can I use in my book project?

My Side of the Mountain

BY JEAN CRAIGHEAD GEORGE

home had no heating system. Without modern technology, how would you cope with the natural world around you?

Most people would have a hard time. But Sam Gribley, the fictional hero of the novel *My Side of the Mountain,* decided to live close to nature. He went to the Catskill Mountains in New York state and built a treehouse in a tall hemlock tree. His only companion was his falcon, Frightful. This excerpt tells how Sam managed during his first winter in the mountains.

Questions to Explore
1. What did Sam learn about nature as he lived alone in a forest in winter?
2. What skills did Sam need to survive alone in the wilderness?

Reach Into Your Background

Has your electricity ever gone out during a storm or a power failure? Suppose you had no electricity at all, or your

hemlock (HEM lahk) *n.* pine trees with drooping branches and short needles
copse (kahps) *n.* a thicket of small trees or shrubs

Connect What would you do to pass the time if you did not have television, radio, or other electronic gadgets?

I lived close to the weather. It is surprising how you watch it when you live in it. Not a cloud passed unnoticed, not a wind blew untested. I knew the moods of the storms, where they came from, their shapes and colors. When the sun shone, I took Frightful to the meadow and we slid down the mountain on my snapping-turtle-shell sled. She really didn't care much for this.

When the winds changed and the air smelled like snow, I would stay in my tree, because I had gotten lost in a blizzard one afternoon and had to hole up in a rock ledge until I could see where I was going. That day the winds

were so strong I could not push against them, so I crawled under the ledge; for hours I wondered if I would be able to dig out when the storm blew on. Fortunately I only had to push through about a foot of snow. However, that taught me to stay home when the air said "snow." Not that I was afraid of being caught far from home in a storm, for I could find food and shelter and make a fire anywhere, but I had become as attached to my hemlock house as a brooding bird to her nest. Caught out in the storms and weather, I had an urgent desire to return to my tree, even as The Baron Weasel returned to his den, and the deer, to their copse.

We all had our little "patch" in the wilderness. We all fought to return there.

I usually came home at night with the nuthatch that roosted in a nearby sapling. I knew I was late if I tapped the tree and he came out. Sometimes when the weather was icy and miserable, I would hear him high in the trees near the edge of the meadow, yanking and yanking and flicking his tail, and then I would see him wing to bed early. I considered him a pretty good barometer, and if he went to his tree early, I went to mine early too. When you don't have a newspaper or radio to give you weather bulletins, watch the birds and animals. They can tell when a storm is coming. I called the nuthatch "Barometer," and when he holed up, I holed up, lit my light, and sat by my fire whittling or learning new tunes on my reed whistle. I was now really into the teeth of winter, and quite fascinated by its activity. There is no such thing as a "still winter night." Not only are many animals running around in the breaking cold, but the trees cry out and limbs snap and fall, and the wind gets caught in a ravine and screams until it dies.

yank (yangk) *v.* the sound made by a nuthatch
barometer (bah RAH muh tur) *n.* an instrument for forecasting changes in the weather; anything that indicates a change
whittle (witl) *v.* to cut or pare thin shavings from wood with a knife
teeth of winter the coldest, harshest time of winter

EXPLORING YOUR READING

Look Back

1. How has Sam's relationship with the weather changed?

Think It Over

2. Sam's relationship with his environment is different from most people's. In places, he talks about wind and trees as if they were alive. Think about your relationship with nature. How is it like Sam's? How is it different?

Go Beyond

3. What things does Sam do without that you take for granted?

Ideas for Writing: Essay

4. How might you decide what to wear to school in the morning without hearing a weather forecast? Write an essay that explains to your classmates how to watch for weather signs.

Cultures of the World

PICTURE ACTIVITIES

Have you ever jumped for joy? The Inuits of Alaska toss one another for joy. People gather in a circle, grab the sides of an animal skin blanket, and use it to toss one another sky-high. The people here are celebrating a whaling festival. The Inuits also toss one another to celebrate the arrival of spring or a religious holiday or a successful hunt.

Look for clues
What can you find out about where the people in this picture live? List the clues you find. Explain what they tell you about the place shown.

Write a letter
Write a letter to someone in this photograph. Describe your thoughts about the tossing ceremony. Tell them about an activity you enjoy. Explain how these two activities are similar and different.

What Is Culture?

BEFORE YOU READ

Reach Into Your Background

You and the people you know have certain ways of doing things. You have a way of celebrating birthdays. You have a way of greeting your friends. You have a way of eating a meal. You have a way of speaking. You have ways of gesturing. Many of the ways you do things are unique to you alone. Others you share with people around you.

Questions to Explore

1. What is culture?
2. How do cultures develop?

Key Terms

culture
cultural trait
technology
cultural landscape
agriculture

"**A**ll right, students," your teacher says, "time to clean the room. Kaitlyn—I'd like you to sweep today. Guy and Keisha, please use these feather dusters to clean our shelves and windowsills. Eric and Bobby, you can do the lunch dishes today. Serena and Zack, please empty the wastebaskets and take out the trash."

Would you be surprised if this happened in your classroom? Would you pitch in—or complain? In Japan, students would pitch in to help keep their classrooms clean. Hard work and neatness are important lessons. Although Japanese schools are similar to American ones, there are differences. Japanese students generally spend more time studying than many American students. In Japan, most children go to school five days a week and often on Saturdays for half a day. Many students do many hours of homework every afternoon and evening and over vacations.

Japanese students, like many American students, also enjoy sports, music, drama, and science. They join teams and clubs. They paint and take photographs. They play baseball, soccer, and tennis. They do karate and judo. They play musical instruments.

▼ These students in Japan are listening closely as their classmate speaks. How is your own classroom like this one? How does it differ?

Culture: A Total Way of Life

What if you met students from Japan? You would probably ask many questions. "How do you feel about cleaning your classroom?" you might ask. When you heard about how much homework they do, you might also ask "How do you find time to have fun?" Later, you might wonder about other things. What do Japanese students eat for lunch? What kinds of music do they like? What makes them laugh?

Answers to these questions will tell you something about the culture of Japan. **Culture** is the way of life of a group of people who share similar beliefs and customs. The language Japanese students speak and the way they dress are both a part of their culture. So are the subjects Japanese students study and what they do after school.

Elements of Culture   Culture includes the work people do, their behaviors, their beliefs, and their ways of doing things. Parents pass these things on to their children, generation after generation. A particular group's individual skills, customs, and ways of doing things are called **cultural traits.** Over time, cultural traits may change, but cultures change very slowly.

Some elements of a culture are easy to see. They include material things, such as houses and other structures, television sets, food, or clothing. Sports, entertainment, and literature are also visible elements of culture. The things you cannot see or touch are also part of culture. They include spiritual beliefs, ideals, government, and ideas about right and wrong. Language is also a very important part of culture.

READ ACTIVELY

Predict What do you think the word *culture* means?

▼ How people live is part of their culture. Different cultures sometimes interact with their environment in similar ways. In mountainous Japan, farmers build terraces on the hillsides to increase the amount of land available for farming. Terrace farming is also used in other cultures, including those in South America and South Asia.

Some aspects of culture, like the clothes people wear, may not seem important. When you visit another country, however, these differences can make you feel like an outsider. This photograph shows children who are watching an international track meet held in Los Angeles. The children are from the Los Angeles area. To make athletes from other countries feel welcome, they dressed in many different national costumes.

People and Their Land   Geographers study culture, especially activities that relate to the environment. These things are part of the theme of human-environment interaction. Geographers want to know how landforms, climate, vegetation, and resources affect culture. For example, fish and seaweed are popular foods in Japan, a nation of islands. These islands are mountainous, with little farmland. Therefore, the Japanese get food from the sea.

Geographers are also interested in the effect people have on their environment. Often the effect is tied to a culture's technology, or tools and the skills people need to use them. People use technology to take advantage of natural resources and change the environment. Technology can mean tools like computers and the Internet. But technology also means stone tools and the ability to make them. Geographers use levels of technology to see how advanced a culture is.

A group's cultural landscape includes any changes to its environment. It also includes the technology used to make the changes. They vary from culture to culture. For example, Bali, in Indonesia, has many mountains. Therefore, people carved terraces in them to create flat farmland. Other regions, such as central India, have much level land. Farmers there would not develop a technology to create terraces.

Think about your culture. What do people eat? What are the houses like? What kind of work do people do? Can you identify some beliefs and values of your culture? In your mind, describe your culture. You may find it is harder to look at your own culture than at someone else's.

Working Together
Sometimes the old ways are best. Two Bolivians, Bonifacia Quispe and Oswaldo Rivera, discovered the ancient Aymara Indians cut terraces into the sides of mountains to create flat farmland. Terraces are easier to irrigate and fertilize than slopes. In 1986, Quispe and Rivera taught the method to today's Aymara farmers. These farmers then grew 28 times more food.

The Development of Culture

Cultures develop over a long time. Geographers say early cultures went through four stages: the invention of tools, the discovery of fire, the growth of **agriculture**, or farming, and the use of writing.

Technology and Weather Forecasting

Technology is a very important part of culture because it changes the way we do things. For thousands of years, people have looked up at the sky to try to forecast the weather. Today, meteorologists—scientists who study the weather—still look up at the sky. However, they use very advanced technology, including various kinds of satellites, to do their job. Our ancestors could do little more than guess about the weather. Modern meteorologists, however, can make highly accurate forecasts about the weather several days into the future. Below is a diagram of a weather tracking satellite system.

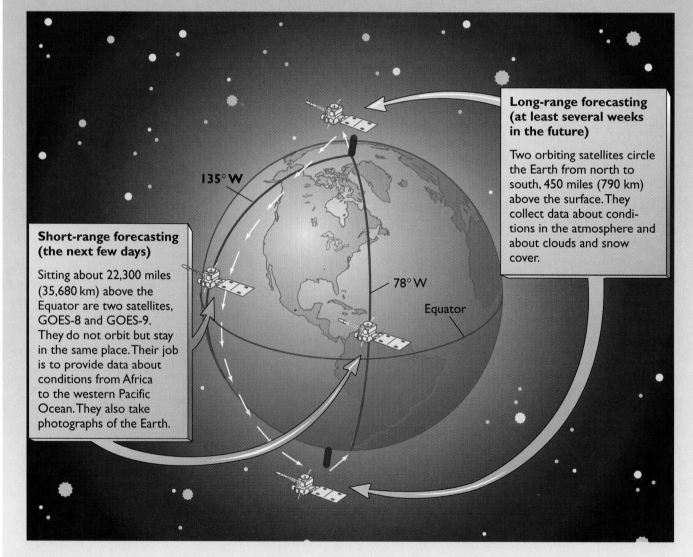

135° W

Long-range forecasting (at least several weeks in the future)

Two orbiting satellites circle the Earth from north to south, 450 miles (790 km) above the surface. They collect data about conditions in the atmosphere and about clouds and snow cover.

Short-range forecasting (the next few days)

Sitting about 22,300 miles (35,680 km) above the Equator are two satellites, GOES-8 and GOES-9. They do not orbit but stay in the same place. Their job is to provide data about conditions from Africa to the western Pacific Ocean. They also take photographs of the Earth.

78° W

Equator

Early Technology For most of human history, people were hunters and gatherers. Traveling from place to place, they collected wild plants, hunted game, and fished. Wood and stone tools and weapons helped them hunt, prepare food, and do other work. Later they learned to make and use fire, so some people began living in colder climates.

The Start of Agriculture Then, people discovered how to grow crops and tame wild animals to use as food or to help them with work. Now people no longer had to spend all their time following herds or moving from campsite to campsite in search of wild plants. Over time, societies relied on farming for most of their food. Historians call this great change the Agricultural Revolution.

By 3,000 years ago, the Agricultural Revolution had changed much of the world. Agriculture provided a steady food supply. Birthrates rose; death rates fell; population increased. Agriculture also led to the creation of cities and complex societies. Some people produced food, and others developed special skills. For example, people became potters, tailors, or metal workers. People began to develop laws and government. To record information, they developed writing. Now, people could store knowledge and pass it on to others. When a culture creates a writing system, it is called a civilization.

Early civilizations also created unique forms of art and music. They organized their beliefs into religions, with priests, temples, and ceremonies. Their roads and canals became features of the landscape. People learned to control and change their environment. Because of technological inventions such as irrigation and terracing, people could grow more and better crops in more areas. People spread over more and more regions. As they moved, they made changes to the Earth's landscape.

The Domestication of Grain Early people gathered the seeds of the wild grains for food. However, about 10,000 years ago, people in Southwest Asia decided to try to plant wild wheat to tide them over. The first crop was poor. But farmers saved seeds from the best plants and tried again the next year. Over time, this led to today's domesticated wheat.

SECTION 1 REVIEW

1. **Define** (a) culture, (b) cultural trait, (c) technology, (d) cultural landscape, (e) agriculture.

2. If someone asked you to describe your culture, what would you tell them?

3. Describe four important developments in human culture. Tell why they are important.

Critical Thinking

4. **Recognizing Cause and Effect** Agriculture encouraged people to settle in one area and provided a steady food supply. How did agriculture lead to civilization?

Activity

5. **Writing to Learn** Find a photograph of a familiar scene in your town or city. List at least ten features of your culture shown in the photograph.

Social Groups, Language, and Religion

Reach Into Your Background

Even if you can't speak a word of Chinese, Italian, French, or Spanish, you can probably get Chinese, Italian, French, or Spanish food. Here is a list of four restaurants: Hoy Hing, Bella Vista, Café de Paris, Casa Mexico. Where would you go for enchiladas? For egg rolls? You know where to go because you connect food and language. Both are parts of culture. What else is part of culture?

Questions to Explore

1. Why is social organization important to cultures?

2. What elements make cultures distinct from one another?

Key Terms

social structure   ethics
nuclear family
extended family

▼ The end of Ramadan means a joyous celebration for these Egyptian Muslims.

It is still dark when the muezzin (moo EZ in) calls the people of Cairo to prayer. Roosters crow. As you wake, you remember that today is the first day of Ramadan (ram uh DAHN). During this religious season, Muslims, followers of the religion of Islam, eat and drink nothing from sunrise to sunset. This year, Ramadan will be special. Young children do not fast during Ramadan, but now you are 12. Now you are old enough to join the fast.

You are excited and a little nervous. You want to fast. It is a way to praise Allah, and it shows you are an adult. Still, you wonder if you can go all day without eating or drinking. You join your family for the *suhoor* (soo HOOR), the meal eaten before daybreak. Your parents and grandparents smile at you proudly. In the evening, you will join them for the *Iftar* (if TAHR), or the meal eaten after dark. That meal will taste especially good. And a month from now, when you celebrate the end of Ramadan, you will be prouder than ever. Every year you receive gifts, but this year they will be very special. You will give the prayers of thanksgiving, knowing you have joined with Muslims all over the world to celebrate Ramadan.

How Society Is Organized

Although the children of Cairo join with Muslims all over the world to celebrate Ramadan, they do so within their own households. Every culture has a **social structure**. This is a way of organizing people into

In the United States, a mother, father, and their two sons enjoy a day in the park (top left). In Malaysia, children join their parents, aunts, uncles, and grandparents to make music (top right). In the mountains of Tibet, a mother leads her child on a yak (bottom). As these pictures show, a family can be as small as two people or as large as a roomful of people.

smaller groups. Each smaller group has particular tasks. Some groups work together to get food. Others protect the community. Still others raise children. Social structure helps people work together to meet the basic needs of individuals, families, and communities.

The family is the basic, most important social unit of any culture. Families teach the customs and traditions of the culture. Through their families, children learn how to dress, to be polite, to eat, and to play.

Kinds of Families All cultures do not define family in the same way. In some cultures, the basic unit is a **nuclear family,** or a mother, father, and their children. This pattern is common in industrial nations such as the United States, Great Britain, and Germany. Adults often work outside the home. They usually have money to buy what they need. They depend on the work of machines like vacuum cleaners and automobiles.

Other cultures have extended families. An **extended family** includes several generations. Along with parents and their children, there may be grandparents, aunts, uncles, cousins, and other relatives who live with them or close by. In extended families, older people are very respected. They pass on traditions. Extended families are less common than they used to be. As rural people move to cities, nuclear families are becoming more common.

Cultures also differ when deciding who is in charge in families. Many cultures have patriarchal (PAY tree ar kal) families. That means men make most family decisions. But some African and Native American cultures have matriarchal (MAY tree ar kal) families. In these, women have more authority than in patriarchies. Today, family organization is changing. Men and women have started to share family power and responsibility.

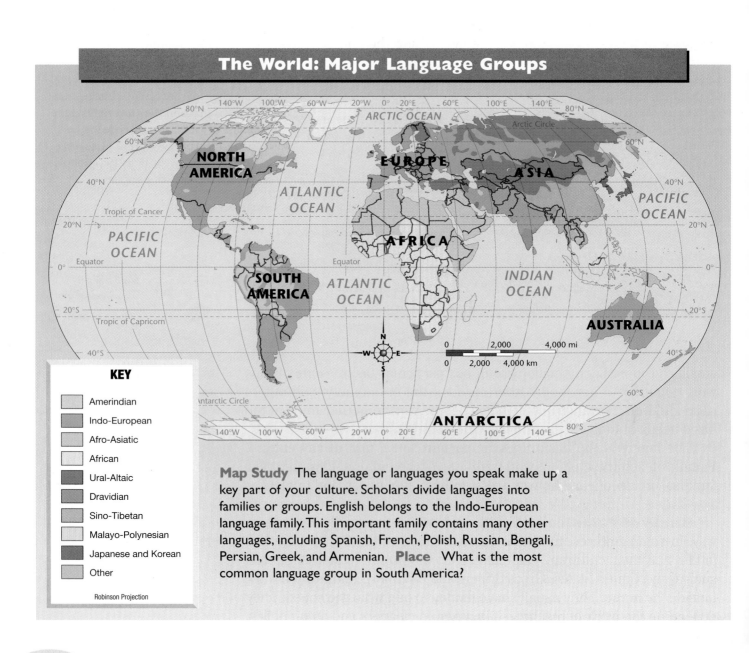

The World: Major Language Groups

KEY

- Amerindian
- Indo-European
- Afro-Asiatic
- African
- Ural-Altaic
- Dravidian
- Sino-Tibetan
- Malayo-Polynesian
- Japanese and Korean
- Other

Robinson Projection

Map Study The language or languages you speak make up a key part of your culture. Scholars divide languages into families or groups. English belongs to the Indo-European language family. This important family contains many other languages, including Spanish, French, Polish, Russian, Bengali, Persian, Greek, and Armenian. **Place** What is the most common language group in South America?

Social Classes   Cultures also have another kind of social organization—social classes. These rank people in a culture. A person's status or position may come from such things as wealth, land, ancestors, or education. In some cultures in the past, it was often hard—or impossible—for people to move from one social class to another. Today, people in many societies can improve their status. They can get a good education, make more money, or even marry someone of a higher class.

Language

Culture is a total way of life. Whoever you are, wherever you live, you are part of the culture of your society. You learn your culture from your family or from others. You also learn a great deal through language. Think of how hard it would be if you had no way to say, "Meet me by the gate after school," or "I'll have a tuna sandwich." How could you learn if you could not ask questions?

All cultures have language. In fact, every culture is based on language. It lets people communicate everything they need to share in their culture. Without language, people could not pass on what they know or believe to their children.

A culture's language reflects the things that its people think are important. For example, English has the word *snow* and several adjectives for the white stuff that falls in some places in winter. But the Inuits of North America have over 13 words for snow. Why? Where the Inuits live, snow covers the ground for a good part of the year. Snow is a more important part of their environment than it is to people of other cultures. The Inuits, therefore, have created words to meet their needs. All cultures have their own unique terms.

In some countries, people speak different languages. For example, the official language of Egypt is Arabic. It is spoken by most Egyptians. But some Egyptians speak Italian, Greek, or Armenian. Canada has two official languages, French and English, and Native Americans there speak a number of languages. People who speak these languages are culturally different in some ways from other people in their country. They may celebrate different festivals, wear different clothes, or have different customs for such things as dating or education.

Ways of Believing

Language is basic to cultures. Other basics are values and religion. At the beginning of this section, you read about Ramadan, a religious celebration of Muslims, followers of the religion of Islam. Ramadan is a very important part of Islam. And Islam is a major part of Egyptian culture. Other religions are important in other cultures.

Religion helps people understand the world. Religion can provide comfort and hope for people facing difficult times. And religion helps answer questions about the meaning and purpose of life. It helps define the values that people believe are important. Religions guide people in **ethics,** or standards of accepted behavior.

Ancient Alphabets The Phoenicians were ancient traders along the Mediterranean Sea. Their alphabet had 22 letters, and they wrote from right to left. The Greeks saw this writing system and based their own alphabet on it—with one difference. The Greeks, like us, wrote from left to right. We owe our alphabet, in part, to these two ancient cultures.

Predict Why are religions an important part of cultures?

The World: Major Religions

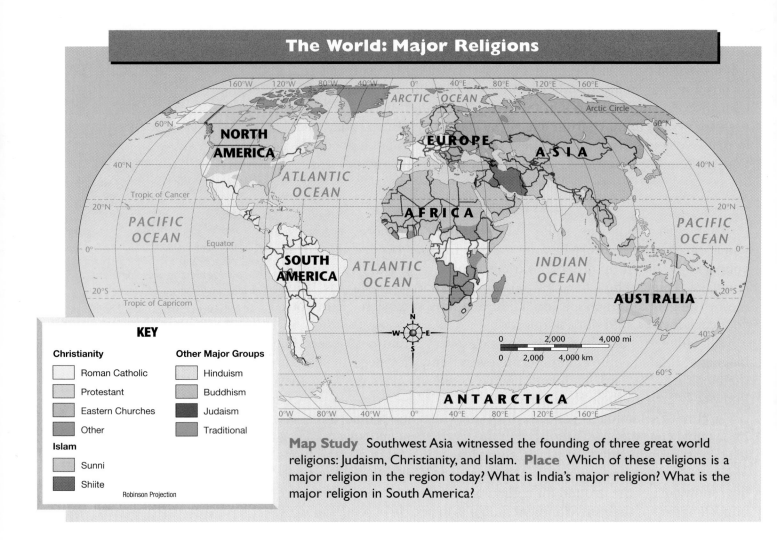

KEY

Christianity
- Roman Catholic
- Protestant
- Eastern Churches
- Other

Islam
- Sunni
- Shiite

Other Major Groups
- Hinduism
- Buddhism
- Judaism
- Traditional

Robinson Projection

Map Study Southwest Asia witnessed the founding of three great world religions: Judaism, Christianity, and Islam. **Place** Which of these religions is a major religion in the region today? What is India's major religion? What is the major religion in South America?

Religious beliefs vary. Some religions such as Islam, Judaism, and Christianity believe in one god. Other religions worship more than one god. But all religions have prayers and rituals. Every religion celebrates important places and times. Most religions expect people to treat one another well and behave properly.

SECTION 2 REVIEW

1. **Define** (a) social structure, (b) nuclear family, (c) extended family, (d) ethics.

2. What is the basic unit of a culture's social structure?

3. What are three important features of a culture?

4. Explain the difference between a matriarchy and a patriarchy.

5. What is the role of religion in a culture?

Critical Thinking

6. **Recognizing Bias** How do you know that one language is not better than another?

Activity

7. **Writing to Learn** Make notes about your own culture. Draw three circles labeled "social structure," "language," and "religion." In each circle, make notes about your own culture's social structure, language, and religion. Include information about others in your family or neighborhood whose culture influences you.

Economic and Political Systems

BEFORE YOU READ

Reach Into Your Background
Many schools are polling places where people vote. You may have seen adults going into the gym or another part of your school to use a voting machine or mark a ballot.

Signs nearby often urge people to vote for a candidate or a certain way on an issue. Perhaps your student body holds elections, too. They are part of the political process in many places in the United States.

Questions to Explore
1. What is an economic system?
2. How do governments differ in their structure?

Key Terms

economy
producer
goods
services
consumer
capitalism
socialism
communism

government
direct democracy
monarchy
constitution
representative democracy
dictator

Muhammad Yunnus is a professor of economics in the country of Bangladesh. Bangladesh (bahng gluh DESH) is a very poor nation in South Asia. Yunnus wanted to understand how the people in his country really lived. His goal was to help them. He knew Bangladeshis ate only one or two meals a day. Though many had not gone to school, they were intelligent. Yunnus knew they were hard-working and could be trusted.

In the early 1970s, Yunnus met Sufiya Khatun. She made bamboo stools. But she earned only two cents a day because she had so few stools to sell. If she had more money for supplies, she could make more. But Sufiya had no way to borrow money to buy supplies. At first, Yunnus thought he would simply give her the small sum she needed. Then he wondered if others in the village were also like Sufiya. He found 42 people that needed to borrow about $26 each for their businesses.

Yunnus was shocked. So little money meant the difference between success and failure. But banks would not

▼ Most of Muhammad Yunnus's customers are women seeking to open small businesses. This woman used her loan to start a weaving shop.

not bother with such small loans. In 1976, Yunnus decided to do something about this situation. He started up a bank to loan small amounts of money only to poor people. Every borrower must join a group of five people. Every group member is responsible for the loans of every other member, so members must all trust and help each other. To build trust, they meet once a week to talk over their problems.

Yunnus's bank is called the Grameen Bank, which means "village bank." Today, the Grameen Bank has more than 1,000 offices and has loaned money to 2 million customers. Its interest rates are fairly high, but 98 percent of its loans are paid back. People in other countries are starting banks like Grameen. There are even some in the United States.

READ ACTIVELY

Connect Think about each member of your family and what he or she does. Is each a consumer, a producer, or both? Explain why.

Economic Systems

Banks like the Grameen help people become productive members of their nation's economy. An **economy** is a system for producing, distributing, and consuming goods and services. Owners and workers are **producers.** They make products, such as bamboo baskets or automobiles. Those products are called **goods.** Some products are really **services** that producers perform for other people. They may style hair, provide hotel rooms, or heal diseases. **Consumers** are people who buy and use the goods and services.

There are two categories of businesses. Basic businesses are essential for a nation to function. They include things like transportation, communication, and electricity. Non-basic industries are "nice but not necessary." They may make products such as compact disks or sports equipment. Services can also be basic or non-basic businesses. Hospitals are basic businesses. Singing telegram companies are non-basic businesses.

◀▼ Neighbors in the New York town of Ithaca have a very interesting system of exchange. Instead of paying dollars, they trade "Ithaca Hours" for goods like fresh bread, as well as for services like baby-sitting. Each hour is worth $10—the average hourly wage in Ithaca. "Prices" depend on the amount of labor involved in producing the good or service.

Capitalism Replaces Communism

This photograph was taken in Berlin shortly after Communist East Germany united with capitalist West Germany. These East German children had never seen so many different school supplies before. The supplies came from the West, where the free market forces businesses to compete for customers.

Cultures choose the way they want to organize their economies. Today, most cultures choose from three basic systems: *capitalism, socialism,* and *communism.*

In **capitalism,** most basic and non-basic businesses are privately owned. Workers produce the goods or services. When a company sells its products, it earns profits, or money. The owners decide how much to pay workers and how to use profits.

The consumer is important in capitalism. Companies make products, but consumers might refuse to buy them. Successful companies supply goods or services that consumers need, want, and can afford. Capitalist countries include the United States, South Africa, and Japan. Capitalism is also called a free-market economy.

In **socialism,** the government owns most basic industries. It runs them for the good of society, not for profit. The government decides how much to pay workers and how much to charge for goods. It uses profits to pay for services such as health and education. Non-basic industries and services follow the capitalist model. They are privately owned, and consumers decide which products to buy. A few countries follow socialism or have socialistic programs. These countries include Spain, Portugal, and Italy.

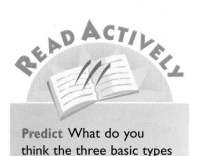

READ ACTIVELY

Predict What do you think the three basic types of economic systems are?

ACROSS THE WORLD

Quebec In Quebec, a province in Canada, many people are descendants of French settlers. So, they speak both French and English. Some residents want Quebec to become a separate nation. This has led to much political debate. Canada is a democracy, so residents of Quebec could vote on the issue. For now, Quebec has decided to remain part of Canada, but the argument continues.

Ask Questions What would you like to find out about different kinds of government?

In **communism,** the central government owns all property, such as farms and factories, for the benefit of its citizens. It controls all aspects of citizens' lives, including prices of goods and services, how much is produced, and how much workers are paid. Today, only a few of the world's nations practice communism. They include Cuba, China, and North Korea.

Hardly any nation has a "pure" economic system. For example, the United States has a capitalistic economy. However, state, local, and federal governments provide educational services, build and repair roads, and regulate product safety. In communist countries, you will find some private businesses such as small farms and special stores.

Political Systems

Small groups of people can work together to solve problems that affect them all. But that is impossible in complex cultures. Still, they also have to resolve conflicts between individuals and social groups. People also need protection from other countries and cultural groups. Communities need laws, leaders, and organizations that make decisions. **Government** is the system that sets up and enforces a society's laws and institutions. Some governments are controlled by a few people. Others are controlled by many.

Lacquer Painting

Olga Loceva
Age 14
Russia
Under communism, traditional Russian arts and crafts, such as lacquer painting of boxes and vases as shown here, were discouraged. Since the collapse of the Soviet Union, many Russians have begun to practice these arts once again. What traditions do you value? How would you feel if the government banned those traditions?

Direct Democracy The earliest governments were probably simple. People lived in small groups and practiced **direct democracy.** That means everyone participated in running the day-to-day affairs of the group. Chiefs or elders decided what was right or what to do. Decisions were based upon the culture's customs and beliefs. Today, government plays much the same role for complex cultures.

Monarchy Until about 100 years ago, one of the most common forms of government was a **monarchy.** In this system, a king or queen rules the government. The ruler inherits the throne by birth. Monarchies still exist today. Sweden, Denmark, Great Britain, Spain, and Swaziland are examples. But the rulers of these countries do not have the power their ancestors did. Instead, they are constitutional monarchs. Their countries have **constitutions,** or sets of laws that define and often limit the government's power. In a constitutional monarchy, the king or queen is often only a symbol of the country.

▲ In Great Britain's constitutional monarchy, the monarch has little authority. The real power is wielded by Parliament, an elected body like our Congress.

Representative Democracy A constitutional monarchy usually is a **representative democracy.** That means citizens elect representatives to run the country's affairs. Democracy comes from the Greek word *demos,* which means "common people." In a representative democracy, the people indirectly hold power to govern and rule. They elect representatives, who create laws. If the people do not like what a representative does, they can refuse to re-elect that person. They can also work to change laws they do not like. This system ensures that power is shared. The United States, Canada, and Israel are examples of representative democracies.

Dictatorship "If I ruled the world. . . . " Have you ever said or heard those words? It's fun to think about. You could give away free ice cream. You could give 12-year-olds the right to vote. Maybe you could end war and poverty.

◀ Josef Stalin was one of the world's cruelest dictators. He ruled the former Soviet Union from 1929 until 1953. He controlled every aspect of Soviet life and jailed or executed anybody who opposed him.

Of course, no one person rules the world. There are some countries, though, where one person rules. A government leader who has almost total power over an entire country is called a **dictator.**

Dictators decide what happens in their countries. They make the laws. They decide if there will be elections. When dictators take over, they often make promises that sound good. They may promise to end crime or to make a country strong. Sometimes they keep their promises. More often, they do not. Either way, people lose the right to make their own decisions.

SECTION 3 REVIEW

1. Define (a) economy, (b) producer, (c) goods, (d) services, (e) consumer, (f) capitalism, (g) socialism, (h) communism, (i) government, (j) direct democracy, (k) monarchy, (l) constitution, (m) representative democracy, (n) dictator.

2. Describe the three main types of economic systems.

3. Which form of government gives power to make decisions to the greatest number of people—a monarchy, a democracy, or a dictatorship?

Critical Thinking
4. Drawing Conclusions You hear on the news an announcement from the newly elected leader of a foreign country. The announcement states that the country's representatives will not meet. It also says that no elections will be held until further notice. What kind of a government does this country have? How do you know?

Activity
5. Writing to Learn You are working on a project to increase voting in your community. A statewide election is approaching. On behalf of your project, write a letter to a newspaper. In it, describe two reasons why people who are eligible to vote should do so.

Cultural Change

BEFORE YOU READ

Reach Into Your Background
If you like to listen to rap, rock, folk, or jazz music, you like music from many different cultures. The rhythms you like might have come from Ireland, Jamaica, or Peru. You probably like some artists from different countries, too. Name some music you like that you think is a cultural blend.

Questions to Explore
1. What causes cultures to change?

2. Why has the rate of cultural change been increasing?

Key Terms
cultural diffusion
acculturation

Most people think that blue jeans are typical American clothes. But many cultures contributed to them. Blue jeans were created in the United States in the 1800s, by Levi Strauss, a German salesman who went to California. He made the jeans with cloth from France, called *serge de Nîmes*. The name was shortened to denim. Strauss dyed the denim with indigo, a plant from India and China. The indigo colored the denim dark blue.

In the 1980s, the Japanese and the French developed stonewashing. It made brand-new denim jeans look worn. Then, an Italian company created acid-washed jeans. Today, jeans are still popular in America. They are also very popular in Britain, the former Soviet Union, India, and parts of Africa. And the name *jeans*? It's French, for Italian sailors who wore sturdy cotton pants. What is more American than jeans?

Always Something New

Just as jeans have changed over time, so, too, has American culture. Cultures change all the time. Because culture is a total way of life, a change in one part changes other parts. Changes in the natural environment, technology, and new ideas affect culture.

▼ Blue jeans are a popular form of casual wear across the world. These blue-jeans clad dancers are from Barcelona, Spain.

◄ Explorers brought crops native to the Americas, such as corn, squash, potatoes, and tomatoes back to Europe. This greatly changed the diet—and life—of Europeans.

A Change in the Environment If the weather changes long enough, the climate will change. That affects the kinds of food people can grow. It affects the kinds of clothes they wear. Changes in climate affect ways of making a living. But other changes can affect a culture, too.

A New Idea New ideas also change a culture. People used to take nature for granted. They thought anyone could use resources without damaging the overall supply. Since the 1950s, people in the United States and all over the world have become concerned about the environment. They recycle and work to protect endangered species and preserve forests. People also realized that we can use up or pollute many natural resources. The desire to save nature is a cultural change.

Technology Equals Change Cultural change has been going on for a long time. New technological discoveries and inventions may have had the most effect on cultures. The discovery of fire helped early people to survive colder climates. When people invented wood and stone tools and weapons, ways of living also changed. Hunters could kill animals such as the mammoth and the giant bear. These animals had been too large to hunt without weapons.

Think of how technology has changed the culture of the United States. Radio and television brought entertainment and news into homes. Such things as TV dinners and instant information are now part of our culture. Computers change how and where people work. Computers even help people live longer. Doctors use computers to treat

Predict What are some changes that technology has made in our culture in modern times?

patients. Radio, television, and computers add new words to our language. *Broadcast, channel surfing,* and *hacker* are three. What other new words can you think of?

Sharing Ideas People are on the move all over the world. People come to the United States from other countries. Americans travel to other countries. In the process, they all bring new things such as clothing and tools with them. They also bring ideas about such things as ways to prepare food, teach children, or worship and govern. Sometimes a culture adopts these new ideas. The movement of customs and ideas is **cultural diffusion.**

The blue jeans story is a good example of cultural diffusion. Jeans were invented in the United States but now are popular around the world. People in other countries made changes to jeans. People in the United States adopted the changes. The process of accepting, borrowing, and exchanging ideas is called **acculturation.**

You can see cultural diffusion and acculturation if you study the history of baseball. It began as an American sport, but today it is played all over the world. That is an example of cultural diffusion. The Japanese love baseball. However, they changed the game to fit their culture. This change is an example of acculturation. Americans value competition. They focus on winning. But in Japan, a game can end in a tie. The

Tuning In to Cyberspace
Many record companies are now on the Internet. They talk about things like a band's latest musical release and upcoming tours. Some let people hear a band's music before buying it. Some bands have even tried live concerts over the Internet. This could be a big cultural change—listening to live performances at home instead of at a concert!

Working in a Canning Factory, 1912

Immigrants to the United States, like these young workers in a New York canning factory, came from many different ethnic backgrounds. The mixing of their various cultures produced a new, American culture.

Ask Questions Imagine you meet someone on the Internet from another culture. What questions would you ask to learn more about his or her culture?

Japanese do not mind a tie game for several reasons. For instance, in Japan, how well you play is more important than winning. Also, people try hard not to embarrass someone.

Technology and the Speed of Change

What's the fastest way to get from your house to Japan? A jet plane? A phone call? A television broadcast? The Internet? A fax? All these answers can be right. It depends on whether you want to transport your body, your voice, a picture, an interactive game, or a sheet of paper.

For thousands of years, cultures changed slowly. People moved by foot or wagon or sailing ship, so ideas and technology also moved slowly. Recently, technology has increased the speed of change. People no longer have to wait for a newcomer to bring changes. Faxes and computers transport information almost instantly. Magazines and television shows bring ideas and information from all over the world to every home. This rapid exchange of ideas speeds up cultural change.

A Global Village A village is a small place where people all know each other. It doesn't take long to get from one place to another. Today, many people call the Earth a "global village." That is because modern transportation and communications tell everyone about faraway people, businesses, and governments almost instantly.

Technology has brought many benefits. Computers let scientists share information about how to clean up oil spills. Telephones let us instantly talk to relatives thousands of miles away. In the Australian Outback, students your age use closed-circuit television and two-way radios to go to school in their own homes.

International Travel

Chart Study More and more people visit foreign countries each year. In 1995, 47 million Americans traveled to other nations. That's nearly as many people as live in California and Texas combined. **Movement** How have today's forms of transportation, such as jet planes, affected international travel? **Critical Thinking** How do you think the increase in international travel has affected the "global village"?

Year	U.S. Travelers to Foreign Countries	Foreign Visitors to the United States
1980	22 million	22 million
1985	35 million	25 million
1990	45 million	40 million
1995	47 million	43 million

In recent years, people across the world have made greater efforts to preserve their traditions. In this picture, for example, young people from 20 Native American nations perform a dance at a gathering near Lake Casitas, California. **Critical Thinking** Why do you think it has become more important in recent years for people to preserve their traditions?

Information Overload? Change can help, but it can also hurt. If things change too fast, people can become confused, and culture is threatened. Valuable traditions can disappear. Once important sources of knowledge are lost, they can never be regained. In many parts of the world, people are working to save their own cultures before it is too late. They do not want to lose what is good in their culture. They understand it is important to remember where they came from if they are to understand where they are going.

SECTION 4 REVIEW

1. **Define** (a) cultural diffusion, (b) acculturation.

2. List three things that can cause a culture to change.

3. Explain the meaning of the term "global village."

Critical Thinking
4. **Distinguishing Fact From Opinion** A friend who has a computer tells you she has an e-mail pal in Singapore. "You learn more by having a pen pal on the Internet than by having one through regular mail," she says. You point out that you get drawings and photos in the mail from your pen pal in Turkey. Which of you has stated a fact? Which has stated an opinion? How do you know?

Activity
5. **Writing to Learn** Interview an older person about what changes she or he has seen in the culture over the years. Write two paragraphs summarizing what they say.

Locating Information

Rhonda was puzzled. "Did you hear that?" she whispered to Denise. "He just told me to shrink the panic! What does he mean?" Rhonda and Denise were staying in the home of a family in Argentina, a country in South America. They had traveled there as exchange students. The family had a mother, a father, a young girl, and a teenage boy. Rhonda had just told the teenage boy that she felt nervous about finding her way around.

That's when he turned to her and said, "Achicar el panico! I'll help you." Rhonda knew "achicar el panico" translated as "shrink the panic" in English. But what did it mean? The boy smiled at her puzzled look. "In Argentina, that's how we say 'chill out!'" he said. Rhonda smiled back.

"I get it," she said. "I guess I also need help learning the slang you use here!"

You know that people in different cultures live lives that are very different from yours. But do you know just how different? Even little things like slang can have completely different meanings. Before you travel to another country, it helps to learn as much about its culture as possible. The trick, believe it or not, is to build a pyramid!

Get Ready

This pyramid is not a real pyramid, of course, but a "pyramid of knowledge." There

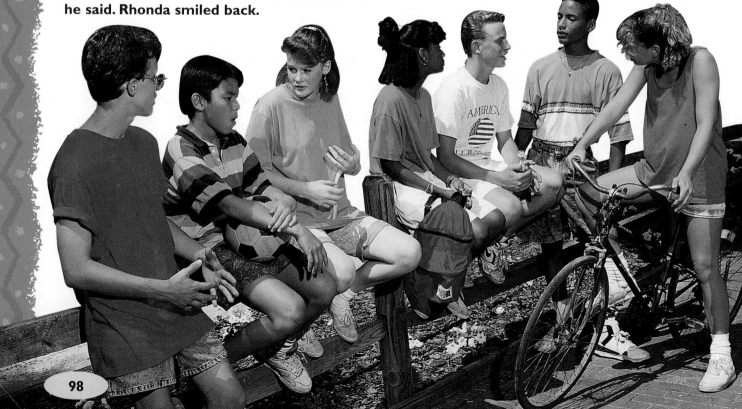

98

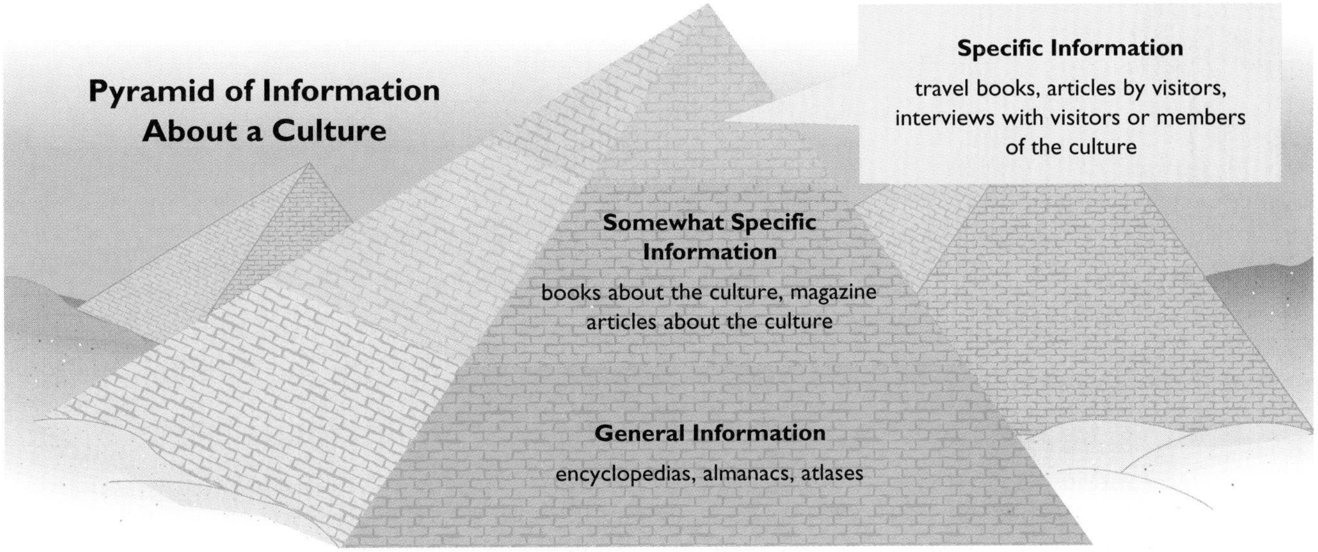

Pyramid of Information About a Culture

Specific Information
travel books, articles by visitors, interviews with visitors or members of the culture

Somewhat Specific Information
books about the culture, magazine articles about the culture

General Information
encyclopedias, almanacs, atlases

are thousands of sources of information about the peoples and cultures of the world. By organizing your search into the form of a pyramid, you can easily learn what you need to know. You will build your pyramid in a library.

Try It Out

Follow the steps below to build a pyramid of knowledge. As you work, refer to the diagram.

A. Choose a culture to learn about. You might choose a culture in a country in Europe, Latin America, Africa, or Asia.

B. Build a base of general information. Pyramids are built from the bottom up. The base of your pyramid of knowledge about a culture is general information. This includes such things as the correct name of a cultural group, its geographic location, the language the people speak, the population, and so on. Find this information by consulting the sources listed in the diagram of the pyramid.

C. Build the middle of the pyramid with more detailed information. The middle of the pyramid is made up of more detailed information about how people live in the culture. What are schools like? What customs are important? What are some common foods? What types of jobs do people have?

D. Build the top with specific information. Complete the pyramid by building the very top. It is made up of specific information about how individuals in the culture interact. Find out, for example, what proper greetings are and what certain gestures mean. Learn how to say basic phrases such as "How do you do?" and "Good-bye" in the language of the culture. Add specific information about anything else that interests you.

You can see you have learned a great deal about the culture in a short time. It takes a lifetime to develop a deep understanding of any culture. But by building a pyramid and continually adding to it, you can add to what you know.

Apply the Skill

Building a "pyramid of knowledge" is as simple as 1-2-3:

1. **Build the base.**
2. **Build the middle.**
3. **Build the top.**

As the pyramid grows, so does your knowledge. Practice applying this skill the next time you have any assignment requiring research. Find general information first, then more detailed information, and then very specific information. Work your way from the bottom to the top.

Review and Activities

Reviewing Main Ideas

1. What is the relationship between the environment people live in and their culture?

2. Describe three developments that have affected human culture.

3. Explain how the technology used in a culture reveals things about the culture's daily life, work, and values.

4. Why was the Agricultural Revolution so important in human history? What changes did it bring about?

5. Explain three important ways in which cultures can differ from one another.

6. Compare the three economic systems described in this chapter: capitalism, socialism, and communism.

7. Explain why people formed governments.

8. Why has culture changed more rapidly in modern times than in the past?

Reviewing Key Terms

Use each key term below in a sentence that shows the meaning of the term.

1. culture
2. technology
3. cultural landscape
4. social structure
5. nuclear family
6. extended family
7. economy
8. producer
9. goods
10. services
11. capitalism
12. socialism
13. government
14. constitution
15. representative democracy
16. dictator
17. cultural diffusion
18. acculturation

Critical Thinking

1. **Identifying Central Issues** Why is no culture exactly like any other culture?

2. **Expressing Problems Clearly** Why do you think people in one culture sometimes do not understand people in another?

Graphic Organizer

Think about how having less fresh water would affect society. Copy this cause-effect organizer. Then consider these topics: social organization, language, economic system, or government. Fill in the boxes, explaining how a water shortage might affect each topic.

Less Fresh Water

Vocabulary Activity

Many terms in this chapter compare and contrast similar ideas or activities. For instance, in capitalism, businesses are run by private individuals, but in communism, businesses are run by government. On a separate sheet of paper, explain how these terms compare and contrast similar ideas or activities.

1. goods and services

2. direct democracy and representative democracy

3. nuclear family and extended family

Writing Activity

Writing a Public Service Message
Your town or city is going to have a culture fair. The fair will introduce people to new cultures. It will also introduce people to different cultures within the United States. Write a public service message for a local radio station. A public service message includes the time, place, and purpose of a cultural event. Your notice should tell people why and how they should get involved with the culture fair.

Internet Activity
Use a search engine to find the **Human-Languages Page.** Click on **Languages and Literature.** Use the dictionaries and common phrases sections to learn how to say and write a greeting in five languages. Write your greetings, and an English translation, on a sheet of construction paper. Hang your greetings on a class "World Greetings" bulletin board.

Skills Review

Turn to the Skills Activity.

Review the steps for locating information. Then complete the following: (a) How can building a pyramid of knowledge help you to locate information? (b) Explain the difference between general information and specific information.

How Am I Doing?

Answer these questions to help you check your progress.

1. Do I understand how environment affects culture and how culture affects environment?

2. Can I list the major elements of culture and the forms that they take?

3. Can I describe the ways that cultures change?

4. What information from this chapter can I use in my book project?

Rough Country

BY DANA GIOIA

BEFORE YOU READ

Reach Into Your Background

Think about the area where you live. It has many characteristics that make it unique. Perhaps there is a flood plain, hills, flat land, or an earthquake fault. Perhaps there are special stores or restaurants in your neighborhood. Perhaps the people who live there speak several languages. Or, perhaps, when you first think about it, you cannot see anything about your neighborhood that is different from anywhere else.

Most people are so used to their surroundings that they do not pay any attention to them. But Dana Gioia goes into great detail to explain why "Rough Country" is a very special place. As you read the poem, notice how Gioia emphasizes the unique nature of "Rough Country."

Questions to Explore

1. What characteristics make the country described in the poem "rough"?
2. What is so special about this spot in the country?

---

glacial (GLAY shul) *adj.* from a glacier; here, rocks left behind by a glacier

bottomlands *n.* low land through which a river flows; flood plain

tendril (TEN drihl) *n.* thread-like part of a climbing plant that supports the plant

---

Rough Country

Give me a landscape made of obstacles,
of steep hills and jutting glacial rock,
where the low-running streams are quick to flood
the grassy fields and bottomlands.
                                        A place
no engineers can master—where the roads
must twist like tendrils up the mountainside
on narrow cliffs where boulders block the way.

Where tall black trunks of lightning-scalded pine
push through the tangled woods to make a roost
for hawks and swarming crows.
                                        And sharp inclines
where twisting through the thorn-thick underbrush,
scratched and exhausted, one turns suddenly
to find an unexpected waterfall,

not half a mile from the nearest road,
a spot so hard to reach that no one comes—

a hiding place, a shrine for dragonflies
and nesting jays, a sign that there is still
one piece of property that won't be owned.

READ ACTIVELY

Visualize What does this place look like in your mind's eye?

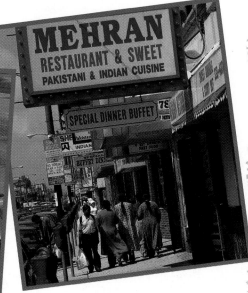

◀▼ Where do you call home? Some people live in the Canadian Rockies, and others live in Washington farmlands. What unique features might you find if you lived in those places?

▲ What might you find if you lived in Chicago, Illinois?

EXPLORING YOUR READING

Look Back

1. What human activities would be difficult or impossible in this place?

Think It Over

2. In the fourth stanza of "Rough Country," the poet describes a hike that suddenly opens onto a waterfall. What makes the waterfall seem especially beautiful to the poet?

Go Beyond

3. In "Rough Country," the poet describes "one piece of property that won't be owned." Antarctica is another place that no one "owns." No country can claim any part of it. Why might people think a place was so important that no one should own it?

Ideas for Writing: Poem

4. Think about the place where you live. Make a list of its characteristics, and draw a picture of it. Then, write a poem about your place. Finally, compare your poem with "Rough Country."

CHAPTER 5

Earth's Natural Resources

PICTURE ACTIVITIES

Think of the power of a waterfall as it tumbles from high places to low ones. Today, dams like this one on the Brazil-Paraguay border create waterfalls. In the process, they harness river power to create electricity for homes and businesses. This helps economies grow. A dam across a river also has a huge effect on the environment. The dam holds back the water of the river. It floods acres of land and creates a lake. Sometimes such lakes flood forests, farmland, and even towns and villages.

Examine both sides of an issue
Think about how this dam changes the natural landscape and how it helps people. Make a list of the advantages and disadvantages of such a project.

Study the picture
Each country has natural resources. From this picture, what resources do you think Brazil has? As you read this chapter, think about how a country's wealth relates to its land and climates.

What Are Natural Resources?

BEFORE YOU READ

Reach Into Your Background

How much do you throw away each day? How much do you recycle? What do you own that is made of recycled material? Jot down your answers.

Questions to Explore

1. What are natural resources?
2. What is the difference between renewable and nonrenewable natural resources?

Key Terms

natural resource
raw material
recyclable resource
renewable resource
nonrenewable resource
fossil fuel

What can we do with the garbage we create? People are searching for answers. Some are unique. In 1995, architect Kate Warner built a house in Martha's Vineyard, Massachusetts. She used materials most people call trash. The builders mixed concrete with ash left over from furnaces that burn trash. Then they used the mixture to make the foundation of the house. To make the frame of the house, they used wood left over from old buildings, not fresh lumber. Warner wanted glass tiles in the bathroom. So she had glassmakers create them out of old car windshields. "We ask people to recycle, but then we don't know what to do with the stuff," Warner says. "By making use of waste materials, the manufacturers of these new building materials are creating exciting new markets and completing a loop." In this loop, materials are used over and over again. Garbage becomes a natural resource.

▼ Factories make new steel for bicycles and buildings by combining iron and other natural resources with recycled or "scrap" steel.

Natural Resources

Kate Warner is one of many people who want to use the Earth's natural resources wisely. These people believe this is the only way for humans to survive. A **natural resource** is any useful material found in the environment. Usually when people talk about natural resources, they mean such things as soil, water, minerals, and vegetation. A natural resource, then, is anything from the Earth that helps meet people's needs for food, clothing, and shelter.

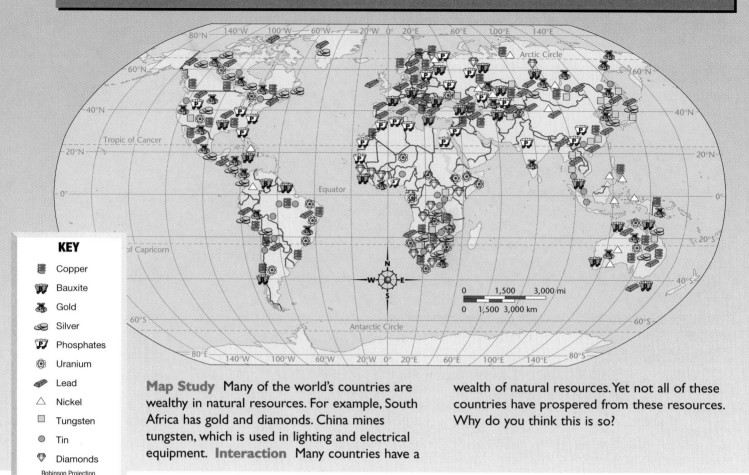

KEY

Copper	
Bauxite	
Gold	
Silver	
Phosphates	
Uranium	
Lead	
Nickel	
Tungsten	
Tin	
Diamonds	

Robinson Projection

Map Study Many of the world's countries are wealthy in natural resources. For example, South Africa has gold and diamonds. China mines tungsten, which is used in lighting and electrical equipment. **Interaction** Many countries have a wealth of natural resources. Yet not all of these countries have prospered from these resources. Why do you think this is so?

All people need food, clothing, and shelter to survive. People drink water. People eat the food that the soil produces. So do the animals that provide eggs, cheese, and meat. People get such things as fish and salt from the ocean. Homes are made from wood, clay, and steel. Every day you benefit from the natural resources in the environment.

People can use some resources just the way they come from nature. Fresh water is one. But most resources must be changed before people use them. For example, people cannot just go out and cut down a tree to make a house. Even if they want to build a log cabin, they must cut the tree into pieces first. For a modern home, the wood must have the bark shaved away. Then the wood is cut into boards of various sizes. Resources that must be altered, or changed, before they can be used are called **raw materials.** Trees are the raw material for paper and wood.

Three Kinds of Resources The environment is full of natural resources. But not all resources are alike. Geographers divide them into three groups. The first group of resources cycle naturally through the environment. They do so because of the way the Earth works. In the water cycle, water evaporates into the air and falls as rain, snow, hail, or sleet. This happens over and over again. Therefore, the Earth has the same amount of water, although there may be too much of it in some places and not enough in others. For this reason, geographers call water a **recyclable resource.** Some other materials that cycle through natural processes as recyclable resources are nitrogen and carbon.

A second group of resources includes trees and other living things on the Earth. These things are different from recyclable resources. It is possible for people to gather plants or hunt animals until they no longer exist. But it does not have to happen. For example, a timber company may cut down all the trees in an area. But the company may then plant new trees to replace the ones they cut. Every day the people of the world eat many chickens and ears of corn. But farmers and chicken ranchers make sure there are always more corn plants and chickens to replace the ones people eat. If a resource can be replaced, it is called a **renewable resource.** If people are careful, they can have a steady supply of renewable resources.

The third group of resources is called **nonrenewable resources.** When they are used up, they cannot be replaced. Most nonliving things, such as minerals, coal, natural gas, and petroleum—or oil—are nonrenewable resources. So are metals. City recycling programs are often eager to recycle aluminum cans and plastic bottles. That is because these cans and bottles are made of nonrenewable resources.

Ancient Energy: Fossil Fuel Often people take some things for granted. Lights turn on when a switch is flicked. The house is warm in winter or cool in summer. The car runs. All of these things require

READ ACTIVELY

Visualize Visualize the world if people do not take care to replace renewable resources. What would your town or city look like?

Rain Forests: A Fragile Resource

Rain forests once covered millions of acres in Asia. Today, the rain forests of Asia are rapidly disappearing. Using heavy equipment to harvest the most valuable woods, loggers often damage huge areas of forest. In this photograph of the Malaysian rain forest, notice the sawmills that process the valuable tropical lumber and the roads that carry the wood out of the area. Once this rain forest is cut down, it will be very difficult to replace.

fossil fuels, which include coal, natural gas, and petroleum. Fossil fuels were created over millions of years from the remains of prehistoric plants and animals. These fuels are no longer being created. As a result, fossil fuels are nonrenewable resources. If people continue using coal, natural gas, and petroleum at today's rate, the Earth will run out of fossil fuels in 100 to 200 years.

A Special Resource: Energy

Imagine that you are in your room, reading your geography book. What items around you require energy? Some are obvious. A clock, a radio, or a lamp all use energy directly, in a form called electricity. Others are not so obvious because they use energy indirectly. Consider a water glass on a dresser or athletic shoes on the floor. These things were manufactured in a factory, and that process uses energy.

What about things made of plastic—a toy, a comb, or a pen? If you have a rug, it may be made of a synthetic material that looks like wool but is really a kind of plastic. These things are manufactured, so they use energy indirectly. But they also use energy directly. The reason is that plastics are made from petroleum, and petroleum is an energy source.

Getting everything to your room required energy, too. Your family bought them at a store, so you used energy to travel back and forth. The store bought them from a manufacturer, which required more energy. It takes a great deal of energy to put a small plastic glass in your room. So it is easy to see why people value energy sources so highly.

World Petroleum Consumption

Country	Percentage
United States	25%
Canada	2.7%
Mexico	1.8%
China	8.5%
Japan	5.3%
India	2.5%
Russia	10.6%
Germany	4.6%
Ukraine	2.8%
France	2.8%
United Kingdom	2.8%
Italy	2.1%

Percentage of World Petroleum Consumption (0, 5, 10, 15, 20, 25, 30)

Chart Study Products made from petroleum are used to provide heat for buildings and power for automobiles, airplanes, and factories. People use so much petroleum that experts think that world supplies will be almost exhausted in 100 to 200 years. **Critical Thinking** What countries consume the most petroleum? Think of some ways that these countries could reduce their consumption of petroleum.

Energy "Have's" and "Have Not's" Everyone in the world needs energy. But energy resources are not evenly spread around the world. Certain areas are rich in some energy resources. Others have very few.

World Petroleum Production

Chart Study Petroleum is a nonrenewable resource, one that cannot be replaced once it is used. As a result, it is very valuable. Countries that have deposits can sell petroleum for a profit. **Critical Thinking** Compare this chart with the one on the previous page. Notice that the United States uses about twice as much petroleum as it produces. How does Russia's production compare with its consumption?

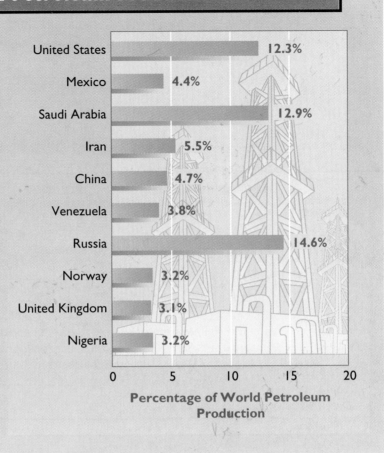

Country	Percentage
United States	12.3%
Mexico	4.4%
Saudi Arabia	12.9%
Iran	5.5%
China	4.7%
Venezuela	3.8%
Russia	14.6%
Norway	3.2%
United Kingdom	3.1%
Nigeria	3.2%

Percentage of World Petroleum Production

Countries like Saudi Arabia and Mexico have huge amounts of oil. Others, like the United States and China, have coal and natural gas. Countries with many rivers, such as the countries of Northwestern Europe, can use water energy to create electricity. Others, such as Japan, have very few energy sources. These countries must buy their energy from other countries.

Growing Needs and the Search for New Supplies In 1973, members of the Organization of Petroleum Exporting Countries (OPEC) decided to sell less of their oil. In the United States, this caused a shortage of gasoline, which is made from oil. When there is a shortage of something, it is more expensive. The price of gas more than doubled. Drivers sat in long lines at gas stations. Companies that used fuel oil to make electricity sent notices to families and businesses. The notices asked people to use as little electricity as possible. How could OPEC members have such an effect on the United States?

The answer is that just because a country uses large amounts of energy does not mean that country has its own large energy resources. The biggest users of energy are industrial countries like the United States and the nations of Western Europe. Japan, which has few petroleum resources of its own, uses over twice as much energy as all of

Connect What things can you and your family do to use fewer fossils fuels in your everyday life?

Oil From Under the Ocean

In the chilly waters of the North Sea, European companies drill deep wells to tap the area's large oil deposits. Increased production of North Sea oil may reduce the world's demand for oil from Southwest Asia. **Critical Thinking** How might technological improvements such as more modern drilling rigs cut the cost of oil?

Africa. If a country does not have enough energy resources of its own, it must buy them from other countries. In the 1970s, the United States used so much energy that it had to buy oil from OPEC members. When they limited the supply of oil, they could charge much more for their product. The United States had to pay whatever the producing country asked. The oil shortages of the 1970s made people see they needed to find more sources of energy, including petroleum.

SECTION 1 REVIEW

1. **Define** (a) natural resource, (b) raw material, (c) recyclable resource, (d) renewable resource, (e) nonrenewable resource, (f) fossil fuel.

2. (a) Name two renewable resources. (b) What are two nonrenewable resources?

3. Name some ways that people use fossil fuels.

4. What is the difference between indirect energy use and direct energy use?

Critical Thinking

5. **Expressing Problems Clearly** Explain why people must be careful about how they use nonrenewable resources.

Activity

6. **Writing to Learn** Early pioneers in North America used forests and grasslands as they pleased. Write a paragraph explaining why it might have been less important then to replace those resources.

How People Use the Land

Reach Into Your Background
How many manufactured, or factory-made, items do you use in a day? What natural resources were used to make them? Make a list of these resources.

Questions to Explore
1. What are the stages of economic development?
2. How do different cultures use land?

Key Terms
manufacturing
developed nation
developing nation
commercial farming
subsistence farming
plantation
foreign aid

"**A**ll this water started flowing, but we were told it was restricted for use only by the oil company and we were not allowed to use it," said Li Lixing, a Chinese farmer. "We had to go at night and secretly take some for our crops." Li Lixing lives in a village by the banks of the Huang He. People have farmed here for hundreds of years. In Li's region, the government wants to help the economy by supporting businesses like the oil company. Farmers, therefore, face problems.

Many countries face problems of limited resources, increasing population, and growing demand. Studying how countries use their natural resources shows three basic patterns of economic activity.

Stages of Resource Development

Water from the Huang He is essential for Chinese farmers like Li. But industry needs resources, too. Which group is more important? In some cultures, industry comes first. In others, farmers do. Geographers study how people in different cultures use land and develop their resources. This tells geographers much about a culture. Geographers also compare land use and resource development all over the world.

First-Level Activities   Geographers study three stages of economic activity. In the first, people use land and resources directly to make products. They may hunt, cut wood, mine, and fish. They also may herd animals and farm. This is the first stage of activities. People are beginning to develop their land. About half the world's population works in first-level activities. In countries like the United States, however, fewer people do this kind of work every year.

Harvesting Corn

Farmers in the midwest United States are part of the first level of economic activity. Before you eat this corn, it may be frozen, canned, or processed. It may be made into corn meal, cornflakes, corn tortillas, grits, or even corn muffins. Then it must be delivered to a store where you can buy it.

READ ACTIVELY

Connect Think about members of your family and friends who work. Do they do first-, second-, or third-level activities?

Second-Level Activities   Suppose a farmer takes his corn crop to a mill and has the miller grind the corn into corn meal. This is an example of the second step in developing a resource. People turn raw materials into things they use. When a product is processed, it is changed from a raw material into a finished product. That process is called **manufacturing.** The farmer can pay the miller for his service and take the corn meal back home. Or the miller can sell the corn meal to someone else for further processing. Manufacturing may turn the farmer's corn crop into cornflakes for your breakfast.

Third-Level Activities   In the third stage, a person delivers boxes of corn flakes to a local grocery store so you can buy one. In this stage, products are distributed to people who want them. People who distribute products do not make them. They produce a service by making sure products are delivered to people who want and need them.

Industrial nations require service industries. Transportation systems carry products from manufacturer to consumer. Communication for people and businesses comes from telephones, computers, and satellites. Other services—doctors' offices, shopping malls, and fast-food stores—are part of everyday living.

Economic Patterns: Developed and Developing Countries

Today, most manufacturing takes place in factories. Two hundred years ago, that was not so. People produced goods in their homes or small shops. Then came a great change. People invented machines to make goods. They built factories to house the machines. They found new sources of power to run the machines. This change in the way people made goods was called the Industrial Revolution.

The Industrial Revolution created a new pattern of economic activity. It separated countries into two groups—those with many industries and those with few. Countries that have many industries are called **developed nations.** Countries with few industries are called **developing nations.** People live differently in developed and developing nations.

Industrial Societies: Providing Goods and Services

Only about one quarter of the people in the world live in developed nations. These nations include the United States, Canada, Japan, Singapore, Australia, and most European countries. People in these nations use goods made in factories. Their industries consume great amounts of raw materials. They also use power-driven machinery. Businesses spend money on technology, transportation, and communications. Factories produce goods for the country's citizens and extra goods to sell to other countries.

▼ In a Detroit factory, a worker carefully assembles the same part on each automobile that comes down the power-driven assembly line.

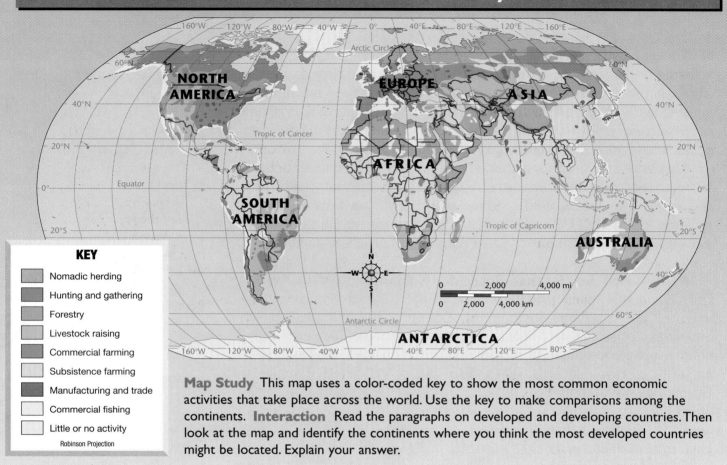

KEY

- Nomadic herding
- Hunting and gathering
- Forestry
- Livestock raising
- Commercial farming
- Subsistence farming
- Manufacturing and trade
- Commercial fishing
- Little or no activity

Robinson Projection

Map Study This map uses a color-coded key to show the most common economic activities that take place across the world. Use the key to make comparisons among the continents. **Interaction** Read the paragraphs on developed and developing countries. Then look at the map and identify the continents where you think the most developed countries might be located. Explain your answer.

READ ACTIVELY

Predict What are the problems of developed nations?

In developed countries, most people live in towns and cities. They work in business and industry. Machines do most of the work. Most people have enough food and water. Most citizens can get a good education and adequate health care.

Developed nations rely on **commercial farming** to produce enough food for their people. Commercial farms are very large. Companies run most of them, not single families. These farms rely on modern technology, so they often need far fewer workers than small traditional farms. Commercial farms are very successful. In the United States, a few million farmers raise enough food to feed more than 250 million people. There is plenty left over to sell to other countries.

People in developed nations depend on each other. Farmers rely on industries for goods and services. City people depend on farmers for food. Anything, like wars and natural disasters, that stops the movement of goods and services can make life hard for everyone.

Developed nations can have some serious problems. Unemployment is a challenge. Not everyone can find a job. Manufacturing can also threaten the environment with air, land, and water pollution. Heavy production uses up natural resources, so shortages develop. Developed nations are working to solve these problems.

Developing Nations It is important to remember that every culture is not like that of the United States. Most of the people of the world live in developing countries. Many of these countries are in Africa, Asia, and Latin America.

Developing countries often do not have great wealth. Many people work at **subsistence farming.** That means farmers raise enough food and animals to feed their own families. The farms require much labor, but they do not yield many crops. Often, the only commercial farms are **plantations.** These farms employ many workers but are owned by only a few people. Plantations usually raise a single crop for export, such as bananas, coffee, sugar cane, or tea.

In some developing countries, certain groups herd animals that provide families with milk, meat, cheese, and skins. In the deserts of Africa and Asia, vegetation and water are scarce. Herders in these regions are nomads. They travel from place to place to find food and water for their animals. In some developing nations, some people live as hunter-gatherers. Such groups are found in the Kalahari Desert in Africa and the Amazon region of South America.

Challenges in Developing Nations Developing countries often face great challenges. These include disease, food shortages, unsafe water, poor education and health services, and changing governments. Farmers often rely on one or two crops. That puts farmers at risk if the crops fail. Thousands move to cities, but jobs there are often scarce.

Some challenges are connected to rapid population growth. It strains resources. For example, in the late 1990s, the supply of fresh water was becoming a problem. As populations grow, they need more water. Larger populations also need more food. This means that farms need more water. Industries also require large amounts of fresh water.

Developing countries are working to improve their people's lives. One way is to use their natural resources or sell them to other countries. Some countries have grown richer by selling natural resources, such as oil and other minerals, to others.

ACROSS THE WORLD

A Nation of Herders The Tuareg of the Sahara in northern Africa herd camels, goats, sheep, and cattle. They travel along the edge of the great desert. Here there are seasonal rains so there is pasture for the herds. Men and women are equals in Tuareg culture. Both can own their own herds of animals and other property.

Construction in Vietnam

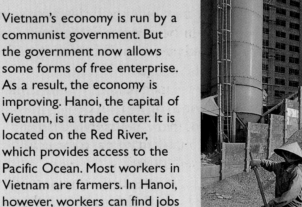

Vietnam's economy is run by a communist government. But the government now allows some forms of free enterprise. As a result, the economy is improving. Hanoi, the capital of Vietnam, is a trade center. It is located on the Red River, which provides access to the Pacific Ocean. Most workers in Vietnam are farmers. In Hanoi, however, workers can find jobs in factories that process food or produce bicycles and farm machinery. Or, like these workers, they can help to construct new buildings as Hanoi expands.

► This woman works in the city of Bangalore, India. In recent years, many Indian businesses have improved their services by using computers.

Developing countries sometimes receive help from developed nations. The help could be in the form of **foreign aid,** or gifts and loans from one government to another or from the United Nations. This aid is often used for special projects, such as building roads to move food and other goods from one area to another. Sometimes conflicts arise when the two governments do not agree on the best way to use foreign aid funds.

Sometimes help comes from businesses in developed countries. They may build factories in developing nations. This provides jobs and money for people. Sometimes building communication systems helps spread new ideas for farming and industries.

SECTION 2 REVIEW

1. **Define** (a) manufacturing, (b) developed nation, (c) developing nation, (d) commercial farming, (e) subsistence farming, (f) plantation, (g) foreign aid.

2. What are the characteristics of a developed nation? Of a developing nation?

3. How is subsistence farming different from commercial farming?

4. How can countries use their natural resources?

5. What challenges face developed nations? Developing nations?

Critical Thinking

6. **Identifying Central Issues** How are developing nations working to improve their people's lives?

Activity

7. **Writing to Learn** People who work at your school have jobs in a service industry. Interview a teacher, a server in the cafeteria, or a receptionist in the office. Find out what that person's duties are and what that person likes about his or her job. Write a brief profile for your school newspaper.

People's Effect on the Environment

Reach Into Your Background

Many of the environmental problems we face are the result of actions people took in the past. Now people pay more attention to environmental issues. Make a list of things you and your community are doing to improve the environment.

Questions to Explore

1. How do people's actions affect the environment?

2. What are people doing to improve the environment?

Key Terms

ecosystem
deforestation
habitat
acid rain
ozone layer
global warming
recycle

Try to picture the United States as one huge desert. Africa's Sahara is even bigger than that. What's more, the Sahara is spreading. Wangari Maathai of Kenya, in East Africa, works to stop it. She heads Africa's Green Belt Movement. It urges people in a dozen African countries to plant trees. Tree roots hold valuable topsoil in place, stopping the spread of the desert. When their leaves fall to the ground, trees add nutrients to the soil. This will make rich soil good for other plants. Since 1977, this organization has planted more than 10 million trees.

▼ Coral reefs, like this one, take millions of years to construct. They can be completely destroyed in a matter of decades by such things as water pollution.

Danger to Land, Water, and Air

Wangari Maathai is saving forests in Africa. Other people around the world are also working to preserve the environment. If we learn to identify environmental problems, we too can protect our world.

The Sahara is a desert. The Amazon River valley is a rain forest. The Great Plains is an area of grasslands. Each of these regions is an ecosystem, a place where living elements depend on one another—and on nonliving elements—for their survival. Living elements are plants and animals. Nonliving elements are water, soil, rocks, and air. Desert birds cannot live in a rain forest. Grassland plants cannot survive in a desert. Living things are tied to their ecosystems.

Death of a Sea The border between Kazakstan and Uzbekistan in western Asia runs through the Aral Sea. Until about 1960, this shallow sea was the fourth largest inland lake or sea in the world. Two rivers fed into the Aral. Then people started diverting the water for irrigation projects. By 1987, the Aral Sea had less than half as much water as before. Its fish were dead. Fishing villages now sat far from the water's edge. Some experts believe it may take 30 years to repair the damage done to the Aral Sea.

If one part of an ecosystem changes, other parts are also affected. For example, ecosystems that have standing water like puddles have mosquitoes. They lay their eggs on the surface of water. A rainy summer produces more standing water. This means that more mosquito eggs will hatch. A dry summer means less water and fewer mosquitoes.

Some changes can destroy an ecosystem. Probably the greatest loss of ecosystems is happening in South America. Rain forests cover more than one third of the continent. They are home for more species, or kinds, of plants and animals than anywhere else in the world. But South Americans need land for farms, so they are cutting down the forests. This process is called **deforestation.** When the forests are gone, many plant and animal species become extinct, or die out.

Protecting Endangered Species How can we prevent species of animals and plants from dying out? One way is through laws. In 1973, Congress passed the Endangered Species Act. It gave the government power to protect not only species that might become extinct but also the places that they live, or their **habitats.** Today, the act protects almost 1,000 kinds of living things in the United States that are threatened, or endangered.

Extinction has many causes. People may build houses or businesses on land that is the habitat of particular animals or plants. The air, soil, or water may be too polluted for a species of plant or animal to survive. Sometimes, a species is hunted until it disappears. Usually, more than one thing threatens a species. The goal of the Endangered Species Act is to stop extinction. But people disagree about the law. Some think humans should be allowed to use natural resources as they need them. Others think people should stop doing things that hurt other species.

Saving the Gray Whale

Temporarily trapped in Alaska's ice, this gray whale may survive to make its yearly journey down the Pacific Coast to Mexico. Whaling nearly destroyed the world's population of gray whales. Protection as an endangered species, however, brought their numbers back up.

Factories and Acid Rain Often, endangered animal species are just one sign of an ecosystem with problems. Visitors to the New York's Adirondack Mountains see an ecosystem in trouble. Its vast forests are centuries old. But today, the needles of the spruce trees are brown, and birch trees have no leaves at all. There are few fish in the rivers. Frogs, certain kinds of birds, and many insects are hard to find. What happened?

According to scientists, **acid rain** is to blame. Acid rain is rain that carries

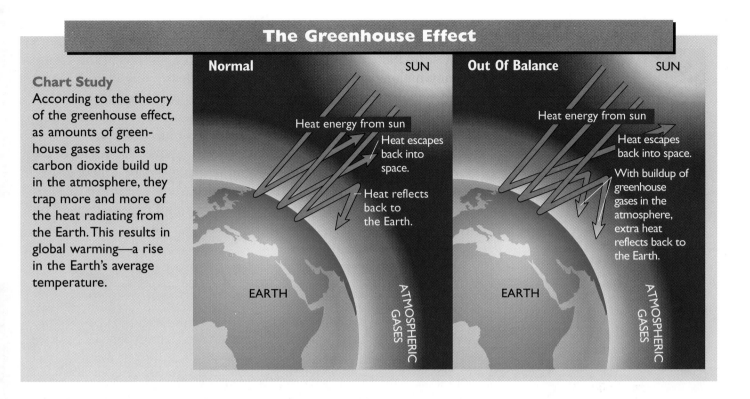

The Greenhouse Effect

Chart Study
According to the theory of the greenhouse effect, as amounts of greenhouse gases such as carbon dioxide build up in the atmosphere, they trap more and more of the heat radiating from the Earth. This results in global warming—a rise in the Earth's average temperature.

Normal   SUN
Heat energy from sun
Heat escapes back into space.
Heat reflects back to the Earth.
EARTH
ATMOSPHERIC GASES

Out Of Balance   SUN
Heat energy from sun
Heat escapes back into space.
With buildup of greenhouse gases in the atmosphere, extra heat reflects back to the Earth.
EARTH
ATMOSPHERIC GASES

dangerous chemicals. The fossil fuels used by industries and automobiles release chemicals into the air. The chemicals combine with water vapor in the air, making the rain as acid as vinegar.

Canada and the United States now have laws to reduce acid rain. Coal-burning electricity plants must cut pollution in half by the year 2000. Factories are installing new devices called filters and scrubbers to clean up the fumes they release. Car makers have added devices to reduce the dangerous chemicals in car exhaust.

Rivers and Sewage Pollution   People have always dumped waste products into rivers, lakes, and oceans. These wastes can harm or destroy living things in the water. They also endanger people. Water creatures take in substances from the water. Little fish eat the creatures, big fish eat the little fish, and animals and people eat the fish. The substances pass from one living thing to another. Some of these substances are poisons.

Fertilizers and pesticides from farms also pollute water. (Pesticides are chemicals that kill insects.) Rainwater washes the substances into lakes and rivers. There, the fertilizers cause water plants to grow too fast, and they use up oxygen needed by fish and other water life.

The Ozone Layer and Ultraviolet Rays   In the 1970s, scientists realized that chemicals called chlorofluorocarbons (CFCs) were destroying the atmosphere's ozone layer. This is a layer of gas in the upper part of our atmosphere. The ozone layer blocks most of the harmful ultraviolet rays from the sun. These rays cause skin cancer in humans. They also damage other forms of life.

Connect What are some things you and your friends could do to protect the environment?

Until recently, aerosol spray cans, refrigerators, and air conditioners used CFCs. In 1985, a United Nations conference discussed the ozone layer. Many nations agreed to get rid of ozone-destroying chemicals by 2000. And scientists are searching for safe chemicals to replace CFCs.

Global Warming   The summer of 1995 in New England was unusually hot and dry. Temperatures stayed above 90 degrees for weeks. Heat and drought caused water shortages and killed crops. Some scientists feared this was the start of **global warming,** a slow increase in the Earth's temperature. Global warming may be caused by

A Sun-Powered House

If you have spent a few hours outside on a hot summer day, then you are well aware of the heating power of the sun. Scientists knew all about it, too. They also knew that if they could find a way to store that power, they would have a cheap, abundant source of energy. The diagram below shows how they solved the problem of storing the heat of the sun.

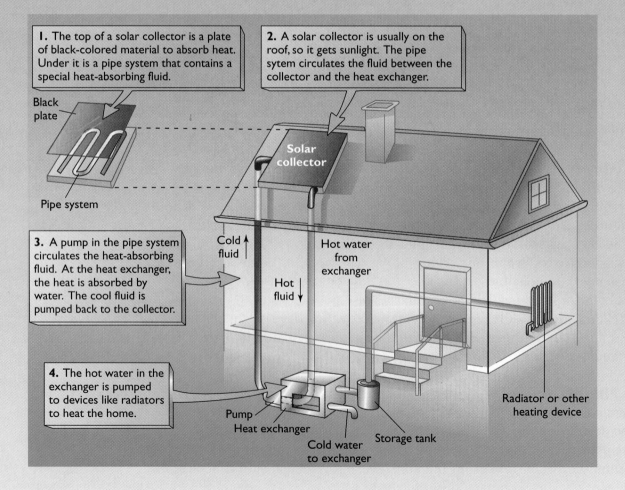

1. The top of a solar collector is a plate of black-colored material to absorb heat. Under it is a pipe system that contains a special heat-absorbing fluid.

2. A solar collector is usually on the roof, so it gets sunlight. The pipe sytem circulates the fluid between the collector and the heat exchanger.

3. A pump in the pipe system circulates the heat-absorbing fluid. At the heat exchanger, the heat is absorbed by water. The cool fluid is pumped back to the collector.

4. The hot water in the exchanger is pumped to devices like radiators to heat the home.

Black plate

Pipe system

Solar collector

Cold fluid

Hot fluid

Hot water from exchanger

Pump

Heat exchanger

Cold water to exchanger

Storage tank

Radiator or other heating device

gases like carbon dioxide that are released into the air. They are called greenhouse gases. Industrial countries produce about 75 percent of these gases. They are released when fossil fuels burn. These fuels produce most of the world's electricity. They also run the world's 550 million cars, buses, and trucks. Developing countries produce these gases when they burn forests to clear land and use wood for heating and cooking.

Normally, heat on the Earth escapes back into space. Some scientists theorize that greenhouse gases trap the heat and reflect it back to Earth. The result is a rise in the Earth's average temperature.

The Challenge of Energy

Because pollution is often tied to using fossil fuels, scientists are exploring other ways to get inexpensive energy. Their research concentrates on nuclear power, water, wind, and the sun. Individuals can protect the environment, too. For example, the United States produces more waste than any other nation in the world. To change that, people now **recycle**, or re-use old materials to make new products. Today, most American cities have recycling programs.

◄ It looks as if a fire burned these trees near the peak of Mount Mitchell in North Carolina. In fact, acid rain killed them.

SECTION 3 REVIEW

3. Why is global warming a problem?

4. What alternatives to fossil fuels are scientists researching?

Critical Thinking

5. **Expressing Problems Clearly** Explain why some species are endangered. Why do people disagree about reserving land for them?

Activity

6. **Writing to Learn** Write a persuasive paragraph explaining why fresh water should be protected. Include facts to support your reasons.

1. **Define** (a) ecosystem, (b) deforestation, (c) habitat, (d) acid rain, (e) ozone layer, (f) global warming, (g) recycle.

2. How do fossil fuels create pollution?

Writing for a Purpose

"SAVE THE EARTH NOT JUST FOR US BUT FOR FUTURE GENERATIONS" ™

Have you ever testified before Congress about pollution? Or stopped a company from pumping poison into a river? Or organized a demonstration to make people more aware of the environment? You may think kids your age do not do such things. But the kids of KAP do.

KAP stands for Kids Against Pollution. These young people work to stop pollution. Nineteen students in Closter, New Jersey, formed KAP in 1987. Today, there are more than 13,000 KAP chapters across the United States and in other countries. KAP's motto is "Save the Earth Not Just For Us But For Future Generations."

One of KAP's main weapons is writing. It can be very powerful. KAP members use the power of persuasive writing, or writing that tries to show other people how their point of view can help solve a problem.

Get Ready

Writing to persuade means taking a stand and trying to convince others to agree with your opinion. There are four basic steps:

1 Decide what your opinion is. Your opinion is the position you plan to take. For example, suppose your opinion is "Our city should make a law to require people to recycle newspapers."

2 Choose your audience. Your audience is the people to whom you will be writing. You might write to a senator or a mayor. You might write to the general public in a magazine article or letter to the editor of a newspaper.

3 Find support for your opinion. Your writing must give reasons for your opinion and the facts to support each reason. For example, the statement "Recycling would prevent burying six tons of paper trash in our town's landfill every month" is a fact that supports an opinion. Find as many facts as you can to support your opinion. They will help make your message stronger.

4 **Write persuasively.** Finally, write a letter or an essay. Present one idea at a time, and defend it with facts. Although persuasive writing emphasizes facts, it often includes an appeal to emotions. Add a sentence or two that does this. KAP's motto, for instance, is an emotional appeal. The combination of facts and emotion can make persuasive writing work.

Try It Out

Suppose you are concerned about the growing amount of litter in a local park. Follow these four steps to write a persuasive letter.

A. **What is your opinion?** Decide upon a plan to solve the park's problem. Should there be stronger anti-litter laws? Should people be urged to litter less, or should they be required to participate in a community cleanup? Choose one of these opinions or develop your own solution.

B. **Who is your audience?** If you want a local law passed, write to a member of your local government. To address your fellow citizens, write to the editor of a local newspaper.

C. **Why do you hold this opinion?** Identify at least two reasons for your opinion. Then support each reason with facts.

D. **How will you persuade your audience to agree with your opinion?** Before you write your letter, make an outline. Start your letter with a catchy opening. Then present your reasons in logical order. In the conclusion, sum up your arguments and appeal to people's emotions.

Apply the Skill

Now, apply the skill to the real world. Choose a topic, and write a persuasive letter about it to the editor of your local newspaper. Try to persuade your fellow citizens to agree with your opinion.

To the Editor:
The time has come to do something about the litter ruining Peace Park. First of all, the Parks Department has released a study that shows littering has increased 10 percent in two years.

Review and Activities

Reviewing Main Ideas

1. (a) Name two natural resources. (b) Describe how they are used.
2. What is the difference between renewable resources and nonrenewable resources?
3. (a) What kind of nation has mainly agricultural activities? (b) What kind of nation has mainly industrial activities?
4. Why is commercial farming part of a developed nation instead of a developing nation?
5. How can foreign aid help a developing nation?
6. Why might one simple change in an ecosystem have many effects in the system?
7. Acid rain hurts forests and lakes. How could acid rain endanger people?
8. What can governments do to protect endangered species?
9. Why is recycling a good use of natural resources?
10. How can people work to prevent global warming?

Reviewing Key Terms

Use each key term below in a sentence that shows the meaning of the term.

1. natural resource
2. raw material
3. recyclable resource
4. renewable resource
5. nonrenewable resource
6. fossil fuel
7. manufacturing
8. developed nation
9. developing nation
10. commercial farming
11. subsistence farming
12. plantation
13. foreign aid
14. ecosystem
15. deforestation
16. habitat
17. acid rain
18. ozone layer
19. global warming
20. recycle

Critical Thinking

1. **Identifying Central Issues** Do you think people should do more to protect the environment? Use facts from the chapter to support your answer.
2. **Recognizing Cause and Effect** Think about the problems that arose during the oil shortage of 1973. It affected the supply of gasoline and heating fuel. Write a paragraph about how a gasoline shortage today would affect the lives of people in your family.

Graphic Organizer

Copy and fill in the table to show how pollution damages the environment and suggest some solutions.

Sources	Damage to Environment	Possible Solutions
Water Pollution		
Land Pollution		
Air Pollution		

Writing Activity

Writing a Letter
Become part of the global community by contacting an organization that works to protect the environment. Two groups are listed here. Describe what you have learned about threats to the environment. Explain how you use natural resources responsibly. Find out if the organization has suggestions for other actions.

Addresses:

Greenpeace
1436 U Street NW
Washington, D.C. 20009

World Wildlife Fund
1250 24th Street, NW
Washington, D.C. 20037

Internet Activity

Use a search engine to find the **U.S. Geological Survey.** Click on **Fact Sheets.** Scroll down and click on **State** to find a USGS program in your area. Click on your state and then choose a program. Write a paragraph that explains the goal of the program and the actions taken to reach the goal.

Skills Review

Turn to the Skills Activity.

Review the steps for writing for a purpose. Then complete the following: (a) Why do you think that it is important to know your audience when you are writing to persuade? (b) Do you think that you need to do research in order to write to persuade? Why or why not?

How Am I Doing?

Answer these questions to help you check your progress.

1. Can I describe natural resources and how different countries use them?
2. Do I understand how the stages of economic development are related to a nation's wealth?
3. Can I identify some threats to the environment?
4. What information from this chapter can I use in my book project?

GEOGRAPHY
TOOLS AND CONCEPTS
PROJECT POSSIBILITIES

*The chapters in this book have some answers
to these important questions.*

☞ **What is the Earth's geography like?**

☞ **Where do the world's people live?**

☞ **What is a culture?**

☞ **How do people use the world's resources?**

Doing a project shows what you know about geography! The knowledge and skills you have gained will help you do a great job.

GEO LEO

Project Menu

Now it's time for you to find your own answers by doing projects on your own or with a group. Here are some ways to make your own discoveries about geography.

The Geography Game
Every place in the world has unique characteristics. Use them to create a geography game with your classmates. Choose a country. Find one fact each about its (1) physical features, (2) climate, (3) population, (4) cultures, and (5) natural resources. These facts will be clues in the game. Practice writing them out until they are short and clear. Clues should not be too easy or too hard. They must provide enough information so that someone can figure out the answer. Now make five playing cards. On one side of each card, write a clue. On the other side, write the name of your country.

Divide into three teams. Each team needs the Atlas in the back of this book. Mix up the cards. Have your teacher or a volunteer pick a card and read the clue to team one. Members have 30 seconds to agree on an answer. If it is correct, the team earns one point. If not, the next team has a chance. Play until the cards are gone. The team with the most points wins.

From Questions to Careers

JOBS IN THE EARTH SCIENCES

People who want to preserve the Earth often have jobs in the sciences. Environmental engineers may figure out how to clean up oil spills or make better use of natural resources. Soil scientists find ways to increase the crops a farmer can grow on a piece of land, or they may work on soil conservation. Ethnobotanists study how certain cultures use plants, especially as medicines. These jobs require a college degree.

Some jobs that help preserve the Earth require less education. People who assist scientists are called technicians. Usually they need only an associate's degree, which takes two years. Technicians may work in agriculture, chemistry, energy, or weather research. All these jobs are vital to helping preserve the environment.

▼ A scientist and technician are shown collecting water quality samples from a stream.

World News Today

Collect newspaper and magazine articles about natural resources, economies, and businesses in countries around the world. Display the clippings on a poster. Choose one country, and study the relationship between its economy and its natural resources. Prepare a five-minute speech to tell your class what you found.

Focus on Part of the Whole

The world and its population are extremely varied. Choose a particular region or country. If you are working with a group, have each person choose a different country on a continent. Learn everything you can about the land's physical geography, the population, and the lifestyles of the people there. Use encyclopedias, almanacs, or other books.

Set up a display based on your research. Prepare a large map that includes important physical features of the land. Add captions that explain how the land's physical geography affects people's lives.

Desktop Countries

What countries did your ancestors come from? Select one and do some research on it. Interview someone, perhaps a relative from there, or read about it. Find a recipe you can prepare to share with the class. Then make a desktop display about your country. Write the name of the country on a card and put it on your desk. Add a drawing of the country's flag or map, or display a souvenir. On place cards, write several sentences about each object. Take turns visiting everyone's "desktop countries."

Reference

TABLE OF CONTENTS

Atlas

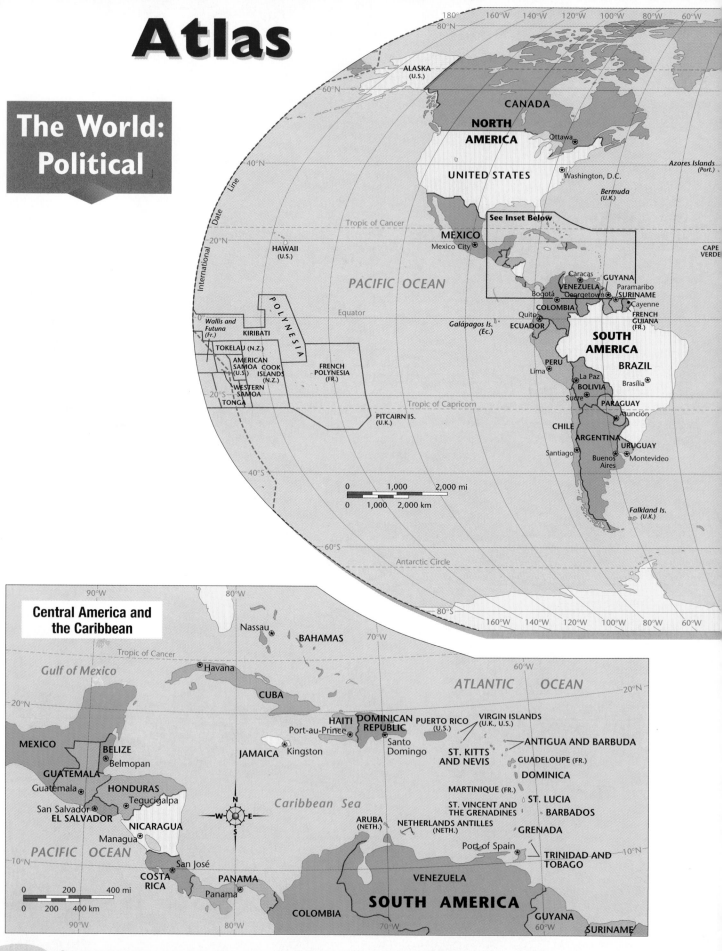

The World: Political

ALASKA (U.S.)

CANADA

NORTH AMERICA

Ottawa ⊛

UNITED STATES

Washington, D.C. ⊛

Azores Islands (Port.)

Tropic of Cancer

MEXICO

Mexico City ⊛

See Inset Below

Bermuda (U.K.)

CAPE VERDE

HAWAII (U.S.)

PACIFIC OCEAN

Caracas ⊛ **GUYANA**

VENEZUELA Paramaribo ⊛

Bogotá ⊛ Georgetown ⊛ **SURINAME**

Cayenne ·

COLOMBIA **FRENCH GUIANA (FR.)**

Equator

Galápagos Is. (Ec.) Quito ⊛ **ECUADOR**

SOUTH AMERICA

Wallis and Futuna (Fr.)

P O L Y N E S I A

KIRIBATI

TOKELAU (N.Z.)

AMERICAN SAMOA (U.S.)

COOK ISLANDS (N.Z.)

WESTERN SAMOA

TONGA

FRENCH POLYNESIA (FR.)

PERU

Lima ⊛ **BRAZIL**

La Paz ⊛ Brasília ⊛

BOLIVIA

Sucre ⊛ **PARAGUAY**

Asunción ⊛

Tropic of Capricorn

PITCAIRN IS. (U.K.)

CHILE

ARGENTINA **URUGUAY**

Santiago ⊛ Buenos Aires ⊛ Montevideo ⊛

0   1,000   2,000 mi

0   1,000   2,000 km

Falkland Is. (U.K.)

Antarctic Circle

Central America and the Caribbean

Nassau ⊛

BAHAMAS

Tropic of Cancer

Gulf of Mexico

Havana ⊛

CUBA

ATLANTIC   OCEAN

MEXICO

BELIZE

⊛ Belmopan

JAMAICA Kingston ⊛

HAITI **DOMINICAN REPUBLIC**

Port-au-Prince Santo Domingo

PUERTO RICO (U.S.)

VIRGIN ISLANDS (U.K., U.S.)

ANTIGUA AND BARBUDA

ST. KITTS AND NEVIS GUADELOUPE (FR.)

GUATEMALA

Guatemala ⊛

HONDURAS

Tegucigalpa ⊛

DOMINICA

San Salvador ⊛

EL SALVADOR

MARTINIQUE (FR.) ST. LUCIA

ST. VINCENT AND THE GRENADINES BARBADOS

Caribbean Sea

NICARAGUA

Managua ⊛

ARUBA (NETH.)

NETHERLANDS ANTILLES (NETH.)

GRENADA

PACIFIC   OCEAN

San José ⊛

Port of Spain ⊛ **TRINIDAD AND TOBAGO**

COSTA RICA

PANAMA

Panama ⊛

VENEZUELA

0   200   400 mi

0   200   400 km

SOUTH AMERICA

COLOMBIA

GUYANA

SURINAME

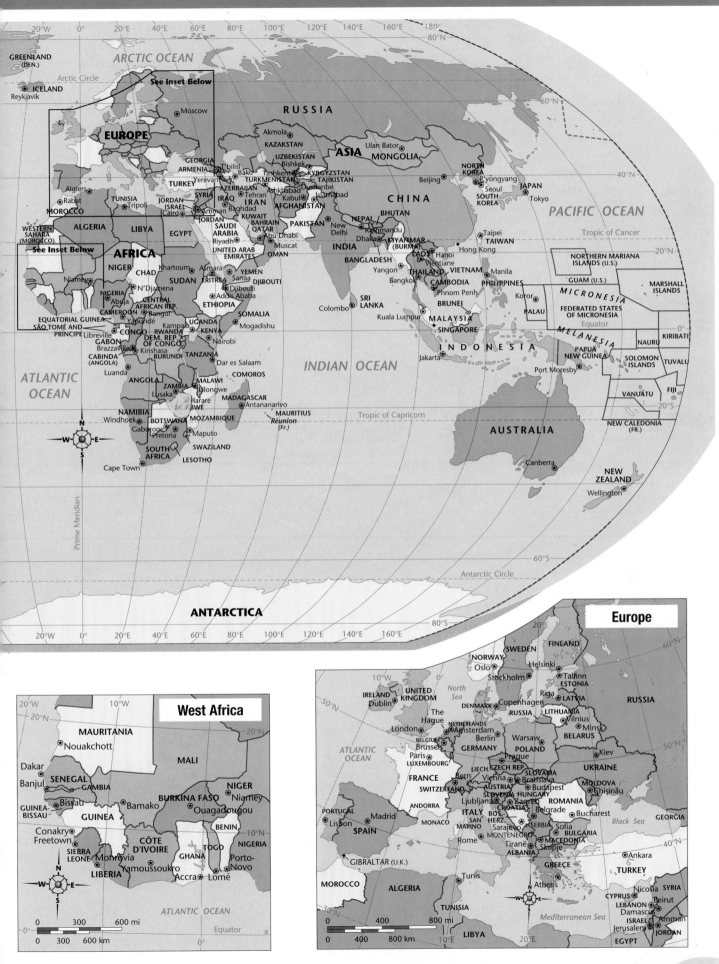

ARCTIC OCEAN

GREENLAND
(DEN.)

Arctic Circle

ICELAND
Reykjavik

⊛ Moscow

See Inset Below

EUROPE

RUSSIA

60°N

40°N

ASIA

KAZAKSTAN

Akmola

⊛ Ulan Bator

MONGOLIA

NORTH
KOREA

⊛ Pyongyang

JAPAN

GEORGIA

⊛Tbilisi

⊛ Baku

UZBEKISTAN

Bishkek

Beijing

Seoul⊛

⊛ Tokyo

ARMENIA

⊛ Yerevan

TURKMENISTAN

Tashkent⊛

KYRGYZSTAN

CHINA

SOUTH
KOREA

Algiers ⊛

TURKEY

AZERBAIJAN

Ashkhabad⊛

TAJIKISTAN

Dushanbe

PACIFIC OCEAN

⊛ Rabat

SYRIA

IRAQ

IRAN

Tehran⊛

Kabul⊛

Islamabad

MOROCCO

JORDAN

⊛Tripoli

ISRAEL

Cairo⊛

Amman⊛

Baghdad

⊛

AFGHANISTAN

NEPAL

BHUTAN

TAIWAN

⊛ Taipei

Tropic of Cancer

WESTERN
SAHARA
(MOROCCO)

ALGERIA

LIBYA

EGYPT

KUWAIT

BAHRAIN

SAUDI
ARABIA

Riyadh⊛

⊛Abu Dhabi

New
Delhi

Kathmandu

⊛

Dhaka⊛

MYANMAR
(BURMA)

Hong Kong

20°N

QATAR

See Inset Below

AFRICA

NIGER

CHAD

Khartoum

Asmara⊛

UNITED ARAB
EMIRATES

OMAN

⊛ Muscat

INDIA

BANGLADESH

LAOS

Hanoi⊛
Vientiane⊛

THAILAND

VIETNAM

Manila

NORTHERN MARIANA
ISLANDS (U.S.)

Niamey⊛

NIGERIA

N'Djamena

SUDAN

ERITREA

YEMEN

Sanaa⊛

DJIBOUTI

Yangon⊛

Bangkok⊛

CAMBODIA

PHILIPPINES

GUAM (U.S.)

MARSHALL
ISLANDS

Abuja⊛

CENTRAL
AFRICAN REP.

⊛ Addis Ababa

⊛ Djibouti

Phnom Penh⊛

BRUNEI

Koror⊛

MICRONESIA

CAMEROON

Bangui⊛

ETHIOPIA

SOMALIA

SRI
LANKA

Colombo⊛

Kuala Lumpur

MALAYSIA

PALAU

FEDERATED STATES
OF MICRONESIA

EQUATORIAL GUINEA
SÃO TOMÉ AND
PRÍNCIPE

Yaoundé⊛

UGANDA

Kampala⊛

KENYA

Mogadishu⊛

SINGAPORE

NAURU

KIRIBATI

0°

Libreville⊛

CONGO

RWANDA

DEM. REP.
OF CONGO

Equator

Nairobi⊛

INDONESIA

MELANESIA

GABON

Brazzaville⊛

BURUNDI

TANZANIA

Jakarta⊛

PAPUA
NEW GUINEA

SOLOMON
ISLANDS

TUVALU

CABINDA
(ANGOLA)

Kinshasa⊛

Dar es Salaam⊛

Port Moresby⊛

ATLANTIC
OCEAN

Luanda⊛

ANGOLA

ZAMBIA

MALAWI

COMOROS

INDIAN OCEAN

VANUATU

FIJI

Lusaka⊛

Lilongwe⊛

MADAGASCAR

⊛Antananarivo

NEW CALEDONIA
(Fr.)

NAMIBIA

BOTSWANA

ZIMBABWE

MOZAMBIQUE

Harare⊛

MAURITIUS
Réunion
(Fr.)

Tropic of Capricorn

20°S

Windhoek⊛

Gaborone⊛

Pretoria⊛

⊛ Maputo

AUSTRALIA

SOUTH
AFRICA

SWAZILAND

LESOTHO

Cape Town⊛

Canberra⊛

NEW
ZEALAND

N
W   E
S

Wellington⊛

60°S

Prime Meridian

Antarctic Circle

ANTARCTICA

80°S

20°W   0°   20°E   40°E   60°E   80°E   100°E   120°E   140°E   160°E

West Africa

MAURITANIA

⊛Nouakchott

MALI

Dakar⊛

SENEGAL

Banjul⊛

GAMBIA

NIGER

⊛Niamey

BURKINA FASO

Bamako⊛

⊛Ouagadougou

GUINEA-
BISSAU

⊛Bissau

GUINEA

BENIN

NIGERIA

Conakry⊛
Freetown⊛

CÔTE
D'IVOIRE

GHANA

TOGO

Porto-
Novo⊛

SIERRA
LEONE

Monrovia⊛

Yamoussoukro⊛

Accra⊛

⊛Lomé

LIBERIA

N
W   E
S

ATLANTIC OCEAN

Equator

0   300   600 mi

0   300   600 km

Europe

NORWAY

SWEDEN

FINLAND

Oslo⊛

Helsinki⊛

Stockholm⊛

Tallinn⊛

ESTONIA

IRELAND

UNITED
KINGDOM

North
Sea

Riga⊛

LATVIA

RUSSIA

Dublin⊛

DENMARK

Copenhagen⊛

LITHUANIA

Vilnius⊛

Minsk⊛

The
Hague

NETHERLANDS

RUSSIA

BELARUS

ATLANTIC
OCEAN

London⊛

Amsterdam⊛

BELGIUM

Berlin⊛

Warsaw⊛

Kiev⊛

Brussels⊛

GERMANY

POLAND

Paris⊛

LUXEMBOURG

Prague⊛

UKRAINE

FRANCE

LIECH.

CZECH REP.

SLOVAKIA

Bern⊛

Vienna⊛

Bratislava⊛

MOLDOVA

⊛Chişinău

SWITZERLAND

AUSTRIA

Budapest⊛

ANDORRA

SLOVENIA

HUNGARY

ROMANIA

Ljubljana⊛

⊛Zagreb

Belgrade⊛

Bucharest⊛

GEORGIA

PORTUGAL

ITALY

CROATIA

SERBIA

Lisbon⊛

Madrid⊛

SAN
MARINO

BOS.
HERZ.

Sarajevo⊛

Sofia⊛

BULGARIA

SPAIN

MONACO

Rome⊛

MONTENEGRO

Tiranë⊛

MACEDONIA

Skopje⊛

Black Sea

GIBRALTAR (U.K.)

ALBANIA

GREECE

TURKEY

Ankara⊛

Tunis⊛

Athens⊛

CYPRUS

Nicosia⊛

SYRIA

MOROCCO

ALGERIA

LEBANON

Beirut⊛

Damascus⊛

Mediterranean Sea

ISRAEL

Jerusalem⊛

Amman⊛

JORDAN

TUNISIA

LIBYA

EGYPT

0   400   800 mi

0   400   800 km

ATLAS   131

The World: Physical

ARCTIC OCEAN

GREENLAND (DEN.)

Beaufort Sea

Yukon R.

Bering Sea

Aleutian Islands

Mackenzie R.

Hudson Bay

NORTH AMERICA

ROCKY MOUNTAINS

GREAT PLAINS

CANADIAN SHIELD

Great Lakes

St. Lawrence R.

Missouri R.

APPALACHIAN MTS.

Mississippi R.

ATLANTIC OCEAN

Hawaiian Islands

Colorado R.

SIERRA MADRE OCCIDENTAL

SIERRA MADRE ORIENTAL

Rio Grande

Gulf of Mexico

West Indies

Tropic of Cancer

P O L Y N E S I A

PACIFIC OCEAN

Caribbean Sea

Orinoco R.

GUIANA HIGHLANDS

AMAZON BASIN

Amazon R.

Equator

SOUTH AMERICA

ANDES MOUNTAINS

BRAZILIAN HIGHLANDS

Tropic of Capricorn

PAMPAS

Rio de la Plata

PATAGONIA

Cape Horn

Drake Passage

ANTARCTIC PENINSULA

Antarctic Circle

KEY

Elevation

Feet	Meters
Over 13,000	Over 3,960
6,500–13,000	1,980–3,960
1,600–6,500	480–1,980
650–1,600	200–480
0–650	0–200
Below sea level	Below sea level

Ice cap

Ice shelf

Robinson Projection

South Pole

ATLANTIC OCEAN

INDIAN OCEAN

QUEEN MAUD LAND

Permanent Ice Pack

Weddell Sea

COATS LAND

ENDERBY LAND

Antarctic Peninsula

Ronne Ice Shelf

Amery Ice Shelf

ANTARCTICA

TRANSANTARCTIC MTS.

Prime Meridian

South Pole

QUEEN MAUD MTS.

Ross Ice Shelf

WILKES LAND

Roosevelt I.

Permanent Ice Pack

Ross Sea

VICTORIA LAND

South Magnetic Pole

PACIFIC OCEAN

International Date Line

0   800 mi

800 km

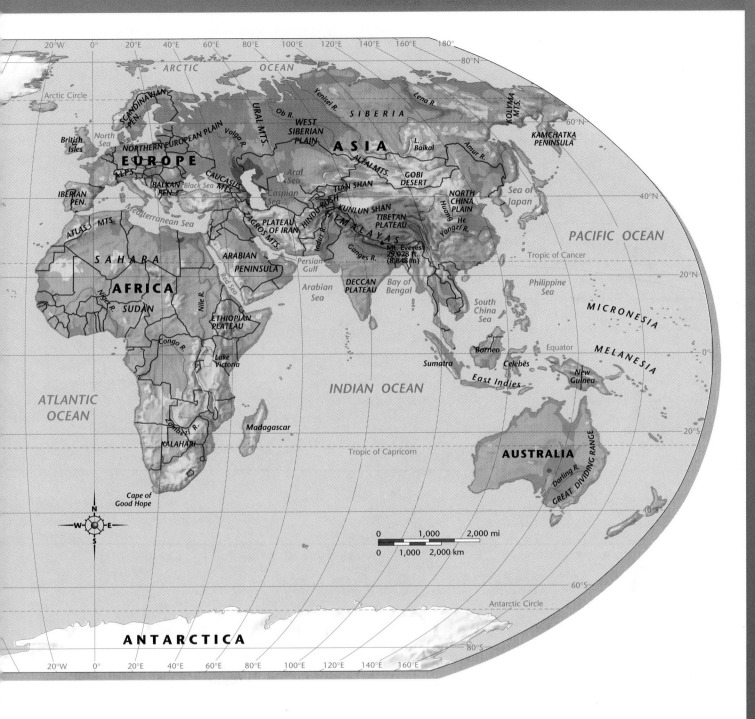

ARCTIC OCEAN
80°N
Arctic Circle
ARCTIC OCEAN
SCANDINAVIAN PEN.
British Isles
North Sea
NORTHERN EUROPEAN PLAIN
EUROPE
ALPS
BALKAN PEN.
IBERIAN PEN.
Black Sea
CAUCASUS MTS.
Caspian Sea
Mediterranean Sea
ATLAS MTS.
URAL MTS.
Volga R.
Ob R.
Yenisei R.
SIBERIA
WEST SIBERIAN PLAIN
ASIA
ALTAI MTS.
TIAN SHAN
Aral Sea
Lena R.
60°N
L. Baikal
Amur R.
GOBI DESERT
KUNLUN SHAN
HINDU KUSH
HIMALAYAS
KAMCHATKA PENINSULA
KOLYMA MTS.
Sea of Japan
40°N
NORTH CHINA PLAIN
PLATEAU OF IRAN
ZAGROS MTS.
TIBETAN PLATEAU
Huang He
Yangzi R.
PACIFIC OCEAN
ARABIAN PENINSULA
Persian Gulf
Indus R.
Ganges R.
Mt. Everest 29,028 ft. (8,848 m)
Tropic of Cancer
SAHARA
Red Sea
Arabian Sea
DECCAN PLATEAU
Bay of Bengal
Philippine Sea
20°N
AFRICA
Niger R.
SUDAN
Nile R.
ETHIOPIAN PLATEAU
South China Sea
MICRONESIA
Congo R.
Lake Victoria
Borneo
Celebes
Equator
MELANESIA
0°
ATLANTIC OCEAN
Sumatra
East Indies
New Guinea
INDIAN OCEAN
Zambezi R.
Madagascar
20°S
KALAHARI
AUSTRALIA
GREAT DIVIDING RANGE
Tropic of Capricorn
Darling R.
Cape of Good Hope
40°S
N W E S
0   1,000   2,000 mi
0   1,000   2,000 km
60°S
Antarctic Circle
ANTARCTICA
80°S
20°W 0° 20°E 40°E 60°E 80°E 100°E 120°E 140°E 160°E

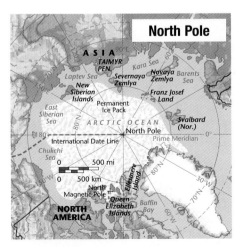

North Pole

ASIA
TAIMYR PEN.
Laptev Sea
Kara Sea
Severnaya Zemlya
Novaya Zemlya
Barents Sea
New Siberian Islands
Franz Josef Land
East Siberian Sea
Permanent Ice Pack
ARCTIC OCEAN
Svalbard (Nor.)
International Date Line
North Pole
Prime Meridian
Chukchi Sea
0   500 mi
0   500 km
North Magnetic Pole
Ellesmere Island
Queen Elizabeth Islands
Baffin Bay
NORTH AMERICA

RUSSIA

ARCTIC OCEAN

Arctic Circle

70°N

70°N

ALASKA

Bering Strait

Yukon

River

CANADA

Anchorage

60°N

60°N

Bering
Sea

Gulf of Alaska

Juneau

0   250   500 mi

0   250   500 km

160°W

140°W

50°N

120°W

110°W

Seattle

Olympia

WASHINGTON

Spokane

Mino

Bismar

Columbia

Missouri River

Portland

Salem

Helena

MONTANA

OREGON

IDAHO

Billings

Boise

Sheridan

Pi

Klamath Falls

Snake River

Jackson

Rapid C

Eureka

40°N

Twin Falls

WYOMING

Winnemucca

Great
Salt Lake

NEBRAS

Cheyenne

Sacramento

Carson City

Salt Lake City

Denver

San Francisco

NEVADA

UTAH

Grand
Junction

COLORADO

Cedar
City

Colorado River

Pueblo

CALIFORNIA

Las Vegas

Ark

PACIFIC

Los Angeles

Santa Fe

OCEAN

Albuquerque

ARIZONA

San Diego

Phoenix

NEW MEXICO

Roswell

Tucson

Rio Grande

El Paso

160°W

155°W

Honolulu

PACIFIC OCEAN

HAWAII

20°N

20°N

Hilo

0   50   100 mi

0   50   100 km

155°W

M E X I C O

Tropic of Cancer

120°W

110°W

CANADA

90°W   80°W   70°W

0   150   300 mi
0   150   300 km

NORTH DAKOTA

MINNESOTA
Duluth
Minneapolis St. Paul

SOUTH DAKOTA

WISCONSIN
Milwaukee
Madison
Chicago
Cedar Rapids

IOWA
Des Moines

Omaha
Lincoln

Lake Superior

Sault Ste. Marie

MICHIGAN

Lansing
Detroit

Lake Michigan

Lake Huron

Lake Erie

Lake Ontario

Buffalo

MAINE
Presque Isle
Augusta
Portland

Montpelier
VERMONT
NEW HAMPSHIRE
Concord
Boston

NEW YORK
Albany

MASSACHUSETTS
Providence
Hartford
New Haven
RHODE ISLAND
CONNECTICUT

40°N

PENNSYLVANIA
Cleveland
Harrisburg
Pittsburgh

New York City
Trenton
NEW JERSEY
Philadelphia

ILLINOIS
Springfield

INDIANA
Indianapolis

OHIO
Columbus

Cincinnati

WEST VIRGINIA
Charleston

Baltimore
Annapolis
Washington, D.C.
Dover
DELAWARE

MARYLAND

Topeka
Kansas City
KANSAS
Wichita

St. Louis
Jefferson City
MISSOURI

Louisville
Frankfort

KENTUCKY

Ohio River

Tennessee River

Richmond
VIRGINIA
Norfolk

Raleigh
NORTH CAROLINA
Charlotte

ATLANTIC OCEAN

OKLAHOMA
Tulsa
Oklahoma City

ARKANSAS
Little Rock
Pine Bluff

Nashville
TENNESSEE
Memphis

Columbia
SOUTH CAROLINA
Charleston

Red River

Missouri River

Mississippi River

Dallas

Birmingham
MISSISSIPPI
Jackson
Hattiesburg

ALABAMA
Columbus
Montgomery

Atlanta
GEORGIA

Savannah

Jacksonville

30°N

TEXAS
Austin
San Antonio

Shreveport

Baton Rouge
LOUISIANA
New Orleans
Houston

Tallahassee

FLORIDA

Tampa
Lake Okeechobee

Miami

Gulf of Mexico

Rio Grande

90°W   80°W

KEY
— National boundary
— State boundary
⊛ National capital
✪ State capital
• Other city
Transverse Mercator Projection

North and South America: Political

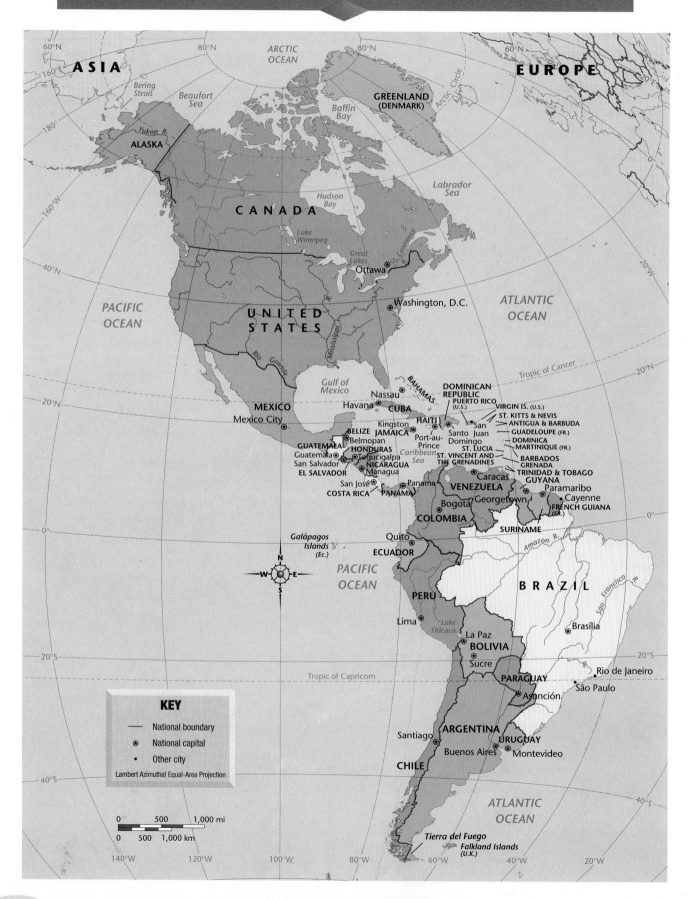

ASIA

ARCTIC OCEAN

EUROPE

Bering Strait

Beaufort Sea

GREENLAND (DENMARK)

Baffin Bay

Yukon R.

ALASKA

Labrador Sea

Hudson Bay

C A N A D A

Lake Winnipeg

Great Lakes

Ottawa ⊛

ATLANTIC OCEAN

PACIFIC OCEAN

U N I T E D S T A T E S

Washington, D.C. ⊛

Rio Grande

Mississippi R.

Tropic of Cancer

Gulf of Mexico

BAHAMAS

Nassau •

DOMINICAN REPUBLIC

PUERTO RICO (U.S.)

MEXICO

Havana ⊛ **CUBA**

VIRGIN IS. (U.S.)

ST. KITTS & NEVIS

Mexico City ⊛

Kingston • **HAITI**

• San Juan

ANTIGUA & BARBUDA

BELIZE JAMAICA

• Belmopan

Port-au-Prince

Santo Domingo

GUADELOUPE (FR.)

DOMINICA

GUATEMALA

HONDURAS

Caribbean Sea

ST. LUCIA

MARTINIQUE (FR.)

Guatemala ⊛

⊛ Tegucigalpa

ST. VINCENT AND

BARBADOS

San Salvador ⊛

NICARAGUA

THE GRENADINES

GRENADA

EL SALVADOR

⊛ Managua

TRINIDAD & TOBAGO

San José ⊛

⊛ Panama

Caracas ⊛

GUYANA

COSTA RICA

PANAMA

VENEZUELA

Paramaribo •

Bogotá ⊛

Georgetown ⊛

Cayenne •

COLOMBIA

FRENCH GUIANA (FR.)

SURINAME

Galápagos Islands (Ec.)

Quito ⊛

Amazon R.

N

W—E

S

PACIFIC OCEAN

ECUADOR

B R A Z I L

São Francisco R.

PERU

Lima ⊛

Lake Titicaca

⊛ Brasília

La Paz •

BOLIVIA

• Rio de Janeiro

• Sucre

Tropic of Capricorn

PARAGUAY

• São Paulo

KEY

—— National boundary

⊛ National capital

• Other city

Lambert Azimuthal Equal-Area Projection

⊛ Asunción

ARGENTINA

URUGUAY

Santiago ⊛

Buenos Aires ⊛

⊛ Montevideo

CHILE

0   500   1,000 mi

0   500   1,000 km

ATLANTIC OCEAN

Tierra del Fuego

Falkland Islands (U.K.)

North and South America: Physical

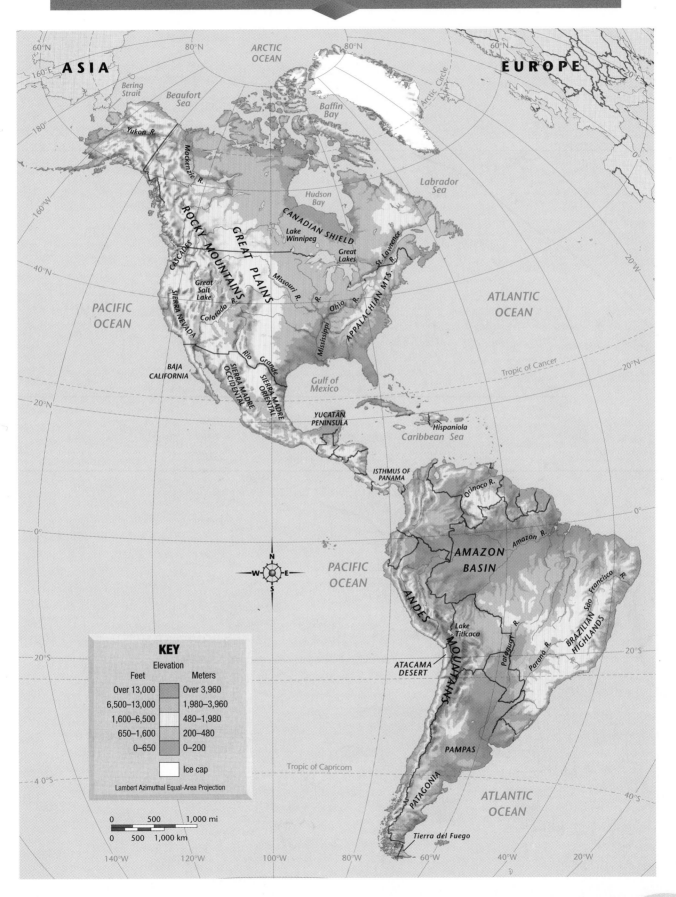

KEY

Elevation

Feet		Meters
Over 13,000		Over 3,960
6,500–13,000		1,980–3,960
1,600–6,500		480–1,980
650–1,600		200–480
0–650		0–200
Ice cap		

Lambert Azimuthal Equal-Area Projection

0   500   1,000 mi

0   500   1,000 km

Europe: Political

KEY

— National boundary
⊛ National capital
• Other city

Lambert Azimuthal Equal-Area Projection

ARCTIC OCEAN

Arctic Circle

Reykjavik ⊛ ICELAND

Faeroe Is. (Den.)

Shetland Is. (U.K.)

ATLANTIC OCEAN

FINLAND

SWEDEN

NORWAY
Lillehammer •

Turku • Helsinki • St. Petersburg

Oslo ⊛ Stockholm ⊛ Tallinn • ESTONIA RUSSIA

Moscow ⊛

Riga ⊛ LATVIA

• Göteborg

North Sea

DENMARK LITHUANIA
Copenhagen ⊛ Vilnius ⊛ BELARUS
RUSSIA Minsk ⊛

IRELAND Gdańsk •
Dublin ⊛ UNITED KINGDOM
• Manchester POLAND
Warsaw ⊛ Kiev ⊛
Amsterdam Berlin ⊛ Łódź •
The Hague ⊛ NETHERLANDS UKRAINE
London ⊛ Katowice •
Brussels ⊛ Cologne • Kraków •
BELGIUM Bonn • Prague ⊛ CZECH
• Frankfurt REPUBLIC MOLDOVA
LUXEMBOURG GERMANY Brno • SLOVAKIA Chişinău ⊛
⊛ Luxembourg Bratislava ⊛
Paris ⊛ Munich • Cluj •
LIECHTENSTEIN Vienna ⊛ Budapest ⊛ ROMANIA
Bern ⊛ AUSTRIA HUNGARY
FRANCE SWITZERLAND Ljubljana ⊛ Bucharest ⊛ Black Sea
Milan • SLOVENIA Zagreb ⊛
Bay of Biscay CROATIA Belgrade ⊛
SAN MARINO BOSNIA & SERBIA BULGARIA
HERZEGOVINA
Marseille • Sarajevo ⊛ Sophia ⊛
PORTUGAL MONACO ITALY Podgorica •
ANDORRA Rome ⊛ MONTENEGRO Skopje ⊛
Corsica VATICAN ALBANIA MACEDONIA
Madrid ⊛ • Barcelona CITY Tiranë ⊛
Lisbon ⊛ Naples • GREECE Aegean Sea
SPAIN Sardinia
Balearic Is. Tyrrhenian Sea Ionian Sea Athens ⊛

Mediterranean Sicily Crete

Strait of Gibraltar GIBRALTAR (U.K.)

Sea MALTA

AFRICA

English Channel

Donube R.

Prime Meridian

Gulf of Bothnia

Baltic Sea

Adriatic Sea

0 250 500 mi
0 250 500 km

Europe: Physical

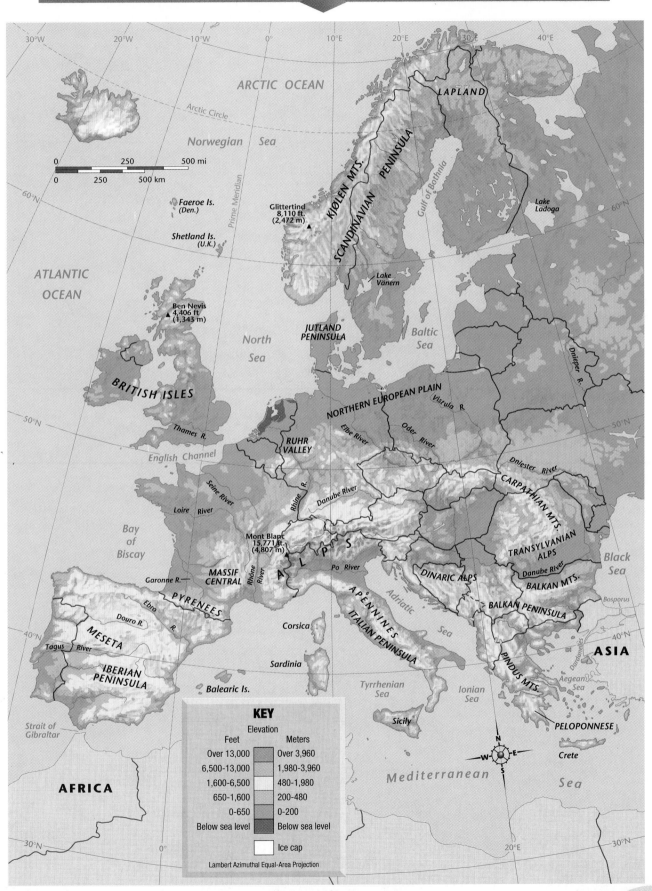

ARCTIC OCEAN

LAPLAND

Norwegian Sea

Arctic Circle

KJØLEN MTS.

SCANDINAVIAN PENINSULA

Gulf of Bothnia

Lake Ladoga

Faeroe Is. (Den.)

Glittertind 8,110 ft. (2,472 m)

Shetland Is. (U.K.)

ATLANTIC OCEAN

Lake Vänern

Ben Nevis 4,406 ft (1,343 m)

JUTLAND PENINSULA

Baltic Sea

North Sea

Dnieper R.

BRITISH ISLES

NORTHERN EUROPEAN PLAIN

Vistula R.

Thames R.

RUHR VALLEY

Elbe River

Oder River

Dniester River

CARPATHIAN MTS.

English Channel

Seine River

Rhine R.

Danube River

Loire River

Mont Blanc 15,771 ft. (4,807 m)

Po River

TRANSYLVANIAN ALPS

Bay of Biscay

MASSIF CENTRAL

Garonne R.

A L P S

Rhône River

DINARIC ALPS

Danube River

BALKAN MTS.

PYRENEES

Ebro R.

A P E N N I N E S

Adriatic Sea

BALKAN PENINSULA

Bosporus

Douro R.

Corsica

ITALIAN PENINSULA

Black Sea

MESETA

Tagus River

Dardanelles

ASIA

IBERIAN PENINSULA

Sardinia

Tyrrhenian Sea

PINDUS MTS.

Aegean Sea

Balearic Is.

Ionian Sea

Strait of Gibraltar

PELOPONNESE

Sicily

Crete

AFRICA

Mediterranean Sea

KEY

Elevation

Feet		Meters
Over 13,000		Over 3,960
6,500-13,000		1,980-3,960
1,600-6,500		480-1,980
650-1,600		200-480
0-650		0-200
Below sea level		Below sea level
Ice cap		

Lambert Azimuthal Equal-Area Projection

Africa: Political

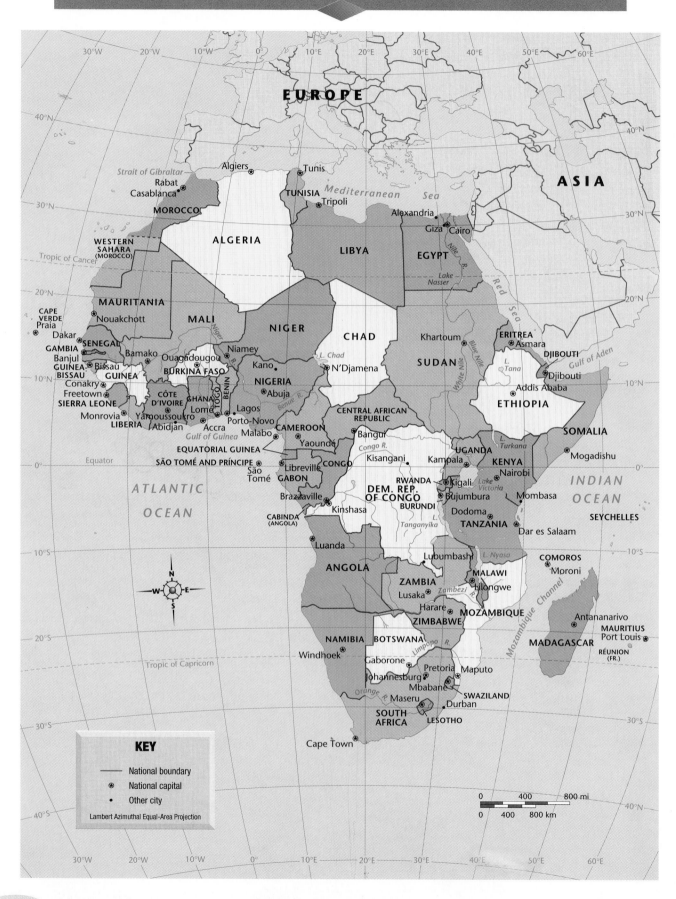

EUROPE

ASIA

Strait of Gibraltar
Algiers ⊛
Tunis ⊛
Rabat •
TUNISIA
Casablanca •
Mediterranean Sea
Tripoli ⊛
Alexandria •
MOROCCO
Giza • ⊛ Cairo

Tropic of Cancer
**WESTERN
SAHARA
(MOROCCO)**
ALGERIA
LIBYA
EGYPT

Lake
Nasser

MAURITANIA
MALI
NIGER
CHAD
Khartoum ⊛
ERITREA
⊛ Asmara
DJIBOUTI

CAPE
VERDE
Praia
Nouakchott ⊛
Niger R.
Niamey ⊛
L. Chad
N'Djamena ⊛
SUDAN
L. Tana
⊛ Djibouti
Addis Ababa •

Dakar •
SENEGAL
Bamako ⊛
Ouagadougou ⊛
Kano •
GAMBIA
Banjul ⊛
GUINEA
Bissau •
BURKINA FASO
NIGERIA
ETHIOPIA
BISSAU
GUINEA
⊛ Abuja

Conakry ⊛
Freetown ⊛
**CÔTE
D'IVOIRE**
GHANA
Lagos •
**CENTRAL AFRICAN
REPUBLIC**
SOMALIA
SIERRA LEONE
Monrovia ⊛
Yamoussoukro ⊛
TOGO
BENIN
Porto-Novo ⊛
Bangui ⊛
UGANDA
LIBERIA
Abidjan •
Accra ⊛
Lomé ⊛
Malabo ⊛
CAMEROON
Congo R.
Kisangani •
Kampala ⊛
Mogadishu •
Gulf of Guinea
Yaoundé ⊛
Nairobi •
EQUATORIAL GUINEA
KENYA
Equator
SÃO TOMÉ AND PRÍNCIPE
São Tomé •
Libreville ⊛
CONGO
Kigali ⊛
L. Turkana
Lake Victoria
GABON
RWANDA
INDIAN OCEAN
Brazzaville ⊛
**DEM. REP.
OF CONGO**
Bujumbura ⊛
Mombasa •
ATLANTIC OCEAN
**CABINDA
(ANGOLA)**
Kinshasa ⊛
BURUNDI
Dodoma ⊛
SEYCHELLES
Luanda ⊛
L. Tanganyika
TANZANIA
Dar es Salaam •
Lubumbashi •
L. Nyasa
COMOROS
• Moroni
ANGOLA
MALAWI
ZAMBIA
Lilongwe ⊛
Lusaka ⊛
Zambezi R.
Antananarivo •
MAURITIUS
Harare ⊛
Port Louis ⊛
MOZAMBIQUE
MADAGASCAR
ZIMBABWE
**RÉUNION
(FR.)**
NAMIBIA
BOTSWANA
Mozambique Channel
Limpopo R.
Windhoek ⊛
Gaborone ⊛
Pretoria ⊛
Maputo ⊛
Johannesburg •
Mbabane ⊛
Orange R.
SWAZILAND
Maseru ⊛
Durban •
**SOUTH
AFRICA**
LESOTHO
Cape Town ⊛

Red Sea
Blue Nile
White Nile
Nile R.
Gulf of Aden

Benue R.

Tropic of Capricorn

KEY

— National boundary
⊛ National capital
• Other city

Lambert Azimuthal Equal-Area Projection

0   400   800 mi
0   400   800 km

Africa: Physical

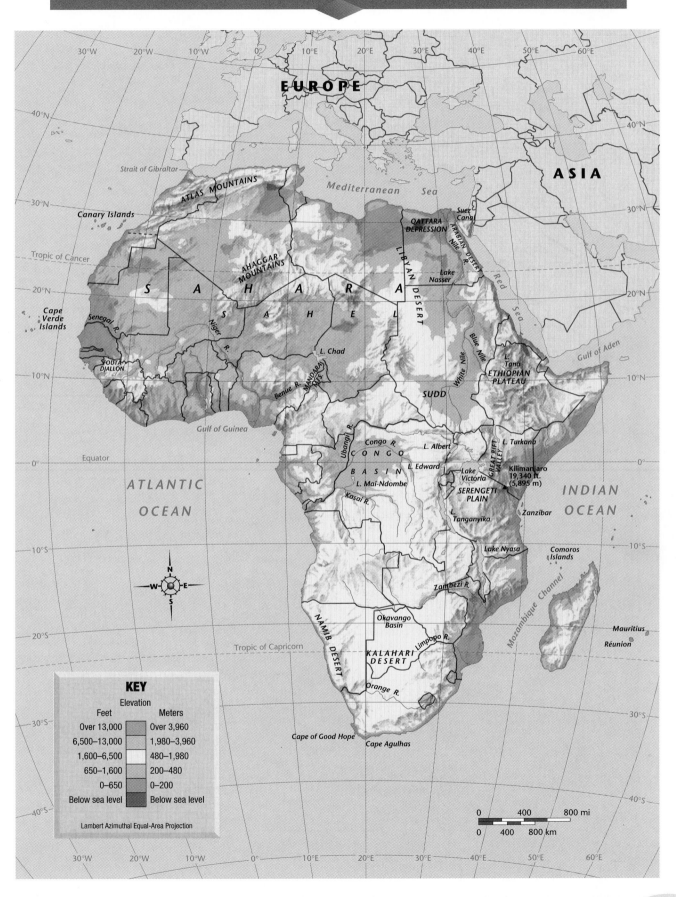

EUROPE

ASIA

Strait of Gibraltar

Mediterranean Sea

ATLAS MOUNTAINS

Canary Islands

Tropic of Cancer

QATTARA DEPRESSION

Suez Canal

ARABIAN DESERT

Nile R.

LIBYAN DESERT

AHAGGAR MOUNTAINS

Lake Nasser

S   A   H   A   R   A

Cape Verde Islands

Senegal R.

S A H E L

Niger R.

Red Sea

L. Chad

MANDARA MTS

Blue Nile

L. Tana

ETHIOPIAN PLATEAU

Gulf of Aden

FOUTA DJALLON

White Nile

Benue R.

SUDD

Gulf of Guinea

Ubangi R.

Congo R.

C O N G O
B A S I N

L. Albert

L. Edward

L. Turkana

GREAT RIFT VALLEY

Kilimanjaro 19,340 ft. (5,895 m)

Equator

Lake Victoria

ATLANTIC OCEAN

L. Mai-Ndombe

SERENGETI PLAIN

INDIAN OCEAN

Kasai R.

Zanzibar

L. Tanganyika

Lake Nyasa

Comoros Islands

Mozambique Channel

Mauritius

NAMIB DESERT

Okavango Basin

Zambezi R.

Réunion

Limpopo R.

Tropic of Capricorn

KALAHARI DESERT

Orange R.

KEY

Elevation

Feet		Meters
Over 13,000		Over 3,960
6,500–13,000		1,980–3,960
1,600–6,500		480–1,980
650–1,600		200–480
0–650		0–200
Below sea level		Below sea level

Lambert Azimuthal Equal-Area Projection

Cape of Good Hope

Cape Agulhas

0   400   800 mi

0   400   800 km

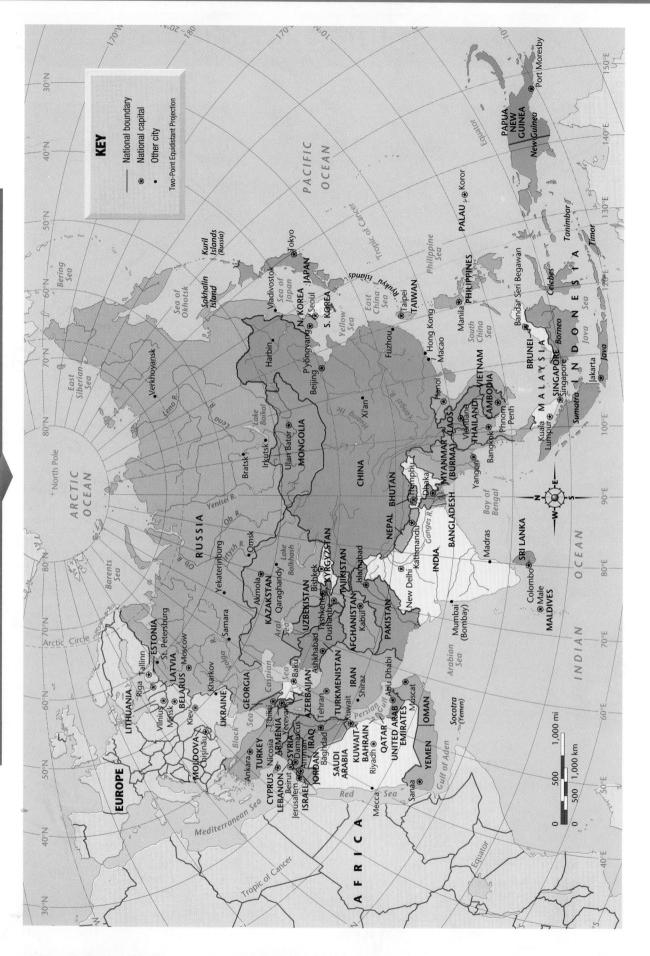

Asia: Political

PACIFIC
OCEAN

ARCTIC
OCEAN

North Pole

Bering
Sea

East
Siberian
Sea

Barents
Sea

Arctic Circle

Verkhoyansk

Sea of
Okhotsk

Sakhalin
Island

Kuril
Islands
(Russia)

Tokyo

Vladivostok

Sea of
Japan

JAPAN

Harbin

Seoul

N. KOREA
S. KOREA

Pyŏngyang

Yellow
Sea

East
China
Sea

Ryukyu Islands

Taipei

TAIWAN

Hong Kong

Macao

Fuzhou

Beijing

Xi'an

Huang He

Yangtze R.

CHINA

South
China
Sea

Philippine
Sea

PHILIPPINES

Manila

PALAU

Koror

PAPUA
NEW
GUINEA

Port Moresby

New Guinea

Equator

RUSSIA

Bratsk

Irkutsk

Lake
Baikal

Lena R.

Ulan Bator

MONGOLIA

Tropic of Cancer

Yenisei R.

Ob R.

Omsk

Yekaterinburg

Irtysh R.

Lake
Balkhash

Akmola

KAZAKSTAN

Qaraghandy

Aral
Sea

BRUNEI

Bandar Seri Begawan

Celebes
Sea

Borneo

INDONESIA

Celebes

Timor

Tanimbar

Java

Java Sea

Jakarta

Sumatra

MALAYSIA

Kuala
Lumpur

SINGAPORE

Singapore

VIETNAM

Hanoi

LAOS

Vientiane

THAILAND

Bangkok

CAMBODIA

Phnom
Penh

MYANMAR
(BURMA)

Yangon

Bay of
Bengal

Bhutan

Thimphu

NEPAL

Kathmandu

Dhaka

BANGLADESH

Ganges R.

INDIA

New Delhi

Madras

SRI LANKA

Colombo

Male

MALDIVES

Mumbai
(Bombay)

Arabian
Sea

Socotra
(Yemen)

INDIAN
OCEAN

Samara

Volga R.

St. Petersburg

Moscow

ESTONIA
Tallinn

LATVIA
Riga

LITHUANIA

Vilnius

BELARUS

Minsk

Kharkov

Kiev

UKRAINE

MOLDOVA

Chişinău

GEORGIA

Tbilisi

Caspian
Sea

Black
Sea

TURKEY

Ankara

ARMENIA

Yerevan

AZERBAIJAN

Baku

Tehran

IRAN

Shiraz

TURKMENISTAN

Ashkhabad

UZBEKISTAN

Tashkent

KYRGYZSTAN

Bishkek

TAJIKISTAN

Dushanbe

AFGHANISTAN

Kabul

PAKISTAN

Islamabad

Persian
Gulf

Kuwait

KUWAIT

BAHRAIN

QATAR

UNITED ARAB
EMIRATES

Abu Dhabi

OMAN

Muscat

Gulf of Oman

YEMEN

Sanaa

Gulf of Aden

SAUDI
ARABIA

Riyadh

Mecca

Red
Sea

IRAQ

Baghdad

SYRIA

Damascus

JORDAN

ISRAEL

Jerusalem

LEBANON

Beirut

CYPRUS

Nicosia

Mediterranean Sea

EUROPE

AFRICA

Tropic of Cancer

Equator

N
W   E
S

1,000 mi

0   500

0   500 1,000 km

1,000 km

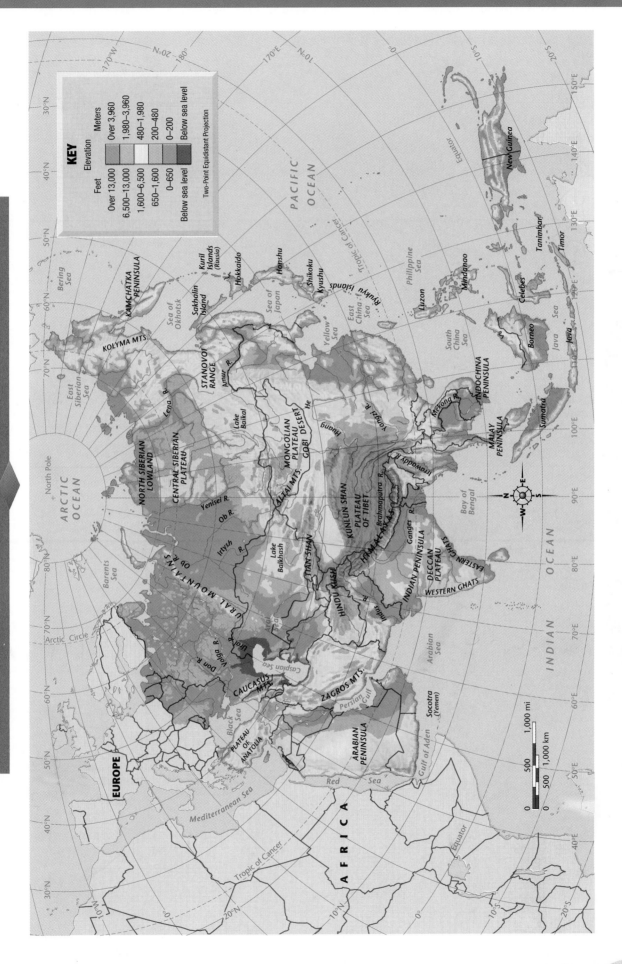

Asia: Physical

KEY

Elevation

Feet	Meters
Over 13,000	Over 3,960
6,500–13,000	1,980–3,960
1,600–6,500	480–1,980
650–1,600	200–480
0–650	0–200
Below sea level	Below sea level

Two-Point Equidistant Projection

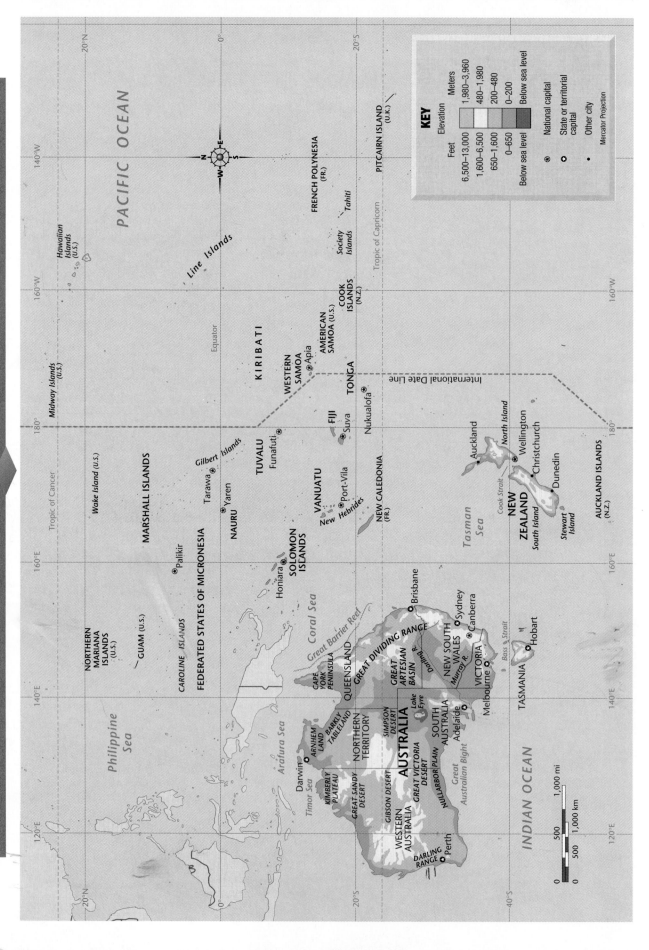

KEY

Elevation	
Feet	Meters
6,500–13,000	1,980–3,960
1,600–6,500	480–1,980
650–1,600	200–480
0–650	0–200
Below sea level	Below sea level

⊛ National capital
⊗ State or territorial capital
• Other city

Mercator Projection

PACIFIC OCEAN

PITCAIRN ISLAND (U.K.)

FRENCH POLYNESIA (FR.)

Tahiti

Society Islands

Tropic of Capricorn

Line Islands

Hawaiian Islands (U.S.)

COOK ISLANDS (N.Z.)

AMERICAN SAMOA (U.S.)

Equator

KIRIBATI

WESTERN SAMOA
⊛ Apia

TONGA
⊛ Nukualofa

Midway Islands (U.S.)

FIJI
Suva

Tropic of Cancer

TUVALU
⊛ Funafuti

Wake Island (U.S.)

MARSHALL ISLANDS

Gilbert Islands

Tarawa
⊛ Yaren

NAURU

VANUATU
⊛ Port-Vila

New Hebrides

NEW CALEDONIA (FR.)

International Date Line

Auckland

North Island
⊛ Wellington
• Christchurch
• Dunedin
South Island

NEW ZEALAND

Cook Strait

Stewart Island

AUCKLAND ISLANDS (N.Z.)

Tasman Sea

NORTHERN MARIANA ISLANDS (U.S.)

GUAM (U.S.)

CAROLINE ISLANDS

FEDERATED STATES OF MICRONESIA

• Palikir

SOLOMON ISLANDS
Honiara

Coral Sea

Philippine Sea

Arafura Sea

Timor Sea

Darwin

Great Barrier Reef

CAPE YORK PENINSULA

QUEENSLAND

GREAT DIVIDING RANGE

• Brisbane

⊛ Sydney
⊛ Canberra

NEW SOUTH WALES

GREAT ARTESIAN BASIN

Darling R.

Murray R.

VICTORIA
Melbourne ⊗

Bass Strait

TASMANIA
⊗ Hobart

ARNHEM LAND

KIMBERLEY PLATEAU

BARKLY TABLELAND

NORTHERN TERRITORY

Lake Eyre

SIMPSON DESERT

SOUTH AUSTRALIA

Adelaide ⊗

GREAT SANDY DESERT

GIBSON DESERT

GREAT VICTORIA DESERT

WESTERN AUSTRALIA

NULLARBOR PLAIN

Great Australian Bight

AUSTRALIA

DARLING RANGE
⊗ Perth

INDIAN OCEAN

1,000 mi

500   1,000 km

0   500   1,000

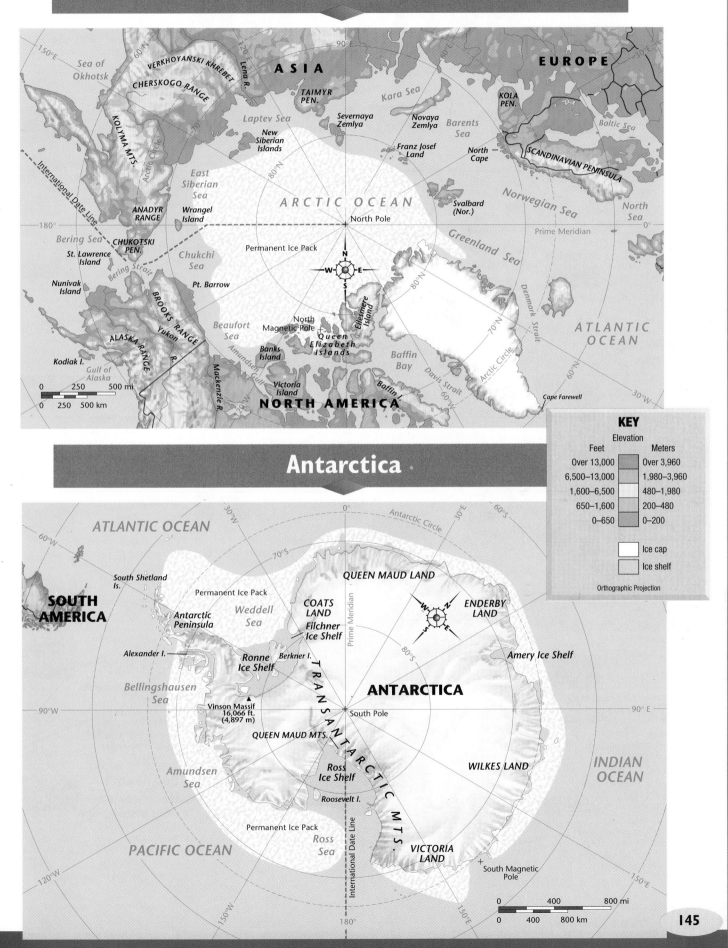

The Arctic

150°E · Sea of Okhotsk · VERKHOYANSKI KHREBET · 60°N · Lena R. · 120°E · 90°E · ASIA · EUROPE · 30°E · CHERSKOGO RANGE · TAIMYR PEN. · Kara Sea · KOLA PEN. · Baltic Sea · KOLYMA MTS. · Laptev Sea · Severnaya Zemlya · Novaya Zemlya · Barents Sea · North Cape · SCANDINAVIAN PENINSULA · 70°N · New Siberian Islands · Franz Josef Land · North Sea · Arctic Circle · East Siberian Sea · 80°N · ARCTIC OCEAN · Svalbard (Nor.) · Norwegian Sea · International Date Line · ANADYR RANGE · Wrangel Island · North Pole · Greenland Sea · Prime Meridian · 0° · 180° · Bering Sea · CHUKOTSKI PEN. · Chukchi Sea · Permanent Ice Pack · N · 80°N · Denmark Strait · North Sea · St. Lawrence Island · Bering Strait · W · E · ATLANTIC OCEAN · Nunivak Island · Pt. Barrow · S · 70°N · Kodiak I. · BROOKS RANGE · Beaufort Sea · North Magnetic Pole · Ellesmere Island · 60°N · ALASKA RANGE · Yukon R. · Banks Island · Queen Elizabeth Islands · Baffin Bay · Davis Strait · Arctic Circle · Gulf of Alaska · Mackenzie R. · Amundsen Gulf · Victoria Island · Baffin I. · 60°N · Cape Farewell · 30°W · 0 250 500 mi · 0 250 500 km · NORTH AMERICA

Antarctica

KEY

Elevation

Feet		Meters
Over 13,000		Over 3,960
6,500–13,000		1,980–3,960
1,600–6,500		480–1,980
650–1,600		200–480
0–650		0–200

Ice cap

Ice shelf

Orthographic Projection

30°W · 0° · Antarctic Circle · 30°E · 60°E · ATLANTIC OCEAN · 60°W · 70°S · QUEEN MAUD LAND · South Shetland Is. · Permanent Ice Pack · COATS LAND · ENDERBY LAND · SOUTH AMERICA · Antarctic Peninsula · Weddell Sea · Filchner Ice Shelf · Prime Meridian · N · Amery Ice Shelf · Alexander I. · Ronne Ice Shelf · Berkner I. · 80°S · W · E · Bellingshausen Sea · TRANSANTARCTIC MTS. · ANTARCTICA · S · 90°E · 90°W · Vinson Massif 16,066 ft. (4,897 m) · QUEEN MAUD MTS. · South Pole · INDIAN OCEAN · Amundsen Sea · Ross Ice Shelf · WILKES LAND · Roosevelt I. · Permanent Ice Pack · Ross Sea · VICTORIA LAND · South Magnetic Pole · PACIFIC OCEAN · International Date Line · 120°W · 150°E · 150°W · 180° · 0 400 800 mi · 0 400 800 km

145

World View

Afghanistan
CAPITAL: Kabul
POPULATION: 24,792,375
MAJOR LANGUAGES: Pashtu, Afghan Persian, Turkic, and 30 various languages
AREA: 250,010 sq mi; 647,500 sq km
LEADING EXPORTS: fruits and nuts, handwoven carpets, and wool
CONTINENT: Asia

Albania
CAPITAL: Tiranë
POPULATION: 3,330,754
MAJOR LANGUAGES: Albanian, Tosk dialect, and Greek
AREA: 11,101 sq mi; 28,750 sq km
LEADING EXPORTS: asphalt, metals and metallic ores, and electricity
CONTINENT: Europe

Algeria
CAPITAL: Algiers
POPULATION: 30,480,793
MAJOR LANGUAGES: Arabic (official), French, and Berber dialects
AREA: 919,626 sq mi; 2,381,740 sq km
LEADING EXPORTS: petroleum and natural gas
CONTINENT: Africa

Andorra
CAPITAL: Andorra La Vella
POPULATION: 64,716
MAJOR LANGUAGES: Catalan (official), French, and Castilian
AREA: 174 sq mi; 450 sq km
LEADING EXPORTS: electricity, tobacco products, and furniture
CONTINENT: Europe

Angola
CAPITAL: Luanda
POPULATION: 10,864,512
MAJOR LANGUAGES: Portuguese (official), Bantu, and various languages
AREA: 481,370 sq mi; 1,246,700 sq km
LEADING EXPORTS: oil, diamonds, and refined petroleum products
CONTINENT: Africa

Anguilla
CAPITAL: The Valley
POPULATION: 11,147
MAJOR LANGUAGE: English (official)
AREA: 35 sq mi; 91 sq km
LEADING EXPORTS: lobster and salt
LOCATION: Caribbean Sea

Antigua and Barbuda
CAPITAL: Saint John's
POPULATION: 64,006
MAJOR LANGUAGES: English (official) and various dialects
AREA: 170 sq mi; 440 sq km
LEADING EXPORTS: petroleum products and manufactures
LOCATION: Caribbean Sea

Argentina
CAPITAL: Buenos Aires
POPULATION: 36,265,463
MAJOR LANGUAGES: Spanish (official), English, Italian, German, and French
AREA: 1,068,339 sq mi; 2,766,890 sq km
LEADING EXPORTS: meat, wheat, corn, oilseed, and manufactures
CONTINENT: South America

Armenia
CAPITAL: Yerevan
POPULATION: 3,421,775
MAJOR LANGUAGES: Armenian and Russian
AREA: 11,506 sq mi; 29,800 sq km
LEADING EXPORTS: gold and jewelry, and aluminum
CONTINENT: Asia

Australia
CAPITAL: Canberra
POPULATION: 18,613,087
MAJOR LANGUAGES: English and various languages
AREA: 2,968,010 sq mi; 7,686,850 sq km
LEADING EXPORTS: coal, gold, meat, wool, and alumina
CONTINENT: Australia

Austria
CAPITAL: Vienna
POPULATION: 8,133,611
MAJOR LANGUAGE: German
AREA: 32,376 sq mi; 83,850 sq km
LEADING EXPORTS: machinery and equipment, and iron and steel
CONTINENT: Europe

Azerbaijan
CAPITAL: Baku
POPULATION: 7,855,576
MAJOR LANGUAGES: Azeri, Russian, Armenian, and various languages
AREA: 33,438 sq mi; 86,600 sq km
LEADING EXPORTS: oil and gas, chemicals, and oil field equipment
CONTINENT: Asia

Bahamas
CAPITAL: Nassau
POPULATION: 279,833
MAJOR LANGUAGES: English and Creole
AREA: 5,382 sq mi; 13,940 sq km
LEADING EXPORTS: pharmaceuticals, cement, rum, and crawfish
LOCATION: Caribbean Sea

Bahrain
CAPITAL: Manama
POPULATION: 616,342
MAJOR LANGUAGES: Arabic, English, Farsi, and Urdu
AREA: 239 sq mi; 620 sq km
LEADING EXPORTS: petroleum and petroleum products
CONTINENT: Asia

Bangladesh
CAPITAL: Dhaka
POPULATION: 127,567,002
MAJOR LANGUAGES: Bangla and English
AREA: 55,600 sq mi; 144,000 sq km
LEADING EXPORTS: garments, jute and jute goods, and leather
CONTINENT: Asia

Barbados
CAPITAL: Bridgetown
POPULATION: 259,025
MAJOR LANGUAGE: English
AREA: 166 sq mi; 430 sq km
LEADING EXPORTS: sugar and molasses, and rum
LOCATION: Caribbean Sea

Belarus
CAPITAL: Minsk
POPULATION: 10,409,050
MAJOR LANGUAGES: Byelorussian and Russian
AREA: 79,926 sq mi; 207,600 sq km
LEADING EXPORTS: machinery and transportation equipment
CONTINENT: Europe

Belgium
CAPITAL: Brussels
POPULATION: 10,174,922
MAJOR LANGUAGES: Dutch, French, and German
AREA: 11,780 sq mi; 30,510 sq km
LEADING EXPORTS: iron and steel, and transportation equipment
CONTINENT: Europe

Belize
CAPITAL: Belmopan
POPULATION: 230,160
MAJOR LANGUAGES: English (official), Spanish, Maya, and Garifuna
AREA: 8,865 sq mi; 22,960 sq km
LEADING EXPORTS: sugar, citrus fruits, bananas, and clothing
CONTINENT: North America

Benin
CAPITAL: Porto-Novo
POPULATION: 6,100,799
MAJOR LANGUAGES: Fon, Yoruba, and at least 6 various languages
AREA: 43,484 sq mi; 112,620 sq km
LEADING EXPORTS: cotton, crude oil, palm products, and cocoa
LOCATION: Atlantic Ocean

Bermuda
CAPITAL: Hamilton
POPULATION: 62,009
MAJOR LANGUAGE: English
AREA: 19.3 sq mi; 50 sq km
LEADING EXPORTS: semitropical produce and light manufactures
LOCATION: Atlantic Ocean

Bhutan
CAPITAL: Thimphu
POPULATION: 1,908,307
MAJOR LANGUAGES: Dzongkha (official), Tibetan dialects, and Nepalese dialects
AREA: 18,147 sq mi; 47,000 sq km
LEADING EXPORTS: cardamon, gypsum, timber, and handicrafts
CONTINENT: Asia

Bolivia
CAPITAL: La Paz
POPULATION: 7,826,352
MAJOR LANGUAGES: Spanish, Quechua, and Aymara
AREA: 424,179 sq mi; 1,098,580 sq km
LEADING EXPORTS: metals, natural gas, soybeans, jewelry, and wood
CONTINENT: South America

Bosnia and Herzegovina

CAPITAL: Sarajevo
POPULATION: 3,365,727
MAJOR LANGUAGE: Serbo-Croatian
AREA: 19,782 sq mi; 51,233 sq km
LEADING EXPORTS: none
CONTINENT: Europe

Botswana

CAPITAL: Gaborone
POPULATION: 1,448,454
MAJOR LANGUAGES: English and Setswana
AREA: 231,812 sq mi; 600,370 sq km
LEADING EXPORTS: diamonds, copper and nickel, and meat
CONTINENT: Africa

Brazil

CAPITAL: Brasília
POPULATION: 169,806,557
MAJOR LANGUAGES: Portuguese, Spanish, English, and French
AREA: 3,286,600 sq mi; 8,511,965 sq km
LEADING EXPORTS: iron ore, soybean, bran, and orange juice
CONTINENT: South America

British Virgin Islands

CAPITAL: Road Town
POPULATION: 13,368
MAJOR LANGUAGE: English
AREA: 58 sq mi; 150 sq km
LEADING EXPORTS: rum, fresh fish, gravel, sand, and fruits
LOCATION: Caribbean Sea

Brunei

CAPITAL: Bandar Seri Begawan
POPULATION: 315,292
MAJOR LANGUAGES: Malay, English, and Chinese
AREA: 2,228 sq mi; 5,770 sq km
LEADING EXPORTS: crude oil and liquefied natural gas
LOCATION: South China Sea

Bulgaria

CAPITAL: Sofia
POPULATION: 8,240,426
MAJOR LANGUAGE: Bulgarian
AREA: 42,824 sq mi; 110,910 sq km
LEADING EXPORTS: machinery and agricultural products
CONTINENT: Europe

Burkina Faso

CAPITAL: Ouagadougou
POPULATION: 11,266,393
MAJOR LANGUAGES: French (official) and Sudanic languages
AREA: 105,873 sq mi; 274,200 sq km
LEADING EXPORTS: cotton, gold, and animal products
CONTINENT: Africa

Burundi

CAPITAL: Bujumbura
POPULATION: 5,537,387
MAJOR LANGUAGES: Kirundi, French, and Swahili
AREA: 10,746 sq mi; 27,830 sq km
LEADING EXPORTS: coffee, tea, cotton, and hides and skins
CONTINENT: Africa

Cambodia

CAPITAL: Phnom Penh
POPULATION: 11,339,562
MAJOR LANGUAGES: Khmer and French
AREA: 69,902 sq mi; 181,040 sq km
LEADING EXPORTS: timber, rubber, soybeans, and sesame
CONTINENT: Asia

Cameroon

CAPITAL: Yaounde
POPULATION: 15,029,433
MAJOR LANGUAGES: 24 various languages, English, and French
AREA: 183,574 sq mi; 475,440 sq km
LEADING EXPORTS: petroleum products and lumber
CONTINENT: Africa

Canada

CAPITAL: Ottawa
POPULATION: 30,675,398
MAJOR LANGUAGES: English and French
AREA: 3,851,940 sq mi; 9,976,140 sq km
LEADING EXPORTS: newsprint, wood pulp, timber, and crude petroleum
CONTINENT: North America

Cape Verde

CAPITAL: Praia
POPULATION: 399,857
MAJOR LANGUAGES: Portuguese and Crioulo
AREA: 1,556 sq mi; 4,030 sq km
LEADING EXPORTS: fish, bananas, and hides and skins
CONTINENT: Africa

Cayman Islands

CAPITAL: George Town
POPULATION: 37,716
MAJOR LANGUAGE: English
AREA: 100 sq mi; 260 sq km
LEADING EXPORTS: turtle products and manufactured goods
LOCATION: Caribbean Sea

Central African Republic

CAPITAL: Bangui
POPULATION: 3,375,771
MAJOR LANGUAGES: French, Sangho, Arabic, Hunsa, and Swahili
AREA: 240,542 sq mi; 622,980 sq km
LEADING EXPORTS: diamonds, timber, cotton, coffee, and tobacco
CONTINENT: Africa

Chad

CAPITAL: N'Djamena
POPULATION: 7,359,512
MAJOR LANGUAGES: French, Arabic, Sara, Songo, and over 100 various languages and dialects
AREA: 495,772 sq mi; 1,284,000 sq km
LEADING EXPORTS: cotton, cattle, textiles, and fish
CONTINENT: Africa

Chile

CAPITAL: Santiago
POPULATION: 14,787,781
MAJOR LANGUAGE: Spanish
AREA: 292,269 sq mi; 756,950 sq km
LEADING EXPORTS: copper and other metals and minerals
CONTINENT: South America

China

CAPITAL: Beijing
POPULATION: 1,236,914,658
MAJOR LANGUAGES: Mandarin, Putonghua, Yue, Wu, Minbei, Minnan, Xiang, and Gan and Hakka dialects
AREA: 3,705,533 sq mi; 9,596,960 sq km
LEADING EXPORTS: textiles, garments, footwear, and toys
CONTINENT: Asia

Colombia

CAPITAL: Bogota
POPULATION: 38,580,949
MAJOR LANGUAGE: Spanish
AREA: 439,751 sq mi; 1,138,910 sq km
LEADING EXPORTS: petroleum, coffee, coal, and bananas
CONTINENT: South America

Comoros

CAPITAL: Moroni
POPULATION: 545,528
MAJOR LANGUAGES: Arabic, French, and Comoran
AREA: 838 sq mi; 2,170 sq km
LEADING EXPORTS: vanilla, ylang-ylang, cloves, and perfume oil
LOCATION: Indian Ocean

Congo (Democratic Republic of)

CAPITAL: Kinshasa
POPULATION: 49,000,511
MAJOR LANGUAGES: French, Lingala, Swahili, Kingwana, Kikongo, and Tshiluba
AREA: 905,599 sq mi; 2,345,410 sq km
LEADING EXPORTS: copper, coffee, diamonds, cobalt, and crude oil
CONTINENT: Africa

Congo (Republic of the)

CAPITAL: Brazzaville
POPULATION: 2,658,123
MAJOR LANGUAGES: French, Lingala, Kikongo, and other languages
AREA: 132,051 sq mi; 342,000 sq km
LEADING EXPORTS: crude oil, lumber, plywood, sugar, and cocoa
CONTINENT: Africa

Cook Islands

CAPITAL: Avarua
POPULATION: 19,989
MAJOR LANGUAGES: English and Maori
AREA: 95 sq mi; 240 sq km
LEADING EXPORTS: copra, fresh and canned fruit, and clothing
LOCATION: Pacific Ocean

Costa Rica

CAPITAL: San José
POPULATION: 3,604,642
MAJOR LANGUAGES: Spanish and English
AREA: 19,730 sq mi; 51,100 sq km
LEADING EXPORTS: coffee, bananas, textiles, and sugar
CONTINENT: North America

Côte d'Ivoire

CAPITAL: Yamoussoukro
POPULATION: 15,446,231
MAJOR LANGUAGES: French, Dioula, and 59 other dialects
AREA: 124,507 sq mi; 322,460 sq km
LEADING EXPORTS: cocoa, coffee, tropical woods, and petroleum
CONTINENT: Africa

Croatia

CAPITAL: Zagreb
POPULATION: 4,671,584
MAJOR LANGUAGE: Serbo-Croatian
AREA: 21,830 sq mi; 56,538 sq km
LEADING EXPORTS: machinery and transportation equipment
CONTINENT: Europe

Cuba

CAPITAL: Havana
POPULATION: 11,050,729
MAJOR LANGUAGE: Spanish
AREA: 42,805 sq mi; 110,860 sq km
LEADING EXPORTS: sugar, nickel, shellfish, and tobacco
LOCATION: Caribbean Sea

Cyprus

CAPITAL: Nicosia
POPULATION: 748,982
MAJOR LANGUAGES: Greek, Turkish, and English
AREA: 3,572 sq mi; 9,250 sq km
LEADING EXPORTS: citrus, potatoes, grapes, wines, and cement
LOCATION: Mediterranean Sea

Czech Republic

CAPITAL: Prague
POPULATION: 10,286,470
MAJOR LANGUAGES: Czech and Slovak
AREA: 30,388 sq mi; 78,703 sq km
LEADING EXPORTS: manufactured goods
CONTINENT: Europe

Denmark

CAPITAL: Copenhagen
POPULATION: 5,333,617
MAJOR LANGUAGES: Danish, Faroese, Greenlandic, and German
AREA: 16,630 sq mi; 43,070 sq km
LEADING EXPORTS: meat and meat products, and dairy products
CONTINENT: Europe

Djibouti

CAPITAL: Djibouti
POPULATION: 440,727
MAJOR LANGUAGES: French, Arabic, Somali, and Afar
AREA: 8,495 sq mi; 22,000 sq km
LEADING EXPORTS: hides and skins, and coffee (in transit)
CONTINENT: Africa

Dominica

CAPITAL: Roseau
POPULATION: 65,777
MAJOR LANGUAGES: English and French patois
AREA: 290 sq mi; 750 sq km
LEADING EXPORTS: bananas, soap, bay oil, and vegetables
LOCATION: Caribbean Sea

Dominican Republic

CAPITAL: Santo Domingo
POPULATION: 7,998,776
MAJOR LANGUAGE: Spanish
AREA: 18,815 sq mi; 48,730 sq km
LEADING EXPORTS: ferronickel, sugar, gold, coffee, and cocoa
LOCATION: Caribbean Sea

Ecuador

CAPITAL: Quito
POPULATION: 12,336,572
MAJOR LANGUAGES: Spanish, Quechua, and various languages
AREA: 109,487 sq mi; 283,560 sq km
LEADING EXPORTS: petroleum, bananas, shrimp, and cocoa
CONTINENT: South America

Egypt

CAPITAL: Cairo
POPULATION: 66,050,004
MAJOR LANGUAGES: Arabic, English, and French
AREA: 386,675 sq mi; 1,001,450 sq km
LEADING EXPORTS: crude oil and petroleum products
CONTINENT: Africa

El Salvador

CAPITAL: San Salvador
POPULATION: 5,752,067
MAJOR LANGUAGES: Spanish and Nahua
AREA: 8,124 sq mi; 21,040 sq km
LEADING EXPORTS: coffee, sugar cane, and shrimp
CONTINENT: North America

Equatorial Guinea

CAPITAL: Malabo
POPULATION: 454,001
MAJOR LANGUAGES: Spanish, Pidgin English, Fang, Bubi, and Ibo
AREA: 10,831 sq mi; 28,050 sq km
LEADING EXPORTS: coffee, timber, and cocoa beans
CONTINENT: Africa

Eritrea

CAPITAL: Asmara
POPULATION: 3,842,436
MAJOR LANGUAGES: Tigre, Kunama, Cushitic dialects, Nora Bana, and Arabic
AREA: 46,844 sq mi; 121,320 sq km
LEADING EXPORTS: salt, hides, cement, and gum arabic
CONTINENT: Africa

Estonia

CAPITAL: Tallinn
POPULATION: 1,421,335
MAJOR LANGUAGES: Estonian, Latvian, Lithuanian, and Russian
AREA: 17,414 sq mi; 45,100 sq km
LEADING EXPORTS: textiles, food products, vehicles, and metals
CONTINENT: Europe

Ethiopia

CAPITAL: Addis Ababa
POPULATION: 58,390,351
MAJOR LANGUAGES: Amharic, Tigrinya, Orominga, Guaraginga, Somali, Arabic, English, and various languages
AREA: 435,201 sq mi; 1,127,127 sq km
LEADING EXPORTS: coffee, leather products, and gold
CONTINENT: Africa

Fiji

CAPITAL: Suva
POPULATION: 802,611
MAJOR LANGUAGES: English, Fijian, and Hindustani
AREA: 7,054 sq mi; 18,270 sq km
LEADING EXPORTS: sugar, clothing, gold, processed fish, and lumber
LOCATION: Pacific Ocean

Finland

CAPITAL: Helsinki
POPULATION: 5,149,242
MAJOR LANGUAGES: Finnish, Swedish, Lapp, and Russian
AREA: 130,132 sq mi; 337,030 sq km
LEADING EXPORTS: paper and pulp, machinery, and chemicals
CONTINENT: Europe

France

CAPITAL: Paris
POPULATION: 58,804,944
MAJOR LANGUAGES: French and regional dialects and languages
AREA: 211,217 sq mi; 547,030 sq km
LEADING EXPORTS: machinery and transportation equipment
CONTINENT: Europe

Gabon

CAPITAL: Libreville
POPULATION: 1,207,844
MAJOR LANGUAGES: French, Fang, Myene, Bateke, Bapounou/Eschira, and Bandjabi
AREA: 103,351 sq mi; 267,670 sq km
LEADING EXPORTS: crude oil, timber, manganese, and uranium
CONTINENT: Africa

The Gambia

CAPITAL: Banjul
POPULATION: 1,291,858
MAJOR LANGUAGES: English, Mandinka, Wolof, Fula, and various languages
AREA: 4,363 sq mi; 11,300 sq km
LEADING EXPORTS: peanuts and peanut products, and fish
CONTINENT: Africa

Georgia

CAPITAL: T'bilisi
POPULATION: 5,108,527
MAJOR LANGUAGES: Armenian, Azeri, Georgian, Russian, and various languages
AREA: 26,912 sq mi; 69,700 sq km
LEADING EXPORTS: citrus fruits, tea, and wine
CONTINENT: Asia

Germany

CAPITAL: Berlin
POPULATION: 82,079,454
MAJOR LANGUAGE: German
AREA: 137,808 sq mi; 356,910 sq km
LEADING EXPORTS: machines and machine tools, and chemicals
CONTINENT: Europe

Ghana

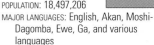

CAPITAL: Accra
POPULATION: 18,497,206
MAJOR LANGUAGES: English, Akan, Moshi-Dagomba, Ewe, Ga, and various languages
AREA: 92,104 sq mi; 238,540 sq km
LEADING EXPORTS: cocoa, gold, timber, tuna, and bauxite
CONTINENT: Africa

Greece

CAPITAL: Athens
POPULATION: 10,662,138
MAJOR LANGUAGES: Greek, English, and French
AREA: 50,944 sq mi; 131,940 sq km
LEADING EXPORTS: manufactured goods, foodstuffs, and fuels
CONTINENT: Europe

Grenada

CAPITAL: Saint George's
POPULATION: 96,217
MAJOR LANGUAGES: English and French patois
AREA: 131 sq mi; 340 sq km
LEADING EXPORTS: bananas, cocoa, nutmeg, and fruits and vegetables
LOCATION: Caribbean Sea

Guatemala

CAPITAL: Guatemala
POPULATION: 12,007,580
MAJOR LANGUAGES: Spanish, Quiche, Cakchiquel, Kekchi, and various languages and dialects
AREA: 42,044 sq mi; 108,890 sq km
LEADING EXPORTS: coffee, sugar, bananas, cardamom, and beef
CONTINENT: North America

Guinea

CAPITAL: Conakry
POPULATION: 7,477,110
MAJOR LANGUAGES: French and various languages
AREA: 94,930 sq mi; 245,860 sq km
LEADING EXPORTS: bauxite, alumina, diamonds, gold, and coffee
CONTINENT: Africa

Guinea-Bissau

CAPITAL: Bissau
POPULATION: 1,206,311
MAJOR LANGUAGES: Portuguese, Criolo, and various languages
AREA: 13,946 sq mi; 36,210 sq km
LEADING EXPORTS: cashews, fish, peanuts, and palm kernels
CONTINENT: Africa

Guyana

CAPITAL: Georgetown
POPULATION: 707,954
MAJOR LANGUAGES: English and various dialects
AREA: 83,003 sq mi; 214,970 sq km
LEADING EXPORTS: sugar, bauxite/alumina, rice, and shrimp
CONTINENT: South America

Haiti

CAPITAL: Port-au-Prince
POPULATION: 6,780,501
MAJOR LANGUAGES: French and Creole
AREA: 8,784 sq mi; 22,750 sq km
LEADING EXPORTS: light manufactures and coffee
LOCATION: Caribbean Sea

Holy See (Vatican City)

CAPITAL: Vatican City
POPULATION: 840
MAJOR LANGUAGES: Italian, Latin, and various languages
AREA: 0.17 sq mi; 0.44 sq km
LEADING EXPORTS: none
CONTINENT: Europe

Honduras

CAPITAL: Tegucigalpa
POPULATION: 5,861,955
MAJOR LANGUAGES: Spanish and various dialects
AREA: 43,280 sq mi; 112,090 sq km
LEADING EXPORTS: bananas, coffee, shrimp, lobsters, and minerals
CONTINENT: North America

Hungary

CAPITAL: Budapest
POPULATION: 10,208,127
MAJOR LANGUAGES: Hungarian and various languages
AREA: 35,920 sq mi; 93,030 sq km
LEADING EXPORTS: raw materials and semi-finished goods
CONTINENT: Europe

Iceland

CAPITAL: Reykjavik
POPULATION: 271,033
MAJOR LANGUAGE: Icelandic
AREA: 39,770 sq mi; 103,000 sq km
LEADING EXPORTS: fish and fish products, and animal products
LOCATION: Atlantic Ocean

India

CAPITAL: New Delhi
POPULATION: 984,003,683
MAJOR LANGUAGES: English, Hindi, Bengali, Telugu, Marathi, Tamil, Urdu, Gujarati, Malayam, Kannada, Oriya, Punjabi, Assamese, Kashmiri, Sindhi, Sanskrit, and Hindustani (all official)
AREA: 1,269,389 sq mi; 3,287,590 sq km
LEADING EXPORTS: clothing, and gems and jewelry
CONTINENT: Asia

Indonesia

CAPITAL: Jakarta
POPULATION: 212,941,810
MAJOR LANGUAGES: Bahasa Indonesia, English, Dutch, Javanese, and various dialects
AREA: 741,052 sq mi; 1,919,251 sq km
LEADING EXPORTS: manufactures, fuels, and foodstuffs
CONTINENT: Asia

Iran

CAPITAL: Tehran
POPULATION: 68,959,931
MAJOR LANGUAGES: Farsi (official) and Turkic languages
AREA: 634,562 sq mi; 1,643,452 sq km
LEADING EXPORTS: petroleum, carpets, fruit, nuts, and hides
CONTINENT: Asia

Iraq

CAPITAL: Baghdad
POPULATION: 21,722,287
MAJOR LANGUAGES: Arabic, Kurdish, Assyrian, and Armenian
AREA: 168,760 sq mi; 437,072 sq km
LEADING EXPORTS: crude oil and refined products, and fertilizers
CONTINENT: Asia

Ireland

CAPITAL: Dublin
POPULATION: 3,619,480
MAJOR LANGUAGES: Irish Gaelic and English
AREA: 27,136 sq mi; 70,280 sq km
LEADING EXPORTS: chemicals and data processing equipment
CONTINENT: Europe

Israel

CAPITAL: Jerusalem
POPULATION: 5,643,966
MAJOR LANGUAGES: Hebrew, Arabic, and English
AREA: 8,019 sq mi; 20,849 sq km
LEADING EXPORTS: machinery and equipment, and cut diamonds
CONTINENT: Asia

Italy

CAPITAL: Rome
POPULATION: 56,782,748
MAJOR LANGUAGES: Italian, German, French, and Slovene
AREA: 116,310 sq mi; 301,230 sq km
LEADING EXPORTS: metals, and textiles and clothing
CONTINENT: Europe

Jamaica

CAPITAL: Kingston
POPULATION: 2,634,678
MAJOR LANGUAGES: English and Creole
AREA: 4,243 sq mi; 10,990 sq km
LEADING EXPORTS: alumina, bauxite, sugar, bananas, and rum
LOCATION: Caribbean Sea

Japan

CAPITAL: Tokyo
POPULATION: 125,931,533
MAJOR LANGUAGE: Japanese
AREA: 145,888 sq mi; 377,835 sq km
LEADING EXPORTS: machinery, motor vehicles, and electronics
CONTINENT: Asia

Jordan

CAPITAL: Amman
POPULATION: 4,434,978
MAJOR LANGUAGES: Arabic and English
AREA: 34,447 sq mi; 89,213 sq km
LEADING EXPORTS: phosphates, fertilizers, and potash
CONTINENT: Asia

Kazakstan

CAPITAL: Akmola
POPULATION: 16,846,808
MAJOR LANGUAGES: Kazakh and Russian
AREA: 1,049,191 sq mi; 2,717,300 sq km
LEADING EXPORTS: oil, and ferrous and nonferrous metals
CONTINENT: Asia

Kenya

CAPITAL: Nairobi
POPULATION: 28,337,071
MAJOR LANGUAGES: English, Swahili, and various languages
AREA: 224,970 sq mi; 582,650 sq km
LEADING EXPORTS: tea, coffee, and petroleum products
CONTINENT: Africa

Kiribati

CAPITAL: Tarawa
POPULATION: 83,976
MAJOR LANGUAGES: English and Gilbertese
AREA: 277 sq mi; 717 sq km
LEADING EXPORTS: copra, seaweed, and fish
LOCATION: Pacific Ocean

Korea, North

CAPITAL: P'yongyang
POPULATION: 21,234,387
MAJOR LANGUAGE: Korean
AREA: 46,542 sq mi; 120,540 sq km
LEADING EXPORTS: minerals and metallurgical products
CONTINENT: Asia

Korea, South

CAPITAL: Seoul
POPULATION: 46,416,796
MAJOR LANGUAGES: Korean and English
AREA: 38,025 sq mi; 98,480 sq km
LEADING EXPORTS: electronic and electrical equipment
CONTINENT: Asia

Kuwait

CAPITAL: Kuwait
POPULATION: 1,913,285
MAJOR LANGUAGES: Arabic and English
AREA: 6,881 sq mi; 17,820 sq km
LEADING EXPORT: oil
CONTINENT: Asia

Kyrgyzstan

CAPITAL: Bishkek
POPULATION: 4,522,281
MAJOR LANGUAGES: Kyrgyz and Russian
AREA: 76,644 sq mi; 198,500 sq km
LEADING EXPORTS: wool, chemicals, cotton, metals, and shoes
CONTINENT: Asia

Laos

CAPITAL: Vientiane
POPULATION: 5,260,842
MAJOR LANGUAGES: Lao, French, English, and various languages
AREA: 91,432 sq mi; 236,800 sq km
LEADING EXPORTS: electricity, wood products, coffee, and tin
CONTINENT: Asia

Latvia

CAPITAL: Riga
POPULATION: 2,385,396
MAJOR LANGUAGES: Lettish, Lithuanian, Russian, and various languages
AREA: 24,750 sq mi; 64,100 sq km
LEADING EXPORTS: oil products, timber, and ferrous metals
CONTINENT: Europe

Lebanon

CAPITAL: Beirut
POPULATION: 3,505,794
MAJOR LANGUAGES: Arabic, French, Armenian, and English
AREA: 4,016 sq mi; 10,400 sq km
LEADING EXPORTS: agricultural products, chemicals, and textiles
CONTINENT: Asia

Lesotho

CAPITAL: Maseru
POPULATION: 2,089,829
MAJOR LANGUAGES: Sesotho, English, Zulu, and Xhosa
AREA: 11,719 sq mi; 30,350 sq km
LEADING EXPORTS: wool, mohair, wheat, cattle, and peas
CONTINENT: Africa

Liberia
CAPITAL: Monrovia
POPULATION: 2,771,901
MAJOR LANGUAGES: English and Niger-Congo
AREA: 43,002 sq mi; 111,370 sq km
LEADING EXPORTS: iron ore, rubber, timber, and coffee
CONTINENT: Africa

Libya
CAPITAL: Tripoli
POPULATION: 5,690,727
MAJOR LANGUAGES: Arabic, Italian, and English
AREA: 679,385 sq mi; 1,759,540 sq km
LEADING EXPORTS: crude oil and refined petroleum products
CONTINENT: Africa

Liechtenstein
CAPITAL: Vaduz
POPULATION: 31,717
MAJOR LANGUAGES: German and Alemannic
AREA: 62 sq mi; 160 sq km
LEADING EXPORTS: small specialty machinery and dental products
CONTINENT: Europe

Lithuania
CAPITAL: Vilnius
POPULATION: 3,600,158
MAJOR LANGUAGES: Lithuanian, Polish, and Russian
AREA: 25,175 sq mi; 65,200 sq km
LEADING EXPORTS: electronics, petroleum products, and food
CONTINENT: Europe

Luxembourg
CAPITAL: Luxembourg
POPULATION: 425,017
MAJOR LANGUAGES: Luxembourgisch, German, French, and English
AREA: 998 sq mi; 2,586 sq km
LEADING EXPORTS: finished steel products and chemicals
CONTINENT: Europe

Macedonia
CAPITAL: Skopje
POPULATION: 2,009,387
MAJOR LANGUAGES: Macedonian, Albanian, Turkish, Serb, Gypsy, and various languages
AREA: 9,781 sq mi; 25,333 sq km
LEADING EXPORTS: manufactured goods and machinery
CONTINENT: Europe

Madagascar
CAPITAL: Antananarivo
POPULATION: 14,462,509
MAJOR LANGUAGES: French and Malagasy
AREA: 226,665 sq mi; 587,040 sq km
LEADING EXPORTS: coffee, vanilla, cloves, shellfish, and sugar
CONTINENT: Africa

Malawi
CAPITAL: Lilongwe
POPULATION: 9,840,474
MAJOR LANGUAGES: English, Chichewa, and various languages
AREA: 45,747 sq mi; 118,480 sq km
LEADING EXPORTS: tobacco, tea, sugar, coffee, and peanuts
CONTINENT: Africa

Malaysia
CAPITAL: Kuala Lumpur
POPULATION: 20,932,901
MAJOR LANGUAGES: Malay, English, Mandarin, Tamil, Chinese dialects, and various languages and dialects
AREA: 127,322 sq mi; 329,750 sq km
LEADING EXPORTS: electronic equipment
CONTINENT: Asia

Maldives
CAPITAL: Male
POPULATION: 290,211
MAJOR LANGUAGES: Divehi dialect and English
AREA: 116 sq mi; 300 sq km
LEADING EXPORTS: fish and clothing
CONTINENT: Asia

Mali
CAPITAL: Bamako
POPULATION: 10,108,569
MAJOR LANGUAGES: French, Bambara, and various languages
AREA: 478,783 sq mi; 1,240,000 sq km
LEADING EXPORTS: cotton, livestock, and gold
CONTINENT: Africa

Malta
CAPITAL: Valletta
POPULATION: 379,563
MAJOR LANGUAGES: Maltese and English
AREA: 124 sq mi; 320 sq km
LEADING EXPORTS: machinery and transportation equipment
LOCATION: Mediterranean Sea

Marshall Islands

CAPITAL: Majuro
POPULATION: 63,031
MAJOR LANGUAGES: English, Marshallese dialects, and Japanese
AREA: 70 sq mi; 181.3 sq km
LEADING EXPORTS: coconut oil, fish, live animals, and trichus shells
LOCATION: Pacific Ocean

Mauritania
CAPITAL: Nouakchott
POPULATION: 2,511,473
MAJOR LANGUAGES: Hasaniya Arabic, Wolof, Pular, and Soninke
AREA: 397,969 sq mi; 1,030,700 sq km
LEADING EXPORTS: iron ore, and fish and fish products
CONTINENT: Africa

Mauritius
CAPITAL: Port Louis
POPULATION: 1,168,256
MAJOR LANGUAGES: English (official), Creole, French, Hindi, Urdu, Hakka, and Bojpoori
AREA: 718 sq mi; 1,860 sq km
LEADING EXPORTS: textiles, sugar, and light manufactures
LOCATION: Indian Ocean

Mayotte
CAPITAL: Mamoutzou
POPULATION: 141,944
MAJOR LANGUAGES: Mahorian and French
AREA: 145 sq mi; 375 sq km
LEADING EXPORTS: ylang-ylang and vanilla
CONTINENT: Africa

Mexico
CAPITAL: Mexico City
POPULATION: 98,552,776
MAJOR LANGUAGES: Spanish and Mayan dialects
AREA: 761,632 sq mi; 1,972,550 sq km
LEADING EXPORTS: crude oil, oil products, coffee, and silver
CONTINENT: North America

Micronesia
CAPITAL: Federated states of Kolonia (on the Island of Pohnpei)
*a new capital is being built about 10 km southwest in the Palikir Valley
POPULATION: 129,658
MAJOR LANGUAGES: English, Turkese, Pohnpeian, Yapese, and Kosrean
AREA: 271 sq mi; 702 sq km
LEADING EXPORTS: fish, copra, bananas, and black pepper
LOCATION: Pacific Ocean

Moldova

CAPITAL: Chisinau
POPULATION: 4,457,729
MAJOR LANGUAGES: Moldovan (official), Russian, and Gagauz dialect
AREA: 13,012 sq mi; 33,700 sq km
LEADING EXPORTS: foodstuffs, wine, and tobacco
CONTINENT: Europe

Monaco
CAPITAL: Monaco
POPULATION: 32,035
MAJOR LANGUAGES: French (official), English, Italian, and Monegasque
AREA: .73 sq mi; 1.9 sq km
LEADING EXPORTS: exports through France
CONTINENT: Europe

Mongolia
CAPITAL: Ulaanbaatar
POPULATION: 2,578,530
MAJOR LANGUAGES: Khalkha Mongol, Turkic, Russian, and Chinese
AREA: 604,270 sq mi; 1,565,000 sq km
LEADING EXPORTS: copper, livestock, animal products, and cashmere
CONTINENT: Asia

Morocco
CAPITAL: Rabat
POPULATION: 29,114,497
MAJOR LANGUAGES: Arabic (official), Berber dialects, and French
AREA: 172,420 sq mi; 446,550 sq km
LEADING EXPORTS: food and beverages
CONTINENT: Africa

Mozambique
CAPITAL: Maputo
POPULATION: 18,641,469
MAJOR LANGUAGES: Portuguese and various dialects
AREA: 309,506 sq mi; 801,590 sq km
LEADING EXPORTS: shrimp, cashews, cotton, sugar, copra, and citrus
CONTINENT: Africa

Myanmar (Burma)
CAPITAL: Rangoon
POPULATION: 47,305,319
MAJOR LANGUAGE: Burmese
AREA: 261,979 sq mi; 678,500 sq km
LEADING EXPORTS: pulses and beans, teak, rice, and hardwood
CONTINENT: Asia

Namibia

CAPITAL: Windhoek

POPULATION: 1,622,328

MAJOR LANGUAGES: English (official), Afrikaans, German, Oshivambo, Herero, Nama, and various languages

AREA: 318,707 sq mi; 825,418 sq km

LEADING EXPORTS: diamonds, copper, gold, zinc, and lead

CONTINENT: Africa

Nauru

CAPITAL: Government offices in Yaren District

POPULATION: 10,501

MAJOR LANGUAGES: Nauruan and English

AREA: 8 sq mi; 21 sq km

LEADING EXPORTS: phosphates

LOCATION: Pacific Ocean

Nepal

CAPITAL: Kathmandu

POPULATION: 23,698,421

MAJOR LANGUAGES: Nepali (official) and 20 various languages divided into numerous dialects

AREA: 54,365 sq mi; 140,800 sq km

LEADING EXPORTS: carpets, clothing, and leather goods

CONTINENT: Asia

Netherlands

CAPITAL: Amsterdam

POPULATION: 15,731,112

MAJOR LANGUAGE: Dutch

AREA: 14,414 sq mi; 37,330 sq km

LEADING EXPORTS: metal products and chemicals

CONTINENT: Europe

New Caledonia

CAPITAL: Noumea

POPULATION: 194,197

MAJOR LANGUAGES: French and 28 Melanesian-Polynesian dialects

AREA: 7,359 sq mi; 19,060 sq km

LEADING EXPORTS: nickel metal and nickel ore

LOCATION: Pacific Ocean

New Zealand

CAPITAL: Wellington

POPULATION: 3,625,388

MAJOR LANGUAGES: English and Maori

AREA: 103,741 sq mi; 268,680 sq km

LEADING EXPORTS: wool, lamb, mutton, beef, fish, and cheese

LOCATION: Pacific Ocean

Nicaragua

CAPITAL: Managua

POPULATION: 4,583,379

MAJOR LANGUAGES: Spanish (official), English, and various languages

AREA: 50,000 sq mi; 129,494 sq km

LEADING EXPORTS: meat, coffee, cotton, sugar, seafood, and gold

CONTINENT: North America

Niger

CAPITAL: Niamey

POPULATION: 9,671,848

MAJOR LANGUAGES: French (official), Hausa, and Djerma

AREA: 489,208 sq mi; 1,267,000 sq km

LEADING EXPORTS: uranium ore and livestock products

CONTINENT: Africa

Nigeria

CAPITAL: Abuja

POPULATION: 110,532,242

MAJOR LANGUAGES: English (official), Hausa, Yoruba, Ibo, and Fulani

AREA: 356,682 sq mi; 923,770 sq km

LEADING EXPORTS: oil, cocoa, and rubber

CONTINENT: Africa

Niue

CAPITAL: (Free association with New Zealand)

POPULATION: 1,800

MAJOR LANGUAGES: Polynesian and English

AREA: 100 sq mi; 260 sq km

LEADING EXPORTS: canned coconut cream, copra, and honey

LOCATION: Pacific Ocean

Norway

CAPITAL: Oslo

POPULATION: 4,419,955

MAJOR LANGUAGES: Norwegian (official), Lapp, and Finnish

AREA: 125,186 sq mi; 324,220 sq km

LEADING EXPORTS: petroleum and petroleum products

CONTINENT: Europe

Oman

CAPITAL: Muscat

POPULATION: 2,363,591

MAJOR LANGUAGES: Arabic (official), English, Baluchi, Urdu, and Indian dialects

AREA: 82,034 sq mi; 212,460 sq km

LEADING EXPORTS: petroleum, re-exports, and fish

CONTINENT: Asia

Pakistan

CAPITAL: Islamabad

POPULATION: 135,135,195

MAJOR LANGUAGES: Urdu (official), English (official), Punjabi, Sindhi, Pashtu, Urdu, Balochi, and other languages

AREA: 310,414 sq mi; 803,940 sq km

LEADING EXPORTS: cotton, textiles, clothing, rice, and leather

CONTINENT: Asia

Palau

CAPITAL: Koror

POPULATION: 18,110

MAJOR LANGUAGES: English (official), Sonsorolese, Angaur, Japanese, Tobi, and Palauan

AREA: 177 sq mi; 458 sq km

LEADING EXPORTS: trochus, tuna, copra, and handicrafts

LOCATION: Pacific Ocean

Panama

CAPITAL: Panama

POPULATION: 2,735,943

MAJOR LANGUAGES: Spanish (official) and English

AREA: 30,194 sq mi; 78,200 sq km

LEADING EXPORTS: bananas, shrimp, sugar, clothing, and coffee

CONTINENT: North America

Papua New Guinea

CAPITAL: Port Moresby

POPULATION: 4,599,785

MAJOR LANGUAGES: English, pidgin English, and Motu

AREA: 178,266 sq mi; 461,690 sq km

LEADING EXPORTS: gold, copper ore, oil, logs, and palm oil

LOCATION: Pacific Ocean

Paraguay

CAPITAL: Asuncion

POPULATION: 5,291,020

MAJOR LANGUAGES: Spanish (official) and Guarani

AREA: 157,052 sq mi; 406,750 sq km

LEADING EXPORTS: cotton, soybeans, timber, and vegetable oils

CONTINENT: South America

Peru

CAPITAL: Lima

POPULATION: 26,111,110

MAJOR LANGUAGES: Spanish (official), Quechua (official), and Aymara

AREA: 496,243 sq mi; 1,285,220 sq km

LEADING EXPORTS: copper, zinc, and fish meal

CONTINENT: South America

Philippines

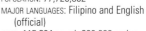

CAPITAL: Manila

POPULATION: 77,725,862

MAJOR LANGUAGES: Filipino and English (official)

AREA: 115,834 sq mi; 300,000 sq km

LEADING EXPORTS: electronics, textiles, and coconut products

CONTINENT: Asia

Poland

CAPITAL: Warsaw

POPULATION: 38,606,922

MAJOR LANGUAGE: Polish

AREA: 120,731 sq mi; 312,680 sq km

LEADING EXPORTS: intermediate goods

CONTINENT: Europe

Portugal

CAPITAL: Lisbon

POPULATION: 9,927,556

MAJOR LANGUAGE: Portuguese

AREA: 35,553 sq mi; 92,080 sq km

LEADING EXPORTS: clothing and footwear, and machinery

CONTINENT: Europe

Qatar

CAPITAL: Doha

POPULATION: 697,126

MAJOR LANGUAGES: Arabic (official) and English

AREA: 4,247 sq mi; 11,000 sq km

LEADING EXPORTS: petroleum products, steel, and fertilizers

CONTINENT: Asia

Romania

CAPITAL: Bucharest

POPULATION: 22,395,848

MAJOR LANGUAGES: Romanian, Hungarian, and German

AREA: 91,702 sq mi; 237,500 sq km

LEADING EXPORTS: metals and metal products, and mineral products

CONTINENT: Europe

Russia

CAPITAL: Moscow

POPULATION: 146,861,022

MAJOR LANGUAGES: Russian and various languages

AREA: 6,952,996 sq mi; 17,075,200 sq km

LEADING EXPORTS: petroleum and petroleum products

CONTINENT: Europe and Asia

Rwanda

CAPITAL: Kigali

POPULATION: 7,956,172

MAJOR LANGUAGES: Kinyarwanda (official), French (official), and Kiswahili

AREA: 10,170 sq mi; 26,340 sq km

LEADING EXPORTS: coffee, tea, cassiterite, and wolframite

CONTINENT: Africa

Saint Kitts and Nevis

CAPITAL: Basseterre
POPULATION: 42,291
MAJOR LANGUAGE: English
AREA: 104 sq mi; 269 sq km
LEADING EXPORTS: machinery, food, and electronics
LOCATION: Caribbean Sea

Saint Lucia

CAPITAL: Castries
POPULATION: 152,335
MAJOR LANGUAGES: English and French patois
AREA: 239 sq mi; 620 sq km
LEADING EXPORTS: bananas, clothing, cocoa, and vegetables
LOCATION: Caribbean Sea

Saint Vincent and the Grenadines

CAPITAL: Kingstown
POPULATION: 119,818
MAJOR LANGUAGES: English and French patois
AREA: 131 sq mi; 340 sq km
LEADING EXPORTS: bananas, and eddoes and dasheen (taro)
LOCATION: Caribbean Sea

Samoa

CAPITAL: Apia
POPULATION: 224,713
MAJOR LANGUAGES: Samoan and English
AREA: 1,104 sq mi; 2,860 sq km
LEADING EXPORTS: coconut oil and cream, taro, copra, and cocoa
LOCATION: Pacific Ocean

San Marino

CAPITAL: San Marino
POPULATION: 24,894
MAJOR LANGUAGE: Italian
AREA: 23 sq mi; 60 sq km
LEADING EXPORTS: building stone, lime, wood, and chestnuts
CONTINENT: Europe

São Tomé and Príncipe

CAPITAL: São Tomé
POPULATION: 150,123
MAJOR LANGUAGE: Portuguese (official)
AREA: 371 sq mi; 960 sq km
LEADING EXPORTS: cocoa, copra, coffee, and palm oil
CONTINENT: Africa

Saudi Arabia

CAPITAL: Riyadh
POPULATION: 20,785,955
MAJOR LANGUAGE: Arabic
AREA: 757,011 sq mi; 1,960,582 sq km
LEADING EXPORTS: petroleum and petroleum products
CONTINENT: Asia

Senegal

CAPITAL: Dakar
POPULATION: 9,723,149
MAJOR LANGUAGES: French (official), Wolof, Pulaar, Diola, and Mandingo
AREA: 75,752 sq mi; 196,190 sq km
LEADING EXPORTS: fish, ground nuts, and petroleum products
CONTINENT: Africa

Serbia and Montenegro

CAPITAL: Belgrade
POPULATION: 11,206,039
MAJOR LANGUAGES: Serbo-Croatian and Albanian
AREA: 39,436 sq mi; 102,350 sq km
LEADING EXPORTS: none
CONTINENT: Europe

Seychelles

CAPITAL: Victoria
POPULATION: 78,641
MAJOR LANGUAGES: English (official), French (official), and Creole
AREA: 176 sq mi; 455 sq km
LEADING EXPORTS: fish, cinnamon bark, and copra
CONTINENT: Africa

Sierra Leone

CAPITAL: Freetown
POPULATION: 5,080,004
MAJOR LANGUAGES: English (official), Mende, Temne, and Krio
AREA: 27,700 sq mi; 71,740 sq km
LEADING EXPORTS: rutile, bauxite, diamonds, coffee, and cocoa
CONTINENT: Africa

Singapore

CAPITAL: Singapore
POPULATION: 3,490,356
MAJOR LANGUAGES: Chinese, Malay, Tamil, and English
AREA: 244 sq mi; 633 sq km
LEADING EXPORTS: computer equipment
CONTINENT: Asia

Slovakia

CAPITAL: Bratislava
POPULATION: 5,392,982
MAJOR LANGUAGES: Slovak and Hungarian
AREA: 18,860 sq mi; 48,845 sq km
LEADING EXPORTS: machinery and transportation equipment
CONTINENT: Europe

Slovenia

CAPITAL: Ljubljana
POPULATION: 1,971,739
MAJOR LANGUAGES: Slovenian, Serbo-Croatian, and various languages
AREA: 7,837 sq mi; 20,296 sq km
LEADING EXPORTS: machinery and transportation equipment
CONTINENT: Europe

Solomon Islands

CAPITAL: Honiara
POPULATION: 441,039
MAJOR LANGUAGES: Melanesian pidgin and English
AREA: 10,985 sq mi; 28,450 sq km
LEADING EXPORTS: fish, timber, palm oil, cocoa, and copra
LOCATION: Pacific Ocean

Somalia

CAPITAL: Mogadishu
POPULATION: 6,841,695
MAJOR LANGUAGES: Somali (official), Arabic, Italian, and English
AREA: 246,210 sq mi; 637,660 sq km
LEADING EXPORTS: bananas, live animals, fish, and hides
CONTINENT: Africa

South Africa

CAPITAL: Pretoria (administrative), Cape Town (legislative), Bloemfontein (judicial)
POPULATION: 42,834,520
MAJOR LANGUAGES: Afrikaans, English, Ndebele, Pedi, Sotho, Swazi, Tsonga, Tswana, Venda, Xhosa, and Zulu (all official)
AREA: 471,027 sq mi; 1,219,912 sq km
LEADING EXPORTS: gold, other minerals and metals, and food
CONTINENT: Africa

Spain

CAPITAL: Madrid
POPULATION: 39,133,996
MAJOR LANGUAGES: Spanish, Catalan, Galician, and Basque
AREA: 194,892 sq mi; 504,750 sq km
LEADING EXPORTS: cars and trucks, and semifinished goods
CONTINENT: Europe

Sri Lanka

CAPITAL: Colombo
POPULATION: 18,933,558
MAJOR LANGUAGES: Sinhala (official) and Tamil
AREA: 25,333 sq mi; 65,610 sq km
LEADING EXPORTS: garments and textiles, teas, and diamonds
CONTINENT: Asia

Sudan

CAPITAL: Khartoum
POPULATION: 33,550,552
MAJOR LANGUAGES: Arabic (official), Nubian, Ta Bedawie, Nilotic, Nilo-Hamitic, and Sudanic dialects
AREA: 967,532 sq mi; 2,505,810 sq km
LEADING EXPORTS: gum arabic, livestock/meat, and cotton
CONTINENT: Africa

Suriname

CAPITAL: Paramaribo
POPULATION: 427,980
MAJOR LANGUAGES: Dutch (official), English, Sranang, Tongo, Hindustani, and Japanese
AREA: 63,041 sq mi; 163,270 sq km
LEADING EXPORTS: alumina, aluminum, and shrimp and fish
CONTINENT: South America

Swaziland

CAPITAL: Mbabane
POPULATION: 966,462
MAJOR LANGUAGES: English (official) and SiSwati (official)
AREA: 6,641 sq mi; 17,360 sq km
LEADING EXPORTS: sugar, edible concentrates, and wood pulp
CONTINENT: Africa

Sweden

CAPITAL: Stockholm
POPULATION: 8,886,738
MAJOR LANGUAGES: Swedish, Lapp, and Finnish
AREA: 173,738 sq mi; 449,964 sq km
LEADING EXPORTS: machinery, motor vehicles, and paper products
CONTINENT: Europe

Switzerland

CAPITAL: Bern
POPULATION: 7,260,357
MAJOR LANGUAGES: German, French, Italian, Romansch, and various languages
AREA: 15,943 sq mi; 41,290 sq km
LEADING EXPORTS: machinery and equipment
CONTINENT: Europe

Syria

CAPITAL: Damascus
POPULATION: 16,673,282
MAJOR LANGUAGES: Arabic (official), Kurdish, Armenian, Aramaic, Circassian, and French
AREA: 71,501 sq mi; 185,180 sq km
LEADING EXPORTS: petroleum, textiles, cotton, and fruits
CONTINENT: Asia

Taiwan

CAPITAL: Taipei
POPULATION: 21,908,135
MAJOR LANGUAGES: Mandarin Chinese (official), Taiwanese, and Hakka dialects
AREA: 13,892 sq mi; 35,980 sq km
LEADING EXPORTS: electrical machinery and electronics
CONTINENT: Asia

Tajikistan

CAPITAL: Dushanbe
POPULATION: 6,020,095
MAJOR LANGUAGES: Tajik (official) and Russian
AREA: 55,253 sq mi; 143,100 sq km
LEADING EXPORTS: cotton, aluminum, fruits, and vegetable oil
CONTINENT: Asia

Tanzania

CAPITAL: Dar Es Salaam
POPULATION: 30,608,769
MAJOR LANGUAGES: Swahili, English, and various languages
AREA: 364,914 sq mi; 945,090 sq km
LEADING EXPORTS: coffee, cotton, tobacco, tea, and cashew nuts
CONTINENT: Africa

Thailand

CAPITAL: Bangkok
POPULATION: 60,037,366
MAJOR LANGUAGES: Thai and English
AREA: 198,463 sq mi; 511,770 sq km
LEADING EXPORTS: machinery and manufactures
CONTINENT: Asia

Togo

CAPITAL: Lome
POPULATION: 4,905,827
MAJOR LANGUAGES: French, Ewe and Mina, Dagomba, and Kabye
AREA: 21,927 sq mi; 56,790 sq km
LEADING EXPORTS: phosphates, cotton, cocoa, and coffee
CONTINENT: Africa

Tonga

CAPITAL: Nukualofa
POPULATION: 108,207
MAJOR LANGUAGES: Tongan and English
AREA: 289 sq mi; 748 sq km
LEADING EXPORTS: squash, vanilla, fish, root crops, and coconut oil
LOCATION: Pacific Ocean

Trinidad and Tobago

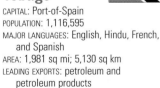

CAPITAL: Port-of-Spain
POPULATION: 1,116,595
MAJOR LANGUAGES: English, Hindu, French, and Spanish
AREA: 1,981 sq mi; 5,130 sq km
LEADING EXPORTS: petroleum and petroleum products
LOCATION: Caribbean Sea

Tunisia

CAPITAL: Tunis
POPULATION: 9,380,404
MAJOR LANGUAGES: Arabic and French
AREA: 63,172 sq mi; 163,610 sq km
LEADING EXPORTS: hydrocarbons and agricultural products
CONTINENT: Africa

Turkey

CAPITAL: Ankara
POPULATION: 65,566,511
MAJOR LANGUAGES: Turkish, Kurdish, and Arabic
AREA: 301,394 sq mi; 780,580 sq km
LEADING EXPORTS: manufactured products, and foodstuffs
CONTINENT: Europe and Asia

Turkmenistan

CAPITAL: Ashgabat
POPULATION: 4,297,629
MAJOR LANGUAGES: Turkmen, Russian, Uzbek, and various languages
AREA: 188,463 sq mi; 488,100 sq km
LEADING EXPORTS: natural gas, cotton, and petroleum products
CONTINENT: Asia

Tuvalu

CAPITAL: Fongafale, on Funafuti atoll
POPULATION: 10,444
MAJOR LANGUAGES: Tuvaluan and English
AREA: 10 sq mi; 26 sq km
LEADING EXPORT: copra
LOCATION: Pacific Ocean

Uganda

CAPITAL: Kampala
POPULATION: 22,167,195
MAJOR LANGUAGES: English, Luganda, Swahili, Bantu languages, and Nilotic languages
AREA: 91,139 sq mi; 236,040 sq km
LEADING EXPORTS: coffee, cotton, and tea
CONTINENT: Africa

Ukraine

CAPITAL: Kiev
POPULATION: 50,125,108
MAJOR LANGUAGES: Ukranian, Russian, Romanian, Polish, and Hungarian
AREA: 233,098 sq mi; 603,700 sq km
LEADING EXPORTS: coal, electric power, and metals
CONTINENT: Europe

United Arab Emirates

CAPITAL: Abu Dhabi
POPULATION: 2,303,088
MAJOR LANGUAGES: Arabic, Persian, English, Hindi, and Urdu
AREA: 29,183 sq mi; 75,581 sq km
LEADING EXPORTS: crude oil, natural gas, re-exports, and dried fish
CONTINENT: Asia

United Kingdom

CAPITAL: London
POPULATION: 58,970,119
MAJOR LANGUAGES: English, Welsh, and Scottish Gaelic
AREA: 94,529 sq mi; 244,820 sq km
LEADING EXPORTS: manufactured goods, machinery, and fuels
CONTINENT: Europe

United States

CAPITAL: Washington, D.C.
POPULATION: 270,311,758
MAJOR LANGUAGES: English and Spanish
AREA: 3,618,908 sq mi; 9,372,610 sq km
LEADING EXPORTS: capital goods and automobiles
CONTINENT: North America

Uruguay

CAPITAL: Montevideo
POPULATION: 3,284,841
MAJOR LANGUAGES: Spanish and Brazilero
AREA: 68,041 sq mi; 176,220 sq km
LEADING EXPORTS: wool and textile manufactures
CONTINENT: South America

Uzbekistan

CAPITAL: Tashkent
POPULATION: 23,784,321
MAJOR LANGUAGES: Uzbek, Russian, Tajik, various languages
AREA: 172,748 sq mi; 447,400 sq km
LEADING EXPORTS: cotton, gold, natural gas, and minerals
CONTINENT: Asia

Vanuatu

CAPITAL: Port-Vila
POPULATION: 185,204
MAJOR LANGUAGES: English, French, pidgin, and Bislama
AREA: 5,699 sq mi; 14,760 sq km
LEADING EXPORTS: copra, beef, cocoa, timber, and coffee
LOCATION: Pacific Ocean

Venezuela

CAPITAL: Caracas
POPULATION: 22,803,409
MAJOR LANGUAGES: Spanish and various languages
AREA: 352,156 sq mi; 912,050 sq km
LEADING EXPORTS: petroleum, bauxite and aluminum, and steel
CONTINENT: South America

Vietnam

CAPITAL: Hanoi
POPULATION: 76,236,259
MAJOR LANGUAGES: Vietnamese, French, Chinese, English, Khmer, and various languages
AREA: 127,248 sq mi; 329,560 sq km
LEADING EXPORTS: petroleum, rice, and agricultural products
CONTINENT: Asia

Yemen

CAPITAL: Sanaa
POPULATION: 16,387,963
MAJOR LANGUAGE: Arabic
AREA: 203,857 sq mi; 527,970 sq km
LEADING EXPORTS: crude oil, cotton, coffee, hides, and vegetables
CONTINENT: Asia

Zambia

CAPITAL: Lusaka
POPULATION: 9,460,736
MAJOR LANGUAGES: English (official) and about 70 various languages
AREA: 290,594 sq mi; 752,610 sq km
LEADING EXPORTS: copper, zinc, cobalt, lead, and tobacco
CONTINENT: Africa

Zimbabwe

CAPITAL: Harare
POPULATION: 11,044,147
MAJOR LANGUAGES: English, Shona, and Sindebele
area: 150,809 sq mi; 390,580 sq km
LEADING EXPORTS: agricultural products and manufactures
CONTINENT: Africa

Glossary of Geographic Terms

basin
a depression in the surface of the land; some basins are filled with water

bay
a part of a sea or lake that extends into the land

butte
a small raised area of land with steep sides

▲ butte

canyon
a deep, narrow valley with steep sides; often has a stream flowing through it

cataract
a large waterfall; any strong flood or rush of water

◀ cataract

delta
a triangular-shaped plain at the mouth of a river, formed when sediment is deposited by flowing water

flood plain
a broad plain on either side of a river, formed when sediment settles on the riverbanks

glacier
a huge, slow-moving mass of snow and ice

hill
an area that rises above surrounding land and has a rounded top; lower and usually less steep than a mountain

island
an area of land completely surrounded by water

isthmus
a narrow strip of land that connects two larger areas of land

mesa
a high, flat-topped landform with cliff-like sides; larger than a butte

mountain
an area that rises steeply at least 2,000 feet (300 m) above sea level; usually wide at the bottom and rising to a narrow peak or ridge

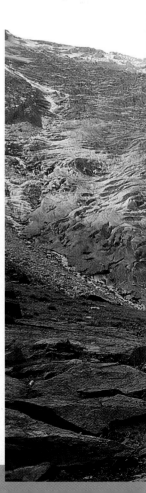

▶ glacier

◀ delta

mountain pass
a gap between mountains

peninsula
an area of land almost completely surrounded by water and connected to the mainland by an isthmus

plain
a large area of flat or gently rolling land

plateau
a large, flat area that rises above the surrounding land; at least one side has a steep slope

river mouth
the point where a river enters a lake or sea

strait
a narrow stretch of water that connects two larger bodies of water

tributary
a river or stream that flows into a larger river

volcano
an opening in the Earth's surface through which molten rock, ashes, and gasses from the Earth's interior escape

▶ volcano

Gazetteer

A

Adirondack Mountains a mountain range of New York State in eastern North America, p. 118

Africa (10°N, 22°E) world's second-largest continent, surrounded by the Mediterranean Sea, the Atlantic Ocean, and the Red Sea, p. 57

Amazon region region of northern South America occupying the drainage basin of the Amazon river, p. 115

Antarctica (80°S, 127°E) the continent located at the South Pole; almost completely covered by an ice sheet, p. 47

Antarctic Circle (66°S) line of latitude around Earth near the South Pole, p. 29

Appalachian Mountains a mountain system in eastern North America, p. 35

Arctic region located at the North Pole, p. 59

Arctic Circle (66°N) line of latitude around Earth near the North Pole, p. 29

Asia (50°N, 100°E) the world's largest continent, surrounded by the Arctic Ocean, the Pacific Ocean, the Indian Ocean, and Europe, p. 57

Australia (25°S, 135°E) an island continent in the Southern Hemisphere; a country including the continent and Tasmania, p. 57

B

Bali (8°S, 115°E) an island of southern Indonesia, p. 79

Bangladesh (24°N, 90°E) a coastal country in South Asia, officially the People's Republic of Bangladesh, p. 87

Bighorn Mountains a mountain range in Wyoming, in western North America, p. 27

C

California Current a southward-flowing oceanic current along the West Coast of North America; flows between 48°N and 23°N, p. 40

Canada (50°N, 100°W) a country in North America, p. 58

Caribbean Sea (14°N, 75°W) part of the southern Atlantic Ocean, p. 41

Central America the part of Latin America between Mexico and South America; includes the seven republics of Guatemala, Honduras, El Salvador, Nicaragua, Costa Rica, Panama, and Belize, p. 65

China (36°N, 93°E) a country occupying most of the mainland of East Asia, p. 90

Cuba (22°N, 79°W) the largest island country in the Caribbean Sea, p. 65

D

Denmark (56°N, 8°E) a country of northern Europe, p. 91

Dominican Republic (19°N, 70°W) a country occupying two thirds of the island of Hispaniola in the Caribbean, p. 65

E

Egypt (27°N, 27°E) a country in North Africa, p. 85

El Salvador (14°N, 89°W) a country in Central America, p. 65

Europe (50°N, 15°E) the world's second-smallest continent, a peninsula of the Eurasian landmass bounded by the Arctic Ocean, the Atlantic Ocean, the Mediterranean Sea, and Asia, p. 57

F

Florida (30°N, 84°W) a state in the southeastern United States that is largely a peninsula, p. 65

G

Galapagos Islands (0.1°S, 87°W) a group of islands located in the eastern Pacific Ocean, part of Ecuador, p. 40

Germany (51°N, 10°E) a country in Europe, p. 83

Grand Bahama Island (26°N, 78°W) one of the Bahama Islands in the Caribbean Sea, p. 18

Great Britain (56°N, 1°W) common name for the United Kingdom, a country in Western Europe including England, Northern Ireland, Scotland, and Wales, p. 83

Great Plains (45°N, 104°W) a dry area of short grasses located in North America, stretching from the Rio Grande at the U.S.-Mexico border in the south to the Mackenzie River Delta in the north, and from the Canadian Shield in the east to the Rocky Mountains in the west, also called "The Great American Desert," p. 46

Greenland (74°N, 40°W) a large, self-governing island in the northern Atlantic Ocean, part of Denmark, p. 16

Greenwich (51°N, 0°) a borough of London, England, and location of the Royal Greenwich Observatory, whose site serves as the basis for longitude and for setting standard time, p. 11

Gulf Stream a warm ocean current in the North Atlantic, flowing northeastward off the North American coast, p. 40

H

Haiti (19°N, 72°W) a country in the Caribbean Sea, on the island of Hispaniola, p. 65

Hanoi (21°N, 106°E) capital of Vietnam, p. 9

I

India (23°N, 77°E) a large country occupying most of the Indian subcontinent in South Asia, p. 37

Indian Ocean (10°S, 40°E) the world's third-largest ocean, lying between Africa, Asia, and Australia, p. 9

Indonesia (4°S, 118°E) a country in Southeast Asia consisting of many islands, including Sumatra, Java, Sulawesi (Celebes), Bali, and the western half of New Guinea, p. 68

Israel (32°N, 34°E) a country in Southwest Asia, p. 91

Italy (44°N, 11°E) a boot-shaped country in southern Europe, including the islands of Sicily and Sardinia, p. 89

J

Jakarta (6°S, 106°E) the capital and largest city of the Republic of Indonesia, p. 68

Jamaica (17°N, 78°W) an island country in the Caribbean Sea, p. 65

Japan (36°N, 133°E) an island country in the Pacific Ocean off the east coast of Asia, consisting of four main islands—Honshu, Hokkaido, Kyushu, and Shikoku, p. 55

K

Kalahari Desert a desert region in southern Africa, p. 115

Kobe (34°N, 135°E) a seaport city in Japan, p. 31

M

Maldives (4°N, 71°E) country consisting of a group of coral islands in the Indian Ocean, formerly known as the Maldive Islands, p. 9

Mexico (23°N, 104°W) a country in North America, p. 41

Milky Way a galaxy consisting of several billions of stars, including the sun, p. 27

Minnesota (46°N, 90°W) a state in the north central part of the United States, p. 65

Morocco (32°N, 7°W) a country in northwestern Africa, p. 67

Mount Everest (28°N, 87°E) highest point on Earth, located in the Great Himalaya Range in Asia, p. 47

Myanmar (Burma) (21°N, 95°E) a country in Southeast Asia, p. 9

N

Nepal (28°N, 83°E) a country in South Asia, p. 47

Nile Valley the fertile land located on both sides of the Nile River in Africa; site of one of the earliest civilizations, p. 59

North America (45°N, 100°W) the world's third-largest continent, consisting of Canada, the United States, Mexico, and many islands, p. 57

North Pole (90°N) northernmost end of Earth's axis located in the Arctic Ocean, p. 39

Norway (63°N, 11°E) country in northwestern Europe occupying the western part of the Scandinavian peninsula, p. 56

P

Pakistan (28°N, 67°E) country in South Asia, between India and Afghanistan, officially the Islamic Republic of Pakistan, p. 63

Pangaea (pan JEE uh) according to scientific theory, a single landmass that broke apart to form today's separate continents; thought to have existed about 180 million years ago, p. 33

Peru Current a cold-water current of the southeast Pacific Ocean; flows between 40°S and 4°S, p. 40

R

Ring of Fire a circle of volcanic mountains that surrounds the Pacific Ocean, including those on the islands of Japan and Indonesia, in the Cascades of North America, and in the Andes of South America, p. 31

Rocky Mountains the major mountain range in western North America, extending south from Alberta, Canada, through the western United States to Mexico, p. 35

S

Sahara largest tropical desert in the world, covers almost all of North Africa, p. 117

San Francisco (37°N, 122°W) a seaport city in California, p. 8

São Paulo (23°S, 46°W) the largest city in Brazil, p. 68

South America (15°S, 60°W) the world's fourth-largest continent, bounded by the Caribbean Sea, the Atlantic Ocean, and the Pacific Ocean, and linked to North America by the Isthmus of Panama, p. 40

South Pole (90°S) southernmost end of Earth's axis, located in Antarctica, p. 29

St. Louis (38°N, 90°W) a city in Missouri, p. 40

Sudan (14°N, 28°E) a country in north central Africa, officially the Republic of Sudan, p. 24

T

Taiwan (23°N, 122°E) a large island country off the southeast coast of mainland China, formerly Formosa; since 1949, the Nationalist Republic of China, p. 9

Tokyo (35°N, 139°E) capital and largest city of Japan, p. 55

Trinidad and Tobago (11°N, 61°W) republic of the West Indies, on the two islands called Trinidad and Tobago, p. 65

Tropic of Cancer (23.5°N) the northern boundary of the tropics, or the band of Earth that receives the most direct light and heat energy from the sun; such a region lies on both sides of the Equator, p. 29

Tropic of Capricorn (23.5°S) the southern boundary of the tropics; see above, p. 29

Turkey (38°N, 32°E) a country located in southeast Europe and southwest Asia, p. 67

V

Vietnam (18°N, 107°E) a country located in Southeast Asia, p. 66

W

Wisconsin (44°N, 91°W) a state in the north central United States, p. 65

Glossary

A

absolute location the exact position of a place on Earth, p. 10

acculturation the process of accepting, borrowing, and exchanging ideas and traits among cultures, p. 95

acid rain rain whose high levels of chemicals can pollute or damage the environment; usually caused by pollutants from the burning of fossil fuels, p. 118

adaptations features plants have that enable them to live in their particular climate, p. 43

agriculture farming; includes growing crops and raising livestock, p. 80

arid hot climate that receives very little rain, with little vegetation, p. 44

atlas a collection of physical and political maps, p. 128

atmosphere the multilayered band of gases that surrounds Earth, p. 35

axis an imaginary line around which a planet turns; Earth turns around its axis which runs between its North and South poles, p. 28

B

barometer an instrument for forecasting changes in the weather; anything that indicates a change, p. 75

basic business an industry that is essential for a nation to function, such as electricity, p. 88

birthrate the number of live births each year per 1,000 people, p. 61

blizzard a very heavy snowstorm with strong winds, p. 42

bottomlands low land through which a river flows; flood plain, p. 102

C

canal a waterway constructed or modified to improve irrigation or drainage, p. 12

canopy a layer of branches and leaves at the tops of trees in a forest, p. 44

capitalism an economic system in which people and privately owned companies own both basic and nonbasic businesses and industries, p. 89

cardinal direction one of the four compass points: north, south, east, and west, p. 19

climate the weather patterns that an area typically experiences over a long period of time, p. 38

commercial farming farming that is done by companies; commercial farms are large and use modern technology; also, the raising of crops and livestock for sale in outside markets, p. 114

communication systems organized ways for people to contact each other, such as mail, telephone, radio, and computers, p. 116

communism a theory of government in which property such as farms and factories is owned by the government for the benefit of all citizens; a political system in which the central government controls all aspects of citizens' lives, p. 90

compass rose a map feature that usually shows the four cardinal directions, p. 19

conformal map a flat map of all of Earth that shows correct shapes but not true distances or sizes; also known as a Mercator projection after geographer Gerhardus Mercator, p. 16

coniferous cone-bearing; referring to trees that bear cones to produce seeds; most have needles which they keep year-round, p. 46

constitution a set of laws that defines and limits a government's power, p. 91

consumer a person who buys goods and services, p. 88

continental United States the geographical area that includes all states of the United States except Alaska and Hawaii, p. 57

copse a thicket of small trees or shrubs, p. 74

crust the outer skin of Earth, p. 33

cultural diffusion the movement of customs and ideas from one culture to another, p. 95

cultural landscape a landscape that has been changed by human beings and that reflects their culture, p. 79

cultural trait a behavioral characteristic of a people, such as a language, skill, or custom, passed from one generation to another, p. 78

culture language, religious beliefs, values, customs, and other ways of life shared by a group of people, p. 78

D

dam a barrier across a waterway to control the level of water, p. 12

death rate the number of deaths each year per 1,000 people, p. 61

deciduous leaf-shedding; referring to trees that lose their leaves each year, p. 46

deforestation the process of clearing land of forests or trees, usually to make room for farms and homes, p. 118

degree a unit of measure used to determine absolute location; on globes and maps, latitude and longitude are measured in degrees, p. 11

demographer a scientist who studies human populations, including their size; growth; density; distribution; and rates of births, marriages, and deaths, p. 56

desert a hot, dry region with little vegetation, p. 12

developed nation a country with a modern industrial society and a well-developed economy, p. 113

developing nation a country with relatively low industrial production, often lacking modern technology, p. 113

dictator a ruler who has complete power over a country, p. 92

direct democracy a system of government in which the people participate directly in decision making, p. 91

distortion a misrepresentation of the true shape; each map projection used by a cartographer produces some distortion, p. 15

E

economy a system for producing, distributing, consuming, and owning goods, services, and wealth, p. 88

ecosystem a community of living things and their environment; the elements of an ecosystem interact with one another, p. 117

energy usable heat or power; capacity for doing work, p. 108

energy resources resources that can be used to produce energy, such as oil, coal, natural gas, water, and wind, p. 108

environment all of the surroundings and conditions that affect living things, such as water, soil, and air, p. 12

equal area map a map showing the correct size of landmasses but with altered shapes, p. 16

Equator an imaginary line that circles the globe at its widest point (halfway between the North and South poles), dividing Earth into two halves called hemispheres; used as a reference point from which north and south latitudes are measured, p. 11

equinox two days in the year on which the sun is directly over the Equator and the days are almost exactly as long as the nights; known as spring and fall equinoxes, p. 29

erosion a process by which water, wind, or ice wears away landforms and carries the material to another place, p. 35

ethics the standards or code of moral behavior that distinguishes between right and wrong for a particular person, religion, group, profession, and so on, p. 85

extended family a family unit that may include parents, children, grandparents, aunts, uncles, cousins, and other relatives, often living with or near each other, p. 84

F

fault cracks in Earth's crust caused by Earth's plates pushing against each other and fracturing, p. 34

fertilized caused to be healthy and capable of producing more plants, p. 9

foreign aid economic and military aid to another country, p. 116

fossil fuel any one of several nonrenewable resources such as coal, oil, or natural gas, created from the remains of plants and animals, p. 108

G

geography the study of Earth's surface and the processes that shape it, the connections between places, and the relationships between people and their environment, p. 10

glacial from a glacier; rocks left behind by a glacier, p. 102

global village term used for the people of Earth; referring to the way people are connected by modern transportation and communication, p. 96

global warming a slow increase in Earth's temperature due to the increasing amount of carbon dioxide in the atmosphere; if there is too much carbon dioxide in the atmosphere, more heat than normal is trapped and temperatures around the world increase, p. 120

globe a round model of Earth that shows the continents and oceans in their true shapes, p. 15

goods products that are made to be sold; cars, baskets, computers, and paper are all examples of goods, p. 88

government the system that establishes and enforces the laws and institutions of a society; some governments are controlled by a few people, and others are controlled by many, p. 90

Green Revolution changes in agriculture since the 1950s that have greatly increased the world's food supply; the Green Revolution's reliance on costly technologies and dangerous pesticides can be both financially and environmentally damaging to nations, p. 61

groundwater water that flows beneath the Earth's surface and is stored in sail and rock, p. 36

H

habitat the area in which a plant or animal naturally grows or lives, p. 118

hemlock a pine tree with drooping branches and short needles, p. 74

herder person who takes care of a group of animals such as sheep and cattle, p. 59

high latitudes the regions between the Arctic Circle and the North Pole and the Antarctic Circle and the South Pole, p. 29

hill a landform that rises above the surrounding land and that has a rounded top; a hill is lower and usually less steep than a mountain, p. 32

human characteristics characteristics of a place that are related to people, p. 25

human-environment interaction how people affect the environment and the physical characteristics of their surroundings and how the environment affects them, p. 10

humid continental climate with moderate to hot summers but very cold winters; supporting grasslands and forests, p. 46

hurricane wind and rain storms that form over the tropics in the Atlantic Ocean and produce huge waves that can destroy towns along the shore, p. 41

hydroponics a method of growing plants in water and nutrients rather than in soil, p. 61

I

immigrant a person who moves to a new country in order to settle there, p. 64

industrial nations countries that have many industries; people in these nations use factory-made goods, consume large amounts of energy and materials, and export goods to other countries, p. 112

interrupted projection type of map that uses gaps to show the size and shape of land accurately; impossible to use this map to figure distances correctly, p. 16

irrigation supplying dry land with water, p. 12

isoline lines drawn on maps to show elevation; also called contour lines, p. 57

K

key the section of a map that explains the symbols for the map features; also called a legend, p. 19

L

landform an area of Earth's surface with a definite shape; mountains and hills are examples of landforms, p. 32

landmass a large area of land, p. 16

latitude lines the series of imaginary lines, also called parallels, that circle Earth parallel to the Equator; used to measure a distance north or south of the Equator in degrees, p. 11

leeward side the side of a mountain away from the wind, p. 40

lichen a plant that is a combination of a fungus and alga that grows and spreads over rocks and tree trunks; found in polar climates, p. 46

life expectancy the number of years that a person may be expected, on average, to live, p. 61

longitude lines the series of imaginary lines, also called meridians, that run north and south from one pole to the other; used to measure a distance east or west of the Prime Meridian in degrees, p. 11

low latitudes the region between the Tropic of Cancer and the Tropic of Capricorn, p. 29

M

magma layer of hot, soft rock underneath Earth's plates, p. 33

manufacturing the process of turning raw materials into a finished product, p. 112

marine west coast moderate climate occurring in mountainous areas cooled by ocean currents; supports more forests than grasses, p. 45

mediterranean moderate climate that receives most of its rain in winter and has hot and dry summers; plants here have leathery leaves that hold water, p. 45

meridian an imaginary line that circles the globe from north to south and runs through both the North and South poles; the lines of longitude on maps or globes are meridians, p. 11

meteorologist scientist who studies the weather, p. 80

middle latitudes the regions between the Tropic of Cancer and the Arctic Circle and the Tropic of Capricorn and the Antarctic Circle, p. 30

migration the movement of people from one country or region to another in order to make a new home, p. 64

mineral a natural resource that is obtained by mining, such as gold, iron ore, or copper, p. 107

moderate a group of climates found in the middle latitudes; marked by medium rainfall, seasonal changes, but temperatures rarely falling below zero, p. 45

monarchy a system of authoritarian government headed by a monarch—usually a king or queen—who inherits the throne by birth, p. 91

mountain usually, a landform that rises more than 2,000 ft (610 m) above sea level and is wide at the bottom and narrow at the peak, p. 32

N

natural resource any useful material found in the environment, p. 105

nonrenewable resource a resource that cannot be replaced once it is used; nonrenewable resources include fossil fuels such as coal and oil, and minerals such as iron, copper, and gold, p. 107

nuclear family a family unit that includes a mother, a father, and their children, p. 83

O

ocean current a fast-moving river-like flow of water in the ocean created by Earth's rotation, p. 40

orbit the path followed by an object in space as it moves around another, such as that of Earth as it moves around the sun, p. 28

Organization of Petroleum Exporting Countries (OPEC) organization of oil-producing countries that agree on how much oil they will sell as well as oil prices, p. 109

ozone layer the layer of gas in the upper part of the atmosphere that blocks out most of the sun's harmful ultraviolet rays, p. 119

P

parallel in geography, any of the imaginary lines that circle Earth parallel to the Equator; a latitude line, p. 11

petroleum an oily substance found under Earth's crust; the source of gasoline and other fuels; an energy resource, p. 107

physical characteristics the natural features of Earth, p. 25

plain a large area of flat or gently rolling land usually without many trees, p. 13

plantation a large estate, usually in a warm climate, on which crops are grown by workers living there; plantations usually raise a single crop for export, p. 115

plate in geography, a huge section of Earth's crust, p. 33

plateau a large, mostly flat area that rises above the surrounding land; at least one side has a steep slope, p. 32

plate tectonics the theory that Earth's crust is made of huge, slowly moving slabs of rock called plates, p. 33

polar climates of the high latitudes that are cold all year with short summers p. 46

population the people living in a particular region; especially, the total number of people in an area, p. 55

population density the average number of people living in a given area, p. 58

population distribution how a population is spread over an area, p. 55

precipitation all the forms of water, such as rain, sleet, hail, and snow, that fall to the ground from the atmosphere, p. 38

Prime Meridian an imaginary line of longitude, or meridian, that runs from the North Pole to the South Pole through Greenwich, England; it is designated 0° longitude and is used as a reference point from which east and west lines of longitude are measured, p. 11

producer a person who makes products that are used by other people, p. 88

projection a representation of the Earth's rounded surface on a flat piece of paper, p. 16

"push-pull" theory a theory of migration that says people migrate because certain things in their lives "push" them to leave, and certain things in a new place "pull" them, p. 65

R

raw material a resource or material that is still in its natural state, before being processed or manufactured into a useful product, p. 106

recyclable resource a resource that cycles through natural processes in the environment; water, nitrogen, and carbon are recyclable resources, p. 107

recycle to reuse materials to make new products, p. 107

region an area with a unifying characteristic such as climate, land, population, or history, p. 12

relative location the location of a place as described by places near it, p. 10

renewable resource a natural resource that the environment continues to supply or replace as it is used; trees, water, and wind are renewable resources, p. 107

representative democracy a system of government in which the people elect representatives to run the affairs of the country, p. 91

revolution one complete orbit of Earth around the sun; Earth completes one revolution every 365 1/4 days, or one year, p. 28

ridge underwater mountains formed by the cooling of magma in the oceans, p. 34

rotation the spinning motion of Earth, like a top on its axis; Earth takes about 24 hours to rotate one time, p. 28

rural area an area with low population density, such as a village or the countryside, p. 68

S

sanitation disposal of sewage and waste, p. 62

scale the size of an area on a map as compared with the area's actual size, p. 15

semiarid hot, dry climate with little rain; supports only shrubs and grasses, p. 44

services work done or duties performed for other people, such as the work of a doctor or of a television repair person, p. 88

smog mixture of dangerous smoke and fog caused by pollution, p. 39

socialism an economic system in which the government owns most basic industries, such as transportation, communications, and banking; nonbasic industries are privately owned, p. 89

social structure the ways in which people within a culture are organized into smaller groups; each smaller group has its own particular tasks, p. 82

subarctic continental dry climate with cool summers and cold winters; supports short grasses, some areas support large coniferous forests, p. 46

subsistence farming farming that provides only enough food and animals for the needs of a family or village, p. 115

summer solstice first day of summer in the Northern Hemisphere, on which the sun shines directly overhead the Tropic of Cancer, p. 29

T

technology tools and the skills that people need to use them; the practical use of scientific skills, especially in industry, p. 79

temperature the degree of hotness or coldness of something, such as water or air, usually measured with a thermometer, p. 38

tendril threadlike part of a climbing plant that supports the plant, p. 102

thunderstorm heavy rain storm with lightning and thunder, and sometimes hail, p. 42

transportation systems means by which products are carried from manufacturers to consumers, p. 112

tundra a region where temperatures are always cool or cold and where only certain plants, such as low grasses, can grow, p. 46

typhoon violent storm that develops over the Pacific Ocean, p. 41

U

urban area an area with a high population density; a city or town, p. 68

urbanization the growth of city populations caused by the movement of people to cities, p. 68

V

vegetation the plants in an area, p. 43

verdant green; covered with growth, p. 9

vertical climate the overall weather patterns of a region as influenced by elevation; the higher the elevation, the colder the climate, p. 47

W

weather the condition of the bottom layer of Earth's atmosphere in one place over a short period of time, p. 37

weathering the breaking down of rocks by wind, rain, or ice, p. 35

wind patterns ways that the wind flows over Earth; affected by the sun, p. 35

windward side side of a mountain from which the wind blows, p. 40

winter solstice first day of winter in the Northern Hemisphere, on which the sun shines directly overhead the Tropic of Capricorn, p. 29

World Bank agency of the United Nations that makes loans to member nations and private investors, encourages foreign trade, and makes investments throughout the world, p. 62

Index

The *italicized* page numbers refer to illustrations. The *m, c, p, t,* or *g* preceding the number refers to maps (*m*), charts (*c*), pictures (*p*), tables (*t*), or graphs (*g*).

A

absolute location, 10, 160
acculturation, 95, 160
acid rain, 118–119, *p 121,* 160
Activity Atlas, 2–7
Activity Shop
   interdisciplinary, 24–25
   lab, 52–53
adaptation, 43, 46, 160
Adirondack Mountains, 118, 156
aerosol spray: effect of, on ozone layer, 120
Afghanistan, *m 2–3,* 4, *m 4, m 5,* 146
Africa, *m 2–3,* 24, 156
   developing nations in, 115
   economic activity, *m 114*
   Green Belt Movement, 117
   language groups of, *m 84*
   limited energy resources of, 109–110
   physical map of, *m 141*
   political map of, *m 140*
   population statistics of, 57, 62
African language group, *m 84*
Afro-Asiatic language group, *m 84*
Agricultural Revolution, 81
agriculture, 80, 160. *See also* farming
air pollution, 39, 114
   chlorofluorocarbons and, 119
   greenhouse effect and, *p 119*
Alaska, *p 118*
   California Current and, 40
Albania, 146
Algeria, 146

Allah, 82. *See also* Islam
alphabets, ancient, 85
Amazon region, 115, 156
Amazon River Valley, 117–118
Amerindian language group, *m 84*
Andorra, 146
Angola, 146
Anguilla, 146
Antarctica, *m 2–3, m 145,* 156
   climate of, *p 46*
   economic activity, *m 114*
   language groups of, *m 84*
Antarctic Circle, 29, *m 29,* 156
Antarctic Ocean, *m 32*
antibiotics, 61
Antigua and Barbuda, 146
Appalachian Mountains, 35, 156
Arabian Sea, *m 4*
Arabic language, 85
Aral Sea, 118
Arctic, *m 145,* 156
Arctic Circle, 29, *m 29,* 156
   wind patterns of, *m 35*
Arctic Ocean, *m 32*
Argentina, 98, 146
arid, 44, 160
Armenia, 146
Asia, *m 2–3, m 32,* 156
   developing nations in, 115
   economic activity, *m 114*
   language groups of, *m 84*
   physical map of, *m 143*
   political map of, *m 142*
   population, 57, 62
astronauts, 9
Atlantic Ocean, *m 13, m 32, m 65*
   hurricanes and, 41
atlas, 128, 160
atmosphere, 35, 160

Australia, *m 2–3,* 67, 146, 156
   economic activity, *m 114*
   land area of, 57
   language groups of, *m 84*
   map of, *m 3, m 144*
   Outback, 96
   population of, 57
Austria, 146
automobile industry, 113, *p 113,* 119
axis, 28, 160
Aymara Indians, 79
Azerbaijan, 146

B

Bahamas, 146
Bahrain, 146
Bali, Indonesia, 79, 156
bamboo, 87, 88
Bangladesh, 4, *m 4, m 5,* 87, 146, 156
Barbados, 146
barometer, 75, 160
baseball: cultural diffusion and, 95
basic business, 88, 160
basin, 154
bauxite, *m 106*
bay, 154
Bay of Bengal, *m 4*
Belarus, 146
Belgium, 146
belief system. See religion
Belize, 146
Benin, 146
Bermuda, 146
Bhutan, *m 4, m 5,* 146
Bighorn Mountains, *p 27,* 156
birthrate, 61, 160
   during the Agricultural Revolution, 81

blizzard, 42, 160
blue jeans, cultural impact of, 93, 95
Bolivia, 146
Bosnia and Herzegovina, 146
Botswana, 147
bottomlands, 102, 160
Botts, Lee 121
Brazil, 147
British Virgin Islands, 147
broadcast, 95
Brunei, 147
Buddhism, m 86
Bulgaria, 147
bullet train, 55, p 55
Burkina Faso, 147
Burma. See Myanmar
Burundi, 147
business, 88
butte, 154, p 154

C

cacti, 43, p 43
Cairo, Egypt, 82
  overcrowding in, p 69
California, 40
  Lake Casitas, p 97
  land area of, 59
  population of, 59
  San Francisco, p 8, 40
California Current, 40, 156
Cambodia, 147
Cameroon, 147
Canada, 113, 147, 156
  laws to reduce acid rain, 119
  Ontario, 37
  petroleum and, g 108
  political system of, 90, 91
  population of, 58
  Quebec, 90
  representative democracy of, 91
canal, 12, 160

canopy, rain forest, 44, 160
canyon, 154
Cape Verde, 147
capitalism, 89, c 89, 160
carbon dioxide, 119, 121
cardinal directions, 19, 160
careers, 127
Caribbean, m 130
Caribbean Sea, 18, 41, 156
Carrying the Fire, 9
cataract, 154, p 154
Catskill Mountains, p 75
Cayman Islands, 147
Census Bureau, 73
Central African Republic, 147
Central America, 65, m 130, 156
central government, 90
CFCs. See chlorofluorocarbons (CFCs)
Chad, 147
channel surfing, 95
Charleston, South Carolina, g 49
Chicago, Illinois, p 103
Chile, 147
China, 147, 156
  economic system of, 90
  farming in, 111
  nonrenewable resources in, 109
  petroleum and, g 108, g 109
  tungsten mining in, m 106
chlorofluorocarbons (CFCs), 119–120
Christianity, 86, m 86
civilization, defined, 81
class. See social classes
clear-cut logging, 45
climate, 38
  arid and semiarid, 44–45
  changes in, 94
  of Charleston, South Carolina, g 49
  continental, 46

defined, 38, 160
differences from weather, 37–38
dry, 44
effect of, on vegetation, 43–47
moderate, 45
polar, 46
regions, m 38–39
of São Paulo, Brazil, g 48
tropical, 43–44
vertical, 47, p 47
closed-circuit television, 96
coal, 107
Collins, Michael, 9, 10
Colombia, 147
commercial farming, 114, 158, 160
communication systems, 94–95, 112, 116, 160
communism, 89, c 89, 90, 161
Comoros, 147
compass rose, m 18, 19, 161
computer
  hacker, 95
  uses of, 94–95
conformal map, 16, 161
Congo, 147
Congo, Democratic Republic of, 147
coniferous, 46, 161
coniferous forest, m 44–45, 46
  vertical climate and, 47
constitution, 91, 161
constitutional monarchy, p 91
consumer, 88, 161
continental United States, 57, 161
continents, movement of, m 2–3. See also Pangaea
contour map, m 57
Cook Islands, 147
copper, m 106
copse, 74, 161
coral reef, p 117
Costa Rica, 147

Acknowledgments

Cover Design

Bruce Bond, Suzanne Schineller, and Olena Serbyn

Cover Photo

Jon Chomitz

Maps

MapQuest.com, Inc.
Map information sources: Columbia Encyclopedia, Encyclopaedia Britannica, Microsoft® Encarta®, National Geographic Atlas of the World, Rand McNally Commercial Atlas, The Times Atlas of the World.

Staff Credits

The people who made up the *World Explorer* team—representing editorial, editorial services, design services, on-line services/multimedia development, product marketing, production services, project office, and publishing processes—are listed below. Bold type denotes core team members.

Barbara Bertell, **Paul Gagnon, Mary Hanisco, Dotti Marshall,** Susan Swan, and Carol Signorino.

Additional Credits

Art and Design: Emily Soltanoff. Editorial: Debra Reardon, Nancy Rogier. Market Research: Marilyn Leitao. Production Services: **Joyce Barisano.** Publishing Processes: **Wendy Bohannan.**

Text

9, Excerpt from *Carrying the Fire* by Michael Collins. Copyright © 1974 by Michael Collins. Reprinted by permission from Farrar, Straus & Giroux, Inc. **27,** Excerpt from *North American Indian Mythology* by Cottie Burland, rev. by Marion Wood. Copyright © 1965 by Cottie Burland, Copyright © renewed 1985 by the Estate of Cottie Burland. Reproduced by permission of Reed Books. **31,** Excerpt from "The Kobe Earthquake: A Chance to Serve," by Megumi Fujiwara, *JAMA,* January 3, 1996, volume 275, p. 79. Copyright © 1996, American Medical Association. Reprinted with permission of the American Medical Association. **74,** From *My Side of the Mountain* by Jean Craighead George. Copyright © 1959 by Jean Craighead George, renewed 1987 by Jean Craighead George. Used by permission of Dutton Children's Books, a division of Penguin Books USA Inc. **102,** "Rough Country" copyright © 1991 by Dana Gioia. Reprinted from *The Gods of Winter* with the permission of Graywolf Press, Saint Paul, Minnesota.

Photos

1 T, © Karen Kasmauski/Woodfin Camp & Associates, **1 BL,** © SuperStock International, **1 BR,** © Paul Chesley/Tony Stone Images, **2 T,** © Ken Graham/Tony Stone Images, **2 B,** Peter Carmichael/Tony Stone Images, **3 T,** © Alan Abromowitz/Tony Stone Images, **3 B,** Robert Frerck/Odyssey Productions, **4,** © Mark Thayer, Boston, **8,** © Baron Wolman/Tony Stone Images, **9,** © Kevin Kelley/Tony Stone Images, **12,** The Rift Valley—Lake Naivasha, by Edwin Rioba, age 16, Kenya. Courtesy of the International Children's Art Museum, **14,** © British Museum, **15 T, M, BL, BR,** © Custom Medical Stock Photo, **20, 21,** © David Young-Wolff/PhotoEdit, **24 L,** © Mike McQueen/Tony Stone Images, **24 R,** © Stephen Studd/Tony Stone Images, **26,** © ESA/TSADD/Tom Stack & Associates, **27,** © Photri, **37,** © David Falconer/Tony Stone Images, **43,** © Rod Planck/Tom Stack & Associates, **46 TR,** © John Beatty/Tony Stone Images, **46 BL,** © Jonathan Nourok/PhotoEdit, **49,** © Grant Taylor/Tony Stone Images, **53,** © David Young-Wolff/PhotoEdit, **54,** © Robert Fox/Impact Visuals, **55,** © Paul Chesley/Tony Stone Images, **56,** © Tony Stone Images, **58 TL,** © Connie Coleman/Tony Stone Images, **58 TR,** © Bill Pogue/Tony Stone Images, **58 B,** SuperStock International, **61,** © Jason Laure'/Laure' Communications, **64,** © Chris Brown/SABA Press Photos, **66,** © Ted Streshinsky/Corbis, **67,** © Mariella Furrer/SABA Press Photos, **69,** © Donna DeCesare/Impact Visuals, **70,** © Earth Imaging/Tony Stone Images, **74,** © Carr Clifton/Carr Clifton Photography, **76,** © Lawrence Migdale/Tony Stone Images, **77,** © Paul Conklin/PhotoEdit, **78,** © Don Smetzer/Tony Stone Images, **79,** © David Young-Wolff/PhotoEdit, **82,** © Donna DeCesare/Impact Visuals, **83 TL,** © David Young-Wolff/PhotoEdit, **83 TR,** © Inga Spence/Tom Stack & Associates, **83 B,** © Andrew Errington/Tony Stone Images, **87,** © Julia Vindasius/Vindasius, **88 T, B,** © Ithaca Money, **89,** © AP/World Wide Photos, **90,** Untitled, by Olga Loceva, age 14, Russia. Courtesy of the International Children's Art Museum, **91,** © Adam Woolfitt/Corbis, **92,** © Hulton Deutsch Collection/Corbis, **93,** © Robert Frerck/Tony Stone Images, **94,** © Felicia Martinez/PhotoEdit, **95,** © The Granger Collection, **97,** © Jose Carrillo/PhotoEdit, **98,** © Billy E. Barnes/PhotoEdit, **103 L,** © Philip & Karen Smith/Tony Stone Images, **103 M,** © Bruce Hands/Tony Stone Images, **103 R,** Peter Pearson/Tony Stone Images, © **104,** © Manfred Gottschalk/Tom Stack & Associates, **105,** © SuperStock International, **107,** © Larry Tackett/Tom Stack & Associates, **110,** © Dennis MacDonald/PhotoEdit, **112 T,** © Paul Conklin/PhotoEdit, **113,** © Andy Sacks/Tony Stone Images, **115,** © Radhika Chalasani/Gamma Liaison International, **116,** © Jean-Marc Giboux/Gamma Liaison International, **117,** © Mike Bacon/Tom Stack & Associates, **118,** © Rich Frishman/Tony Stone Images, **121,** © David M. Dennis/Tom Stack & Associates, **122,** © Jonathan Nourok/PhotoEdit, **123,** © Michael Newman/PhotoEdit, **126,** © Mark Thayer, Boston, **127,** © Roger Chester/Trip Photographic, **154 T,** © A & L Sinibaldi/Tony Stone Images, **154 B,** © John Beatty/Tony Stone Images, **155 T,** © Hans Strand/Tony Stone Images, **155 BL,** © Spencer Swanger/Tom Stack & Associates, **155 BR,** © Paul Chesley/Tony Stone Images.